T0290523

Systems Thinking
in Museums

Systems Thinking in Museums

Theory and Practice

EDITED BY

Yuha Jung and Ann Rowson Love

ROWMAN & LITTLEFIELD
Lanham • Boulder • New York • London

Published by Rowman & Littlefield
A wholly owned subsidiary of The Rowman & Littlefield Publishing Group, Inc.
4501 Forbes Boulevard, Suite 200, Lanham, Maryland 20706
www.rowman.com

Unit A, Whitacre Mews, 26-34 Stannary Street, London SE11 4AB

British Library Cataloguing in Publication Information Available

Library of Congress Cataloging-in-Publication Data
Names: Jung, Yuha, 1981– author. | Love, Ann Rowson, 1967– author.
Title: Systems thinking in museums : theory and practice / Yuha Jung and
    Ann Rowson Love.
Description: Lanham, Maryland : Rowman & Littlefield, 2017. | Includes
    bibliographical references and index.
Identifiers: LCCN 2017024560 (print) | LCCN 2017027490 (ebook) |
    ISBN 9781442279254 (ebook) | ISBN 9781442279230 (cloth : alk. paper) |
    ISBN 9781442279247 (pbk. : alk. paper)
Subjects: LCSH: Museums—Management. | System theory.
Classification: LCC AM121 (ebook) | LCC AM121 .J66 2017 (print) |
    DDC 069/.068—dc23
LC record available at https://lccn.loc.gov/2017024560

∞™ The paper used in this publication meets the minimum requirements of American
National Standard for Information Sciences—Permanence of Paper for Printed Library
Materials, ANSI/NISO Z39.48-1992.

Printed in the United States of America

Contents

Foreword

In 1993, as the recently appointed director of the Division of Public Programs at the National Endowment for the Humanities (NEH) and newly minted member of the federal government's Senior Executive Service (SES), I could access, for the first time in my career, some serious executive leadership training. In one of my Office of Personnel Management courses, I encountered Peter Senge's *The Fifth Discipline: The Art and Practice of the Learning Organization*, originally published in 1990.[1] Senge's focus on the critical attributes of *learning organizations*, where people grow personally and professionally, solve challenging problems, and achieve meaningful results together, made sense to me in my new leadership role. His approach, emphasizing effective teamwork, personal mastery, building a shared vision, and systems thinking provided a fresh and useful framework for managing funding programs and navigating the other NEH divisions. Seeing the agency as an interconnected system with a shared mission of strengthening our democracy by promoting excellence in the humanities helped hone public humanities strategies in support of the agency's mandate.

When I left NEH in 1996 to assume the presidency of Conner Prairie, a living history museum outside of Indianapolis, I quickly realized the importance of seeing the museum within its broader and ever-changing demographic context. As we began working on a new strategic plan, I learned that the previous summer a confidential planning document, suggesting that one corner of the Conner Prairie acreage might become an RV park, had been leaked and had gotten the attention of local media and nearby neighborhood residents, who instigated a NIMBY protest. To them, Conner Prairie was a large and highly visible community presence, and they wanted a voice in its planning efforts. We therefore made sure that our plan identified and responded to community concerns, assets, and needs. We had listening sessions with local residents, educators, business people, community leaders, and foundation representatives and incorporated many of their suggestions as we proceeded with the plan and its programmatic implementation. We forged new partnerships, made new relationships, created new programs, found new funding, and reframed our public and community role.

After my time at Conner Prairie and when I became the first director for Strategic Partnerships at the Institute of Museum and Library Services (IMLS), a systems approach remained part of my professional toolbox. In 2008, as stakeholders recognized that the challenges of the new technology-driven, global economy would require new competencies, we worked with a museum and library task force and other education leaders to create *Museums, Libraries, and 21st Century Skills*, a report to help museums and libraries respond to these challenges, encouraging such essential skills as collaboration, critical thinking, self-direction, and social and cultural awareness that are aligned with systems thinking.[2]

In each of these cases we considered how our agency or organization, remaining faithful to our legislative mandate or mission, could align with strategic partners and community needs to have greater systemic impact. This approach required new roles and relationships among staff and with our partners. We needed to shift our frame and mindset and adjust our understanding of the challenges to be addressed and the mechanisms by which we could address them and move beyond individual departments and programs. While the work was challenging, as we developed trust among the partners and community members, many benefits followed—in our own learning; in nurturing new community and partner relationships; in building organizations' visibility; in attracting new resources for the organizations and their constituents; and in reaching more individuals and communities with new learning opportunities.

Systems Thinking in Museums: Theory and Practice, the first volume to provide multiple, museum-grounded perspectives on this approach, is therefore a much-needed and valuable resource for museums that recognize that they are better off when they operate as open and dynamic learning systems as opposed to traditional, compartmentalized, and hierarchical organizations. Yuha Jung and Ann Rowson Love cover the waterfront with sections on systems theory and specific museum examples. In her book, *Thinking in Systems: A Primer* (2208), Donella H. Meadows noted that systems thinking "gives us the freedom to identify root causes of problems and see new opportunities."[3] In this book, Jung and Love and their many contributors show how systems thinking can enhance the ability of a museum to fulfill its public service mission, including service to (and relationships with) individual learners and larger communities. Moreover, this approach can also be applied to internal challenges, improving staff satisfaction, work processes, business operations, and contributing to a more solvent and sustainable organization.

Our interconnected world, powered by massive advances in technology and witnessing exponential change, is not going away. Our challenges, known and unforeseen, require new systems approaches. *Systems Thinking in Museums* enriches our sector's conversations on ways museums can achieve organizational effectiveness, enhance their public value, and serve as vital community resources for the greater good.

Marsha L. Semmel, principal of Marsha Semmel Consulting

NOTES

1. Peter Senge, *The Fifth Discipline: The Art and Practice of the Learning Organization* (New York: Doubleday, 1990).

2. Institute of Museum and Library Services, *Museums, Libraries and 21st Century Skills* (Washington, DC: Institute of Museum and Library Services, 2009).

3. Donella Meadows, *Thinking in Systems: A Primer*, ed. Diana Wright (White River Junction, VT: Chelsea Green, 2008), 2.

Preface

Systems thinking applied to museums is about interconnectedness and interdependence—collaborative organizational structure, shared authority, and strong community engagement. Mary Mattingly's contemporary art installation *Floating World*, an ecosystem featured on the cover of this book, embodies systems thinking in museums.[1] Her work comprises organic networks of interconnected materials and flowering seedlings that cannot maintain their beauty and function without being interactive with different parts of the sum and the natural environment as a whole. The importance of interconnections among fragile and constantly changing parts made within the natural world is expressed in this intricate installation.

In addition, *Floating World* featured in *Collective Actions*, an exhibition at the Southeast Center for Contemporary Art, represents systems thinking applied in practice; this work is created in collaboration with the museum professionals and community partners promoting shared authority and community engagement (read more about the exhibition in chapter 10). The work encourages audiences and participants to act in order "to consider how we inhabit our planet and to co-create living systems."[2] Museums are complex and sometimes fragile institutions that aim to find the right combination of networks to support and sustain them. Like Mattingly's work, they are in constant and fluctuating circumstances that need to promote and engage in practices that make their systems stronger and more connected within their organizations and with their communities. This artwork offers a unique metaphor for the ideas presented in this book.

This book came about when Yuha Jung, coeditor, had an initial correspondence with Charles Harmon at Rowman & Littlefield about the publisher's potential interest in a book focused on systems thinking in museums. He greeted the request with great enthusiasm and encouraged us to write a formal proposal. Generally speaking, publications focused specifically on elucidating complex theory in museum practice have few venues. However, it is undeniable that we do our everyday work in museums with underlying assumptions and theoretical orientations in place. Over the past couple of decades, we have seen major shifts in museum practice from more object-centric to visitor-centric orientations, or re-orientations.[3] Likewise, we have seen a surge of publications on creating meaningful, empathic, and relevant museums that provide shared authority and promote social change—worthy goals for all museums. We believe that awareness with specific museum examples of systems thinking will help readers make headway into achieving those goals. Many publications share theory without actual practical implementation and the reverse is also true—publications share practice-based examples without making the empirical connections to theory. We need both. We strive to deliver both in this book. The editorial board at Rowman & Littlefield, thankfully, agreed with us. It's time for a book to actively demonstrate how theory translates into practice across departments and including community partners that form social ecosystems together.

We wanted to focus on sharing the ways in which the theory of systems thinking operates in real museums every day—or in some instances how systems thinking could greatly assist museums and their practices when closed models fail. Failures to be inclusive, collaborative, and engaging in meaningful community partnerships may leave museums floundering. We strive in this book to promote how systems thinking changes museums in real and impactful ways. The chapters in the book show various entry points to use systems thinking in museums—some museums are further along than others, but all the examples in the book tie specific systems thinking to museum work.

The twenty chapters in this book are contributed by authors from many parts of the world, featuring museums and perspectives from the United States, Australia, Canada, Brazil, Italy, the United Kingdom, and more. We organized these chapters into ten different parts: (1) introduction to systems thinking, (2) paradigm change in museum functions, (3) management and leadership, (4) personnel management, (5) exhibition and program development, (6) external communications, (7) community engagement, (8) fundraising and financial sustainability, (9) physical museum spaces, and (10) conclusion and next steps. We placed two chapters in each part of the book demonstrating how systems thinking is used in the specific conceptual and functional area with different strategies. By deliberately structuring the book this way, we hope readers will see various entry points for starting or continuing to embed systems thinking approaches in their museums.

We coeditors have been engaged in researching, evaluating, and practicing systems thinking for years. We have presented together and have supported each other through research and conversation. We firmly believe that the included authors and museums have valuable lessons to share with museum practitioners, volunteers including board members, community partners, educators, researchers, and students regardless of discipline—art, history, science, natural history, anthropology, and others.

Ann Rowson Love, coeditor
Yuha Jung, coeditor

NOTES

1. Mary Mattingly, *Floating World*, in *Collective Actions* (Winston-Salem, NC: Southeast Center for Contemporary Art, 2015).

2. "Mary Mattingly," SECCA, accessed March 12, 2017, http://collectiveactions.secca.org/mattingly/.

3. Stephen Weil, "From Being *about* Something to Being *for* Somebody: The Ongoing Transformation of the American Museum," *Daedelus* 128, no. 3 (1999): 229–58.

Acknowledgments

We, Yuha Jung and Ann Rowson Love, wish to acknowledge each other in the process of conceptualizing the book and editing chapters and being critical and supportive of each other. We thank the authors for contributing excellent and inspiring chapters that made this book possible. We also thank our mentors, Mary Ann Stankiewicz and Pat Villeneuve, who academically and professionally pushed us to be where we are today. We appreciate our colleagues and spouses who provided emotional support throughout the process. Yuha appreciates the faculty and staff (Rachel, Geri, Andrea, Joe, and Jill) of the Department of Arts Administration at the University of Kentucky for providing moral support and reassurance for the importance of the project. Yuha thanks her beloved husband, Michael Johnson, for supporting her in every way possible. Ann would like to thank the faculty of the Department of Art Education (Jeff, Antonio, Rachel, Dave, Marsha, Sara, Pat, Theresa, and Scott) at Florida State University for their ongoing support and cheering her on, especially her chair, David Gussak. She thanks the dean of the College of Fine Arts at Florida State, Peter Weishar, for supporting this research and resulting publication. She is grateful for receiving an FSU research grant from the Committee on Faculty Research Support (COFRS) that provided summer support funding for this project. Ann thanks her husband, Eric Love, for his endearing support over the past year and a half as head chef, household project manager, and general life coach. We could not have completed this project without Sarah Grainger and Morgan Szymanski, who provided tremendous editorial and administrative support—thank you! Last but not least, we thank Charles Harmon for selecting systems thinking in museums as an important topic and agreeing to publish it through Rowman & Littlefield.

CHAPTER AUTHORS

Randi Korn would like to thank Stephanie Downey for her thoughtful comments on the manuscript, Amanda Krantz and Cathy Sigmond for applying their visual sensibilities to the graphics, and Erin Lindsey for attending to the publisher's guidelines when preparing the manuscript for publication.

Paul Bowers, Patrick Greene, and Kathy Fox acknowledge the staff of Museums Victoria for contributions to continuous improvement of our culture and exhibition development process.

Doug Worts is grateful to the staff of the Georgia O'Keeffe Museum, especially its director Rob Kret and research center director Eumie Imm Stroukoff, for all their support during his 2014 research fellowship at the museum.

Swarupa Anila, Amy Foley, and Nii Quarcoopome express deep gratitude to their colleagues at the Detroit Institute of Arts and in the field for their willingness to bend institutional practices to support visitors in their museum experiences.

Susan Mann wishes to express her love and gratitude to her husband, Michael, who makes her laugh and holds the ladder so that she can climb onto the shoulders of Bill, Hazel, and Alice. She would steal a bunny for him.

Ana Flávia Machado, Diomira M. C. P. Faria, Sibelle C. Diniz, Bárbara F. Paglioto, Rodrigo C. Michel, and Gabriel Vaz de Melo would like to thank CNPq (National Research Agency) and FAPEMIG (Minas Gerais Research Agency) for supporting their research.

Part I

ABOUT SYSTEMS THINKING
IN MUSEUMS

This first part of the book introduces systems thinking as a theoretical concept and establishes museums as social ecosystems that are part of larger environmental systems. Therefore, the first two chapters in Part I provide broad theoretical and background perspectives for other chapters included in this book. This book includes ten parts, initiated with part introductions, the current part introduction being one of them, to provide more contextual information about each part by adding non-examples of systems-thinking–based museum practices and to introduce the two chapters in each part in depth. The non-examples are based on a fictional museum and will present contemporary problems many museums face today. This fictional museum, based on a real museum, is simply referred as *The Museum* and is located in a blue-collar community in a medium-sized city in the United States. The museum has about fifteen full-time staff members and its annual budget is around $3 million. It follows a traditional museum management paradigm that is top-down, rigid, and compartmentalized and relies on a lone director who is in charge of making most major decisions. It is also considered an elitist and isolated institution by most community members; it serves traditional museum audiences (white, wealthy, and well educated), focuses on academic knowledge without proper interpretation, and is considered an uncomfortable place for people with lower socioeconomic status. As a result, it does not provide services (e.g., exhibitions and programs) relevant to local people and culture. More detailed stories of this museum are placed in the remaining part introductions, illustrating its challenges and failures as connected to its traditional and hierarchical structure and methods, ultimately leading to paradigmatic changes described in the Part X introduction.

In chapter 1, which serves as an introduction to systems thinking and the entire book, the editors, Yuha Jung and Ann Rowson Love, discuss how they became

1

interested in this theoretical concept leading to the creation of this book, explain the theory in depth by including various theoretical views and scholars, and briefly describe characteristics of systems-thinking–based museum practices. This chapter also explains how the book is organized and introduces each chapter.

Neville Vakharia, author of chapter 2, provides a broader understanding of the museum field as an ecosystem using the concept of business ecosystem and network. In order to map the scope and size of the museum ecosystem in the United States, he created the Museum Universe Data File, comprehensive data sources on museums, expanding the limited definitions of a museum and providing more accurate and updated numbers and data on museums. To make this data file more useful to the field, he also created a web-based tool called MuseumStat that can provide additional community-based data around specific museums he identified in the Museum Universe Data File. By utilizing both (File and MuseumStat), museums can truly understand their role in the diverse communities that they serve and understand.

1

Systems Thinking and Museum Ecosystem

Yuha Jung and Ann Rowson Love

This book is a collaborative effort among the two editors, Yuha Jung and Ann Rowson Love, and many authors and museums from different parts of the world to demonstrate how systems thinking works in museum practices. It includes diverse perspectives and ideas from nineteen different groups of authors (including the editors) who are scholars, consultants, educators, museum practitioners, and graduate students. The premise of *systems thinking*, or systems theory, can be summed up in this simple phrase: *the whole is bigger than the sum of its parts.* Systems thinking sees the world as open and interconnected to and interdependent with all parts of the world; the parts are situated in context, shaping the whole, which is better understood by examining dynamic interrelationships among its parts.[1] Our premise is that museums will be better off when they operate as open, dynamic, and learning systems as a whole as opposed to closed, stagnant, and status quo systems that are compartmentalized and hierarchical. In systems thinking, the word *system* is not used to mean a machine (e.g., computer system) or controlled mechanism (e.g., government system) although it may trigger some people to think about a system in a narrow sense.[2] Rather, it refers to a complex, interdependent, and open web of things, people, and relationships that reside within the larger social, cultural, and natural environment that is continually in a state of flux.[3] While the concept of systems thinking is quite simple, applying it to day-to-day museum operations and management widely takes a different mindset and creates challenges along with new opportunities, some of which are demonstrated in this book.

We have three overall goals for this book. First, we introduce the concept of systems thinking as applied to the field of museums, geared toward practitioners, researchers, and students. Second, we elaborate on the practical implication of this new paradigm using real-life museum examples to illuminate various entry points of implementation. Third, we suggest ways to apply systems thinking to museum work with hopes that more museums would employ systems thinking to become more relevant and sustainable.

Although there are discussions of systems thinking in the museum field,[4] they tend to be theoretical and their applicability in real-life settings is relatively absent. An extensive literature review found that few professionals and scholars discuss systems thinking in the museum context. One of these, Darren Peacock, presents systems thinking as an organizational metaphor in the museum setting that helps understand the complex, emergent, and chaotic nature of changes that are not only happening within the organization but outside it.[5] Therefore, having a holistic and comprehensive organizational theory in museums becomes critical for them to be effective internally and socially relevant in the external environment. Perhaps the most comprehensive example of systems thinking applied to a museum context is demonstrated in Robert Janes' book *Museums and the Paradox of Change*, an in-depth case study of the transformation of the Glenbow Museum.[6] It is a seminal work in museum management that recorded how this specific museum was able to change based on a learning organizational model as well as the collective leadership that encouraged empowerment and continuous learning, despite the chaotic nature of change.[7] Like the Glenbow Museum, more museums and professionals are moving toward practices that are aligned with systems thinking such as soft and organic management and organizational models that value networks of ideas rather than traditional hierarchies and compartmentalization.[8] The concept of the *mindful museum* advocated by Robert Janes urges museums to be more focused on their communities and interconnection among departments and its audiences, suggesting that new ways of managing and organizing museums should be in the forefront when museums want to be relevant to the changing needs and interests of audiences.[9]

This book seeks to encourage these new ways of managing and organizing museums by helping fill the gap between theory and practice and act as a resource for implementation. It contributes to that new paradigm shift based on systems thinking and provides insights and best practices for museums to critically think about their current practice and contextualize and revise it to meet their specific museum and community's needs.

Below, we discuss how we became interested in this theory leading to conceptualization of this book and go in depth to explain systems thinking, including theorists and scholars who influenced our understanding of it and describing what systems-thinking–based museum practices would look like. Lastly, we will explain the organization of the book and briefly introduce each chapter.

JOURNEYS THROUGH SYSTEMS THINKING

In this section, we share our independent journeys through systems thinking during our doctoral studies, then the collaborative journey that led to the conceptualization of this book.

Yuha Jung's Journey

I stumbled into systems thinking while exploring theoretical frameworks for my doctoral dissertation in museum education and management at Penn State.[10] My mentor Charles Garoian[11] recommended I read the book *Steps to an Ecology of Mind* by Gregory Bateson,[12] a well-known systems theorist and cyberneticist. This book helped me understand that almost everything is an open system made up of network of interactions and things, and the human mind works the same way. Bateson showed how this thinking can be applied to many different disciplines such as sociology and organizational studies.

My understanding of systems thinking applied to organizations became clearer when I was given the book *The Fifth Discipline*[13] by my former mentor, David Ebitz,[14] whom I respected deeply. When we think about organizations that are run by people and are part of a larger environment, it makes sense that a museum is a system that is open and is influenced by its actions internally and externally. I felt that museums should be viewed as open interconnected systems and encouraged to be learning entities.[15] Yet, museum literature in general does not include or utilize organizational research and behavior; thus there was a niche for me to connect the obvious dots. I eventually applied systems thinking as a theoretical framework for my dissertation in examining an art museum in the midwestern United States. This museum followed what I would consider a traditional museum structure where all departments were separately getting their own work done rather than working as a team to produce cohesive management, exhibitions, and programs. This structure led the museum's workplace culture to be siloed and non-collaborative and hindered the museum from paying attention to what the community wanted from the museum experience. Instead the museum decided what it thought the community needed and wanted.

In my study and subsequent publications[16] the museum staff acknowledged the benefits of teamwork and community partnerships, to name two examples of a systems approach, but could not fully operationalize it in the day-to-day practices. While there could be other influencing factors, I concluded that it happened because the museum was not a healthy, growing, and learning organization. The museum followed the tradition of what has been done and accepted as standard practice of the field rather than critically examining its environment and interconnectivity among its parts and with its community. Because of its closed nature, the museum attracted a certain group of people who tended to be white, wealthy, and well educated and was therefore deemed to be elitist among community members. This, in turn, reinforced the closed nature of the museum as it then increased focus on its existing constituencies; they already care about the museum and give time and money to it. It thereby solidified a closed system between the museum and that small portion of the community. In order to expand its interconnection to the wider community and suggest an alternative way to conceptualize museum management and structure that mimics an interconnected network, I explored the concept of *ecosystem* and how the museum, its departments and staff, its community, and its external environment coexist forming a web of life, as suggested by Capra.[17] After this study, I concluded that many museums, including this museum, needed an alternative organizational structure and workplace culture that value collaboration, communication with the larger community, and institutional learning in order to create a different reality where museums are seen as inclusive and relevant by many publics.

Ann Rowson Love's Journey

Like Yuha, I was first introduced to systems thinking during my doctoral studies in art education at Florida State University, where I also earned a program evaluation certificate. Prior to entering my doctoral program, I spent fifteen years working in art museums as a museum educator, curator, and administrator. For a few years, I also worked for a national arts education center as a professional development facilitator and curriculum specialist.[18] Based on my extensive museum experience and background in evaluation, I have seen some organizations repeating what they have always done, expecting to get different results, and felt that it was due to lack of transformative practice based on a new paradigm. Systems thinking aligns with my practice-based beliefs about organizational change—that co-learning, teamwork, shared leadership, and strategic community engagement enhanced organizational planning and change. Peter Senge's[19] ideas from the field of business management put a theoretical name, so to speak, to what I already believed museums could do as learning organizations.

When starting my initial dissertation research, my mentor and doctoral committee chair, Pat Villeneuve, who is also one of the chapter coauthors in this book (chapter 4), encouraged me to apply a framework that would help me better understand my research interest in curatorial collaboration during exhibition development. Although I was interested in Senge's work, I hoped to find an evaluative approach. My quest to find the best-fitting approach for my art museum and research ensued. Hallie Preskill and Rosalie Torres articulated a program evaluation approach holistically applied to organizations that considered themselves learning organizations.[20] Although they published *Evaluative Inquiry for Learning in Organizations* in 1999, I discovered the approach in 2007 as I was just starting to formulate my ideas for studying a curatorial team, where I was also a co-learner and facilitator. As a program evaluation approach, which nods to Senge's *Fifth Discipline*,[21] this was not a theoretical framework in and of itself, but more like an advanced organizer for planning organizational cultural change and applied learning based on collaboration. This is done by having teams work together and contribute their dialogues, reflections, and actions back to their organization in a continuous cycle of learning.

While working on my dissertation, I was also the founding director of graduate museum studies at a midwestern university based in an art museum, which allowed me to incorporate systems thinking into educating emerging museum professionals.[22] I wanted to see systems theory in practice to show students how theory moves into practice. After six years directing museum studies, I returned to Florida State to help start a new master's and doctoral program that blends museum education and visitor-centered exhibitions, the first of its kind in the United States and the only

PhD degree offered currently in museum studies. Working with Pat Villeneuve, we coined the term *edu-curator* to focus on the hybrid and interconnected functions of education and exhibitions.[23] Our notion of edu-curation is based on ecofeminist systems theory as articulated by Anne Stephens.[24] An ecofeminist systems approach focuses on inclusion of marginalized voices and promotes social action. We newly applied this systems theory to museums to be inclusive of the many voices of museum professionals in the edu-curation process.

Journey to the Book

We met at a museum conference in Istanbul, Turkey, in 2010, where we each presented research explorations into systems thinking in museums.[25] Our shared interests in systems thinking led to several years of discussion and collaboration. We continued to research and address systems thinking theories, yet noted that we have not seen very much in our expanding literature in museum studies pertaining to systems thinking in practice. We decided to create a book, bringing together both academics and professionals, to help fill that void and act as a resource to professionals, researchers, and students. Museum practitioners do not need to wait until they are taking graduate coursework to consider how theory influences practice, but that does often seem to be the opportunity for many of us to have the time to really think about it as demonstrated by our stories. This book would help many to be exposed to the new paradigm without taking an advanced theory class and allow them to apply these theories at their museums, leading to more inclusive, responsive, and connected museums.

UNDERSTANDING SYSTEMS THINKING

The authors in the book apply various systems theories to their museum practices. Although systems thinking is relatively new to museum studies, its application to research and human understanding of phenomena has been around for decades. With roots in the field of biology, systems thinking has been used and popularized in business administration and organizational theories in public and nonprofit sectors as articulated by Russell Ackoff, Jamshid Gharajedaghi, John Seddon, and Peter Senge, to name a few.[26] It was also heavily used and developed in the fields of information technologies, cybernetics, and engineering. Perhaps systems thinking, as we use it in this book, is best described as a worldview or a paradigm as defined by Ludwig von Bertalanffy[27] rather than a confined theory in a single discipline.

Von Bertalanffy[28] conceptualized general systems thinking in the 1930s and articulated it further throughout his career. In general systems thinking, the sum of its parts no longer represent the whole and these complex systems cannot be sufficiently understood as compartmentalized parts as assumed in the classical science tradition of reductionism.[29] "Reductionism generates knowledge and understanding of phenomena by breaking them down into constituent parts and then studying these simple elements in terms of cause and effect."[30] In order to sufficiently understand them, we have to see both the whole and any interconnections among its parts, while also attending to internal changes and what is happening externally. When we see museums through the lens of systems thinking, they are networked systems composed of many interconnected parts and their interrelationships define what they are—but the systems will look different from museum to museum because they are always contextual.

In the 1940s and 1950s, positivism influenced systems thinking. This scientific and quantitative tradition of systems thinking is called *hard systems thinking*, which is referred as the first wave of systems thinking.[31] Hard systems thinking assumes that there are systems to be discovered in the world and these existing systems sometimes do not work well. In these cases, hard systems thinking believes that non-working systems can be fixed with the right engineering.[32] Hard systems thinking is not synonymous to closed systems approach, however; hard systems thinking still understands a system as open, influencing and being influenced by its external environment. Closed system by its definition does not have a place in systems thinking; there is rarely a closed system in the world.

The second wave of systems thinking came in the 1970s and valued more interpretive, subjective, and participatory models.[33] The second wave of systems thinking challenged hierarchical power structures and focused on getting feedback from all involved parts and participants of systems.[34] Soft systems thinking represents this second wave of systems thinking and assumes that the world is "very complex, problematic, mysterious."[35] In order to understand the complexities and problems of the world, in soft systems thinking, the word *system* is applied to the process of understanding and solving problems.[36] As there is not a set or objective system of processes to address a problem, as it depends on the context, the process is described as a learning system.[37] Developed in the last two decades, the third wave of systems thinking is more critical and values marginalized voices as embodied in critical systems thinking and feminist systems thinking, focusing on social improvement, issues of oppression, and gender issues.[38]

While chapters in this book mostly utilize second- and third-wave systems thinking, hard systems thinking could be a useful conceptual tool in analyzing past social networks for financial opportunities as seen in Susan Mann's chapter (chapter 15). In addition, most chapters used systems thinking applied in business administration and organizational theories. For example, many chapters in this book used or are aligned with Senge's idea of systems thinking, looking at organizations and their processes as open and organic systems and embracing the idea of a learning organization "where people continually expand their capacity to create the results they truly desire, where new and expansive patterns of thinking are nurtured, where collective aspiration is set free, and where people are continually learning how to learn together."[39] A learning organization acknowledges that organizations are complex and interconnected and can be better managed with team-learning, shared vision, decentralization, and non-hierarchical structure.[40]

When museums are run based on the systems thinking paradigm, it encourages an organic and team-based network model to operate and manage museums as well as the sharing of ideas internally and externally with communities rather than focusing on compartmentalized and mechanical systems. This leads to more inclusive, responsive, and relevant practices in museums. In addition, hierarchies of people and departments, which are often rigid structures of dominance and control,[41] can be replaced with networks where all involved parties are equally valued and their input and perspectives are reflected in major decision-making processes. For example, an art museum does not exist in a vacuum; it is necessarily a part of the larger community in terms of economic, cultural, political, educational, and social systems.[42] Therefore, it tends to provide services and programs that are more visitor centered than solely museum centered; it includes the perspectives of visitors, trying to be a relevant and useful part of its larger community. The interconnection also exists within the museum. All people who work in the museum are interconnected and interdependent, and all departments coexist to meet the shared mission and vision of the museum. When these connections are ignored (i.e., seeing museums as closed systems) and not successfully utilized, a museum can be dysfunctional. This happens through not applying its resources toward a unified goal or ignoring its connection to the larger community and not maximizing various backgrounds and ideas from all involved individuals, and therefore becoming a less relevant organization or even elitist when seen by the public. A hierarchical or mechanical museum still exists within a larger social ecosystem and is itself a system, but not a healthy one. An unhealthy ecosystem can cause failure, even as extreme as permanent museum closure.

THE ORGANIZATION OF THE BOOK

In conceptualizing the book, we wanted to include museum-based practices that were initiated across museum functions. We organized the book based on many vantage points where museums can start applying systems thinking in their practices and eventually expand its application to the entire museum. The multiple vantage points include management structure and leadership, personnel management, communications, exhibitions and programs, community engagement, fundraising and financial sustainability, physical spaces, and future museum professional preparation. While we separate chapters into sections, we do not see these vantage points or management functions as independent; in reality they are all interconnected and inform each other. The book has a total of ten sections and each vantage point is organized into a section. Each section contains two chapters demonstrating how systems thinking is used in that specific area and affects other internal and external parts of the museum.

Sometimes non-examples are a poignant way to introduce ideas in a concrete manner. As a reader, it would be powerful to see a lost opportunity, even a failure, to think about possibilities and strategies for success.[43] Thus we decided to introduce each section with case study vignettes, written by Yuha, showing a fictional museum less successfully trying to address some of the contemporary issues facing museums. It will sound familiar to a lot of readers, especially as it is based on a real museum. This fictional museum represents the compartmentalized, hierarchical, and controlled museum management system and structure. This is also a non-example of a learning organization. This museum will simply be called *The Museum* in each section introduction.

We also included a practical reflection for taking action at the end of each section, written by Ann, where museum teams or students could take on a set of activities. As a professional museum development facilitator and career-long educator, Ann has long been attracted to providing opportunities to interrupt reading with reflective and active participation, trying out ideas with others. Based on the chapters in each section, she will summarize the zest of each chapter and suggest reflective and practical questions and action steps, providing action-based opportunities to think through practices and challenges. Co-learning and team-based reflection challenges readers to be active rather than passive.

SECTION AND CHAPTER INTRODUCTIONS

This chapter begins Part I, where we introduce characteristics and various understandings of systems thinking. Chapter 2, written by Neville Vakharia, is also part of this section; it provides a broader conceptualization of the museum field as an ecosystem. Using the concept of business ecosystem, Vakharia considers broad implications of museum external communities and shows how the field of museums is like a network and how this network is also part of the larger social ecosystem. He maps the scope and number of museums and provides a tool (MuseumStat) for understanding local communities for more relevant services.

In Part II, we paired two chapters that provide strong perspectives about systems thinking as a theory moving toward practice. Victoria Eudy, doctoral student and author of chapter 3, presents the perspective of an emerging professional grappling with making sense of systems thinking in her career. She presents systems thinking in a lively, yet no-nonsense approach using popular culture metaphors such as Dr. Seuss and the Beatles to illustrate key concepts and application of the theory in her own research. In chapter 4, Pat Villeneuve and Juyeon Song introduce the path leading to paradigm change in museum practices. They apply Checkland's soft systems methodology to suggest possibilities to plan for changes in museums.

Then we enter the individual museum functional areas. In Part III, we focus on management structure and leadership. Randi Korn in chapter 5 emphasizes intentional and reflective practice in museum management, planning, evaluating, reflecting, and aligning museum work to achieve intentional impact on its audience and adopting an attitude of a learning organization that continuously reflects on and improves its work. In chapter 6, Patrick Greene, Paul Bowers, and Kathy Fox from Museums Victoria, a large-scale complex of national museums of Australia, discuss their networked museum approach to leadership and management structure and resultant organizational culture that values collective vision, mutual trust, delegated leadership, and empowered teams.

Part IV discusses how museums can apply systems thinking in personnel development and training and eventually affecting the whole museum change. In chapter 7, Amy Gilman and Lynn Miller talk about how the Toledo Museum of Art in Toledo, Ohio, adopted a systems thinking approach to enterprise risk management and talent management to develop more engaged staff and sustainable organization. Douglas Worts discusses in chapter 8 how he facilitated a sustainability workshop at the Georgia O'Keefe Museum in Santa Fe, New Mexico, fostering the museum's cultural relevance to its surrounding communities.

In Part V, two different systems thinking approaches are applied to exhibition development; both blend the roles of curatorial and education, while embracing community. Caroline Angel Burke and Monica Parker-James in chapter 9 apply a team-based approach to large-scale exhibition development at science centers, the Museum of Science, Boston, and the Edward M. Kennedy Institute for the Senate, also located in Boston. In chapter 10, Cora Fisher and Deborah Randolph explain how they used Buckminster Fuller's systems approach in developing socially inclusive and collective art exhibition and community engagement programs at the Southeastern Center for Contemporary Art in Winston-Salem, North Carolina.

Part VI focuses on systems thinking approaches applied to museum communications with the external constituencies. Jonathan Paquette and Robin Nelson, in chapter 11, consider how museums use social media to communicate with their communities when their physical spaces are closed temporarily for various reasons (e.g., remodeling). Using the concept of an open system and Deleuze and Guattari's idea of de-territorialization, the authors analyze seven different case museums' social media marketing campaigns and conclude that these strategies are used for communicating institutional change and transformation, shaping communities' perception of the museums. In chapter 12, Ana Flávia Machado, Diomira M. C. P. Faria, Sibelle C. Diniz, Bárbara F. Paglioto, Rodrigo C. Michel, and Gabriel Vaz de Melo share their study of a cultural complex in Brazil, Circuito Liberdade (CL). In order to find out how visitors and non-visitors value CL and then to incorporate their feedback in improving CL's management and programs, the authors completed visitor and non-visitor studies. They suggest that regularly conducting these studies, knowing visitors and non-visitors and their cultural habits, and incorporating these findings back into practice can help the cultural institutions to be learning organizations that constantly learn and improve.

Part VII shares how museums can use systems thinking based strategies in engaging with their communities in a profound and meaningful manner. Chapter 13, written by Guido Ferilli, Sendy Ghirardi, and Pier Luigi Sacco, suggests that museums adopt a year-round community engagement practice to become a cultural hub and asset for local communities in addressing local cultural and social issues. They share two successful examples of museum community engagement in the Israel Museum of Jerusalem in Israel and the Castello di Rivoli in Turin, Italy, and further analyze these cases using the *action workflow* model, interpreting the museums' participatory processes as a homeostatic interaction that generates intangible assets. Swarupa Anila, Amy Hamilton Foley, and Nii Quarcoopome share the process of engaging community in Asian permanent collection reinstallation at the Detroit Institute of Arts (DIA) in chapter 14. The process was team based and visitor centered, actually involving community members as paid consultants in rethinking and designing the reinstallation process at the DIA.

In Part VIII, we pair two authors, in discussing how systems thinking is used in fundraising and financial sustainability, one about a museum that closed its doors for good due to missed opportunities for funding and supportive connections and another examining an internationally successful museum model. Susan Mann in chapter 15 uses a hard systems thinking approach of game theory to examine the lost opportunities for expanding fundraising connections and community resources when a museum is a closed system. In chapter 16, Natalia Grincheva analyzes a successful global model of the Guggenheim Foundation in seeing it as an open, networked system with its many branches in the world and utilizing external museum environment, especially economy and neoliberal tendency for fundraising. By closely examining the Bilbao branch, she demonstrates how external environment affects museum fundraising and how museums in turn affect their local economy.

In Part IX, we explore how systems thinking contributes to rethinking physical museum spaces. Ann Rowson Love and Morgan Szymanski wrote chapter 17, exploring the changing concepts of spaces in museums. They juxtapose the applicability of the *third eye* (quiet spaces for contemplation) with the *third place* (active spaces of community) in museum spaces and discuss how traits of third places are connected to feminist systems thinking, which they apply to reconceptualize museum spaces for inclusion and social change. They use two examples to demonstrate how their adopted feminist systems thinking (with third places principles) can be applied to museum spaces, the Tate Exchange at the Tate Modern in London and the Target Studio for Creative Collaboration at the Weisman Art Museum in Minnesota. In chapter 18, Tom Duncan applies systems thinking to illustrate visitor experience as a system that can be enriched through including their perspectives in the redesigning process of Vischering Castle, a heritage site in Muensterland in Germany. As an architect and consultant to the remodeling process, he performed a series of innovative workshops with the project team and volunteer tour guides at the site that engaged workshop participants in thinking through the lens of visitors, using strategies of emotional mapping of visitors over time and role playing.

Part X is the conclusion of the book and contains two chapters. Chapter 19, written by Kiersten F. Latham and John E. Simmons, discusses the theory of systems thinking, in both content and pedagogical approaches, applied to teaching museums studies, a concentration in the School of Library and Information Science at Kent State University in the United States. The program is designed to help students gain a holistic understanding of museums as systems and their context in society. This approach helps educate future museum professionals and scholars to be systems thinkers who understand museums as open systems and can lead to heathier museums. Chapter 20, written by Yuha Jung, concludes the book and summarizes the concepts and ideas of systems thinking collectively utilized in chapters and explores possibilities for future museum practice, training, and research.

Systems thinking reflects the changing and underlying theoretical approaches to everyday museum practice from shared leadership, to networked structure, to team-based staff interaction, to in-depth community engagement, and more. This book provides an entry for exploring theory in action, while at the same time offering tools for effecting change in museums. We hope that this new paradigm for museums leads to alternative organizational structures and workplace cultures, thereby generating impactful results for these museums and their communities, envisioned as inclusive, responsive, sustainable, and learning museums.

BIBLIOGRAPHY

Ackoff, Russell L. *Systems Thinking for Curious Managers: With 40 New Management F-Laws.* Axminster, UK: Triarchy, 2010.

Bateson, Gregory. *Steps to an Ecology of Mind.* Chicago: University of Chicago Press, 2000.

Bergeron, Anne, and Beth Tuttle. *Magnetic: The Art and Science of Engagement.* Washington, DC: American Alliance of Museums, 2013.

Capra, Fritjof. *The Web of Life: A New Scientific Understanding of Living Systems.* New York: Anchor, 1996.

Checkland, Peter. "Soft Systems Methodology: A Thirty Year Retrospective." *Systems Research and Behavioral Science* 17, no. S1 (2000): 11–58.

Flood, Robert Louis. "The Relationship of 'Systems Thinking' to Action Research." *Systemic Practice and Action Research* 23, no. 4 (2010): 269–84.

Fopp, Michael A. *Managing Museums and Galleries.* London: Routledge, 1997.

Gharajedaghi, Jamshid. *Systems Thinking: Managing Chaos and Complexity: A Platform for Designing Business Architecture.* Burlington, MA: Morgan Kaufmann, 2011.

Helgesen, Sally. *The Web of Inclusion: A New Architecture for Building Great Organizations.* New York: Doubleday, 1995.

Janes, Robert R. "The Mindful Museum." *Curator* 53, no. 3 (2010): 325–38.

———. *Museums in a Troubled World: Renewal, Irrelevance or Collapse?* Abingdon, UK: Routledge, 2009.

Jung, Yuha. "The Art Museum Ecosystem: A New Alternative Model." *Museum Management and Curatorship* 26, no. 4 (2011): 321–38.

———. "Building Strong Bridges Between the Museum and Its Community: An Ethnographic Understanding of the Culture and Systems of One Community's Art Museum." *International Journal of the Inclusive Museum* 6, no. 3 (2014): 1–11.

———. "Micro Examination of Museum Workplace Culture: How Institutional Changes Influence the Culture of a Real-World Art Museum." *Museum Management and Curatorship* 31, no. 2 (2016): 159–77.

Latham, Kiersten F., and John E. Simmons. *Foundations of Museum Studies: Evolving Systems of Knowledge*. Santa Barbara, CA: Libraries Unlimited, 2014.

Lencioni, Patrick. *The Five Dysfunctions of a Team: A Leadership Fable*. San Francisco: Jossey-Bass, 2002.

Lord, Gail, and Ngaire Blankenberg. *Cities, Museums, and Soft Power*. Washington, DC: American Alliance of Museums, 2015.

Meadows, Donella, *Thinking in Systems: A Primer* (White River Junction, VT: Chelsea Green, 2008).

Moore, Kevin. "Introduction: Museum Management." In *Museum Management*, edited by Kevin Moore, 1–14. London: Routledge, 1994.

Peacock, Darren. "Making Ways for Change: Museums, Disruptive Technologies and Organisational Change." *Museum Management and Curatorship* 23, no. 4 (2008): 333–351.

Preskill, Hallie, and Rosalie Torres. *Evaluative Inquiry for Learning in Organizations*. Thousand Oaks, CA: Sage, 1999.

Seddon, John. *Systems Thinking in the Public Sector: The Failure of the Reform Regime and a Manifesto for a Better Way*. Axminster, UK: Triarchy, 2008.

Senge, Peter. "Being Better in the World of Systems." Speech at the 30th Anniversary Seminar of the Systems Analysis Laboratory, Aalto University, Finland, November 2014, https://www.youtube.com/watch?v=0QtQqZ6Q5-o.

———. *The Fifth Discipline: The Art and Practice of the Learning Organization*. New York: Doubleday, 1990.

Stephens, Anne. *Ecofeminism and Systems Thinking*. New York: Routledge, 2013.

Stephens, Anne, Chris Jacobson, and Christine King. "Towards a Feminist-Systems Theory." *Systemic Practice and Action Research* 23, no. 5 (2010): 371–86.

Villeneuve, Pat, and Ann Rowson Love. *Visitor-Centered Exhibitions and Edu-Curation in Art Museums*. Lanham, MD: Rowman & Littlefield, 2017.

Von Bertalanffy, Ludwig. "The History and Status of General Systems Theory." *Academy of Management Journal* 15, no. 4 (1972): 23–29.

———. *Modern Theories of Development: An Introduction to Theoretical Biology*. Oxford: Oxford University Press, 1933.

NOTES

1. Fritjof Capra, *The Web of Life: A New Scientific Understanding of Living Systems* (New York: Anchor, 1996); Gregory Bateson, *Steps to an Ecology of Mind* (Chicago: University of Chicago Press, 2000); Donella Meadows, *Thinking in Systems: A Primer* (White River Junction, VT: Chelsea Green, 2008); Peter Senge, *The Fifth Discipline: The Art and Practice of the Learning Organization* (New York: Doubleday, 1990).

2. Peter Checkland, "Soft Systems Methodology: A Thirty Year Retrospective," *Systems Research and Behavioral Science* 17, no. S1 (2000): 11–58.

3. Peter Senge, "Being Better in the World of Systems," speech at the 30th Anniversary Seminar of the Systems Analysis Laboratory, Aalto University, Finland, November 2014, https://www.youtube.com/watch?v=0QtQqZ6Q5-o; Sally Helgesen, *The Web of Inclusion: A New Architecture for Building Great Organizations* (New York: Doubleday, 1995).

4. Michael A. Fopp, *Managing Museums and Galleries* (London: Routledge, 1997); Yuha Jung, "The Art Museum Ecosystem: A New Alternative Model," *Museum Management and Curatorship* 26, no. 4 (2011): 321–38; Kiersten F. Latham and John E. Simmons, *Foundations of Museum Studies: Evolving Systems of Knowledge* (Santa Barbara, CA: Libraries Unlimited, 2014); Peacock, Darren, "Making Ways for Change: Museums, Disruptive Technologies and Organisational Change," *Museum Management and Curatorship* 23, no. 4 (2008): 333–351.

5. Peacock, "Making Ways for Change."

6. Janes, Robert R., *Museums and the Paradox of Change* (Abingdon, UK: Routledge, 2013).

7. Ibid.

8. Anne Bergeron and Beth Tuttle, *Magnetic: The Art and Science of Engagement* (Washington, DC: American Alliance of Museums, 2013); Robert R. Janes, *Museums in a Troubled World: Renewal, Irrelevance or Collapse?* (Abingdon, UK: Routledge, 2009); Gail Lord and Ngaire Blankenberg, *Cities, Museums, and Soft Power* (Washington, DC: American Alliance of Museums, 2015); Kevin Moore, "Introduction: Museum Management," in *Museum Management,* ed. Kevin Moore (London: Routledge, 1994), 1–14.

9. Robert R. Janes, "The Mindful Museum," *Curator* 53, no. 3 (2010): 325–38.

10. Yuha Jung's terminal degree is in art education but she specialized in art museum education and management.

11. Charles Garoian is professor of art education in the School of Visual Arts at Penn State.

12. Bateson, *Steps to an Ecology of Mind.*

13. Senge, *Fifth Discipline.*

14. As former head of education at the J. Paul Getty Museum and director of the John and Mable Ringling Museum of Art, David Ebitz was associate professor of art in the School of Visual Studies at Penn State when Yuha Jung met him. He helped shape Jung's research in tremendous ways and she can't thank him enough.

15. Senge, *Fifth Discipline.*

16. Jung, "The Art Museum Ecosystem"; Yuha Jung, "Building Strong Bridges Between the Museum and Its Community: An Ethnographic Understanding of the Culture and Systems of One Community's Art Museum," *International Journal of the Inclusive Museum* 6, no. 3 (2014): 1–11; Yuha Jung, "Micro Examination of Museum Workplace Culture: How Institutional Changes Influence the Culture of a Real-World Art Museum," *Museum Management and Curatorship* 31, no. 2 (2016): 159–77.

17. Capra, *Web of Life.*

18. During her twenty-five-year career, Ann has worked in small, mid-sized, and large art museums in the midwestern and southeastern United States including the Spencer Museum of Art, University of Kansas; the Morris Museum of Art in Augusta, Georgia; the Nelson-Atkins Museum of Art in Kansas City; and the Ogden Museum of Southern Art in New Orleans. She also directed the visual arts institute at the Southeast Center for Education in the Arts at University of Tennessee–Chattanooga.

19. Senge, *Fifth Discipline.*

20. Hallie Preskill and Rosalie Torres, *Evaluative Inquiry for Learning in Organizations* (Thousand Oaks, CA: Sage, 1999).

21. Senge, *Fifth Discipline.*

22. Ann was the founding director of graduate museum studies at Western Illinois University–Quad Cities from 2008 to 2014. The program is based at the Figge Art Museum in Davenport, Iowa.

23. Pat Villeneuve and Ann Rowson Love, *Visitor-Centered Exhibitions and Edu-Curation in Art Museums* (New York: Rowman & Littlefield, 2017).

24. Anne Stephens, *Ecofeminism and Systems Thinking* (New York: Routledge, 2013).

25. The editors first met at the International Conference of the Inclusive Museum in Istanbul, Turkey.

26. Russell L. Ackoff, *Systems Thinking for Curious Managers: With 40 New Management F-Laws* (Axminster, UK: Triarchy, 2010); Jamshid Gharajedaghi, *Systems Thinking: Managing Chaos and Complexity: A Platform for Designing Business Architecture* (Burlington, MA: Morgan Kaufmann, 2011); John Seddon, *Systems Thinking in The Public Sector: The Failure of the Reform Regime and a Manifesto for a Better Way* (Axminster, UK: Triarchy, 2008); Senge, *Fifth Discipline*.

27. Ludwig von Bertalanffy, "The History and Status of General Systems Theory," *Academy of Management Journal* 15, no. 4 (1972): 23–29.

28. Ludwig von Bertalanffy, *Modern Theories of Development: An Introduction to Theoretical Biology* (Oxford: Oxford University Press, 1933); Von Bertalanffy, "General Systems Theory."

29. Von Bertalanffy, "General Systems Theory."

30. Robert Louis Flood, "The Relationship of 'Systems Thinking' to Action Research," *Systemic Practice and Action Research* 23, no. 4 (2010): 269.

31. Anne Stephens, Chris Jacobson, and Christine King, "Towards a Feminist-Systems Theory," *Systemic Practice and Action Research* 23, no. 5 (2010): 371–86.

32. Checkland, "Soft Systems Methodology."

33. Stephens, Jacobson, and King, "Towards a Feminist-Systems Theory."

34. Ibid.

35. Checkland, "Soft Systems Methodology," 17.

36. Ibid.

37. Ibid.

38. Stephens, Jacobson, and King, "Towards a Feminist-Systems Theory."

39. Senge, *Fifth Discipline*, 3.

40. Ibid.

41. Capra, *Web of Life*.

42. Jung, "The Art Museum Ecosystem"; Jung, "Building Strong Bridges."

43. Patrick Lencioni, *The Five Dysfunctions of a Team: A Leadership Fable* (San Francisco: Jossey-Bass, 2002). This book is good example of a business leadership story told through powerful non-examples.

2

Mapping the Museum Universe

A Systems Approach

Neville K. Vakharia

Museums exist to serve multiple purposes and constituencies, playing a crucial role in education, research, community engagement, and economic development. Museums also need to adapt to their current environments, ensuring that they remain relevant and sustainable to multiple stakeholders. How can museums better understand their role as part of an organizational ecosystem within their own communities and nationally? How can museum leaders understand evolving needs of those they seek to serve? This chapter will outline how a research-driven and systematic approach led to a better understanding of the museum ecosystem in the United States as well as the development of powerful tools to help museum leaders, researchers, and advocates understand community needs and assets.[1]

Using the frameworks of systems thinking and business ecosystems, it is vital that museums understand how they fit into a broader group of stakeholders that collaborate and compete to satisfy customer needs and remain innovative. If museums are to truly be "learning organizations" that can use systems thinking to find the interrelationships among those inside and outside the institution, they must be able to leverage data and information to create institutional knowledge.[2] Going further, museums should strive to be "knowledge-centric organizations," whereby people, departments, and programs use collective knowledge to advance organizational goals.[3] A knowledge-centric organization creates a culture of learning and views knowledge as an institutional asset. Knowledge-centric organizations are able to gather and leverage disparate sources of data and information to create knowledge, and knowledge creation is a core value. More importantly, organizations that prioritize the acquisition and use of knowledge gain a competitive edge through increased levels of innovation and effectiveness as well as the ability to respond more quickly to changes in the environment.[4]

Museums must also be able to view themselves as part of a business ecosystem, a group of interacting organizations and individuals that continuously coevolve to align themselves with the needs of their constituents.[5] Using the biological metaphor of an ecosystem, museums need to have a symbiotic relationship with the communities in which they operate and create effective programs and services for those they intend to serve. This requires insights and knowledge on the individuals and communities around them as a means to be a participant in a healthy ecosystem.

While these systems-based approaches are common in the business and public sectors, there is a need for increased study of this approach within the museum sector. This need can begin to be addressed by improving the current lack of comprehensive data sources on museums combined with broadening the limited definitions of a museum. Without reliable information on the scope and reach of museums, the museum sector is unable to demonstrate its collective impact, advocate for its needs, and truly understand its role in the diverse communities it serves.

DEFINING THE SCOPE OF THE MUSEUM UNIVERSE

Prior to the start of this research effort in 2014, there was no comprehensive data source on all museums in the United States; existing sources were either incomplete or very specialized. A key reason for this lack of comprehensive data is the lack of an inclusive and flexible definition of a museum. The definition of a museum varies significantly based on the entity that is defining it, with most definitions being restrictive rather than broadly accommodating. The Museum and Library Services Act (MLA), enacted by the United States Congress in 1996, defined a museum specifically as "a public or private nonprofit agency or institution organized on a permanent basis for essentially educational or aesthetic purposes, that utilizes a professional staff, owns or utilizes tangible objects, cares for the tangible objects, and exhibits the tangible objects to the public on a regular basis."[6] While this definition provides clarity on the organizational structure of a museum, it self-imposes limitations on the type of organization and the specific manner in which a museum operates. Because the MLA sought to improve how museums and libraries received federal funds and services, this specific definition may be suitable. However, it is clear that there are many museums that fall outside of this definition. On a global scale, the International Council of Museums, an international service organization that provides professional standards, programs, and resources to museums and museum leaders in more than 100 countries, defines a museum somewhat similarly to the MLA, as "a non-profit, permanent institution in the service of society and its development, open to the public, which acquires, conserves, researches, communicates and exhibits the tangible and intangible heritage of humanity and its environment for the purposes of education, study and enjoyment."[7] Again, this self-limiting definition neglects to include a large number of museums throughout the world.

Using rigid definitions of a museum, such as the examples above, to create a data source of all museums in the United States would only continue to propagate the exclusion of many museums throughout the country that provide valuable education and enjoyment experiences to their visitors and communities. Limiting museums to only those that are nonprofit institutions does a disservice to museums that are incorporated through other business structures, including many major institutions as well as novel, idiosyncratic entities that serve niche audiences. A museum definition that requires a museum to utilize a "professional staff" dismisses many vernacular museums that were created by those without professional training, but who instead have a deep knowledge of the culture and traditions they preserve. The use of the term "permanent institution" is both limiting and vague, imposing potentially un-realistic standards on a museum. Using these restricted definitions would eliminate from consideration institutions such as the City Museum in St. Louis, Missouri; the Harley-Davidson Museum in Milwaukee, Wisconsin; the Oz Museum in Wamego, Kansas; and many other unique, vibrant, and esoteric entities that play an important role in their communities.

To avoid the limitations of existing definitions, this research effort defined the museum universe as the broadest range of museum-related organizations and entities that incorporate one or more elements of exhibition, education, collections, research, and public access. Using this broad-based definition of the museum universe, two phases of research and development efforts were undertaken. The first phase sought to gather and compile all relevant and current sources on museum data to assess the total population, location, and category of museums, creating the first-ever compre-hensive source of all museum entities in the United States. The second phase sought to develop a geographic information system (GIS)-based, online tool that would utilize this new data and incorporate important community metrics (e.g., individual- and household-level demographics including income, education, race/ethnicity, and others), providing museum leaders, researchers, and advocates with easily accessible information to better understand their communities, inform their programming, and assess their place within the museum ecosystem locally and nationally.

PHASE 1: DATA GATHERING AND CREATING THE MUSEUM UNIVERSE DATA FILE

Data on museums in the United States were gathered from a variety of public and proprietary sources to ensure the widest possible universe of data from which to work. This would also ensure that the data gathered complied with the broad defini-tion of the museum universe.

A range of public data sources was compiled and analyzed, beginning with the In-ternal Revenue Service's (IRS's) Business Master File of data on nonprofit museums as identified by its National Taxonomy of Exempt Entities code.[8] This broad set of data included the full range of museums including art museums, history museums and societies, botanical gardens and arboreta, zoos, children's museums, and science museums. Added to this were data on any museum that had received funding from the Institute of Museum and Library Services (IMLS), which IMLS provides as a public data source. This data was used to cross-validate and supplement the IRS data.

Added to these public sources of data were data acquired from the Foundation Center's database of grants to museums by a group of 1,000 independent and corporate grantmaking foundations, including donor-advised funds and community foundations. A variety of museum-specific membership organizations, such as the International Planetarium Society and the American Public Gardens Association, provided data on their constituents to further expand the list of museums. In order to gather data on a large number of museums that are part of academic institutions, which would not be gathered through any other means, data from the Integrated Postsecondary Education Data System (IPEDS) was acquired, identifying approximately 2,700 museums and museum-related entities within academic institutions that were previously not identified.

To truly create a database of our broadly defined museum universe, it was critical to find museums that were not solely incorporated as nonprofit organizations and those that would not appear in publicly available data sources. To do this, data were acquired from a commercial data aggregator that maintains a database of more than twenty-one million local businesses and places of interest in the United States. This data is aggregated and procured from multiple sources including third-party contributions and volunteered geographic information (via social media and other outlets), and is run through a proprietary machine-learning process that cleans, categorizes, and resolves locations for each place of interest. This data source added thousands of records that were not part of any other data source, essentially identifying a wide range of undercounted museums.

Compiling all of the data from these multiple sources created a very large and cumbersome database with multiple duplicates and a large number of irrelevant records. While some of the data could be cleaned in an automatic manner, a team of research assistants reviewed each record using a specified protocol, identifying any records that did not comply with the broad museum universe definition or those that appeared to be no longer in existence.

The initial data gathering and cleaning effort was completed in the summer of 2015; it determined that there were 33,072 museums in the United States, almost doubling any previous estimate. While this figure will continue to be revised on a regular basis, it represents a more meaningful count of the museum ecosystem in the United States. This data can now be analyzed by location, museum type, and other related measures to better understand the range and scope of museums in the country. Known as the Museum Universe Data File, the data are now publicly accessible via the Institute for Museum and Library Services (IMLS) data catalog.[9] This figure is now being cited by IMLS, the American Alliance of Museums, and others as the full count of museums in the United States. Plans are being developed to determine a way to update the file on an annual basis.

PHASE 2: TECHNOLOGY DEVELOPMENT
AND CREATING MUSEUMSTAT

While a first-ever comprehensive database of museums is a vital resource, in order for it to be truly beneficial to the field, it must be easily accessible and incorporate additional community-based data as context. To understand how such a database and other community metrics could most benefit museum leaders, researchers, and advocates, a series of ten stakeholder interviews were conducted with senior leadership from museums, museum service organizations, academic museum studies programs, and museum technologists. These semi-structured interviews identified a range of challenges faced in the museum sector when attempting to use data and information to inform decision making. Museum leaders were seeking easy-to-use tools that would provide data on their communities and constituents to inform their programs and services and to cultivate new visitors. Museum service organizations were seeking aggregate data on their members and the overall scope of the museum field. Museum advocates and researchers were seeking ways to quickly identify and visualize important measures of museums and communities within specific geographic areas. All stakeholders interviewed cited a clear need for more data and information tools that could improve their decision making and strategies.

To address the clear needs identified by the museum stakeholders, a software development project was initiated in the fall of 2015 to create a GIS-based online mapping tool to visualize the Museum Universe Data File and incorporate information on important community metrics and demographics on individuals and households. Data on community metrics and demographics would be accessed from the American Community Survey of the United States Census Bureau. Unlike the decennial census, the American Community Survey is an ongoing, annual survey that gathers vital information about people and households in all 65,443 census tracts in the United States.

The online software tool was designed so that museums and their locations would appear as points on a map, with a range of individual and household metrics visualized onscreen. The types of individual and household metrics are shown in table 2.1.

Additionally, the software can show shaded gradients (called choropleths) on the map to visualize the ranges of median household income, families in poverty, adults with no high school diploma, and children with disabilities. These were determined by stakeholders as important measures of community health that could inform the programs and services offered by a museum.

The resulting online software, called MuseumStat,[10] is a free, publicly accessible tool that serves as a powerful means for museum leaders to see their museum as part of an organizational ecosystem as well as understand the communities around them. The power of this tool is that it requires no technical expertise and provides immediate access to information that is actionable and relevant to the museum field. Museum leaders can use this tool to inform their programming and outreach efforts, understand demographic indicators to seek new donor bases, and view their location

Table 2.1. Individual and Household Metrics Provided by MuseumStat

Individual Metrics (for selected area)	Household Metrics (for selected area)
Total population	Total number of households
Total population 18 years and under	Median household income
Total population in poverty	Median home value
Race	Year moved in (owners and renters)
Gender	Household type (family or non-family)
Median age	Languages spoken at home
Employment status	
Per capita income	

Source: Author.

within context of other museums. Researchers and advocates can use the tool to assess the overall scope and reach of museums in a region or nationally, making the case for the important role that museums play. Figures 2.1, 2.2, and 2.3 show some examples of the many types of data visualizations and information provided through MuseumStat.

USING MUSEUMSTAT

MuseumStat is now a free, publicly available web tool, accessible through any major web browser. Users can easily use this tool by visiting the "Getting Started" link, or simply by entering a museum name, city, or zip code into the search bar. When searching for a museum, users can immediately see the museum on a map, with all of the individual and household data visualized below. When searching for a city or a zip code, a map will be displayed showing all the museums within the city or zip code. On all maps, users can add demographic layers, view individual and household data for custom geographies (by drawing a boundary on the map or selecting a specific radius), and expand the map view to explore the interface. For more in-depth research needs, data on the museums in selected geographies or the entire Museum Universe Data File can be downloaded for offline analysis.

CONCLUSION

In a fast-paced, knowledge-driven society, museums must be able to rapidly understand their evolving roles within their communities. Taking a systems approach and understanding the business ecosystem in which they operate are critical to their sustainability and relevance. A knowledge-centric museum can leverage data and information to create new knowledge and use that knowledge strategically.

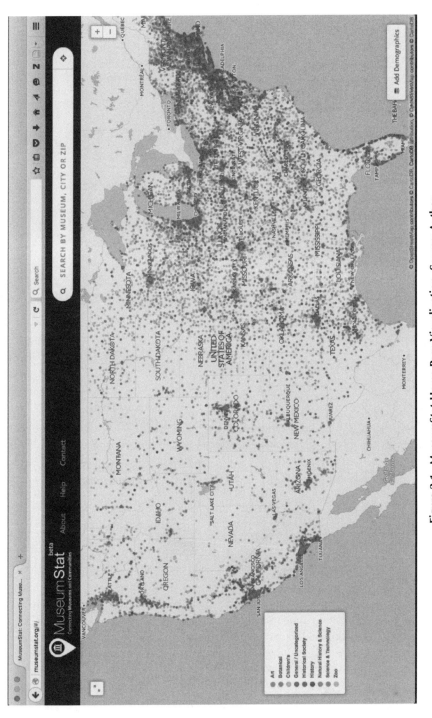

Figure 2.1. MuseumStat Home Page Visualization. *Source:* Author.

Figure 2.2. MuseumStat Displaying Median Household Income Maps for Selected Geography. *Source: Author.*

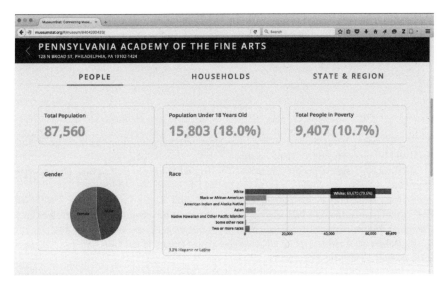

Figure 2.3. A Portion of MuseumStat's Visualization of Demographic Data.
Source: Author.

With the creation of the first-ever comprehensive database of museums, the Museum Universe Data File, the field now has a repository that demonstrates the scope, range, and reach of museums in the United States. With MuseumStat, which combines this data with important community metrics into a powerful, publicly accessible, and GIS-based analytical tool, museum leaders, researchers, and advocates can now make informed decisions based on the full ecosystem of museums and the communities they support. Ultimately, the findings of this research and development effort serve to demonstrate how new sources of information and new data-driven tools can help ensure that museums are able to place themselves within their local and national environments, ultimately creating a more robust and sustainable sector.

BIBLIOGRAPHY

Crawford, Kate, Helen Hasan, Leoni Warne, and Henry Linger. "From Traditional Knowledge Management in Hierarchical Organizations to a Network Centric Paradigm for a Changing World." *Emergence: Complexity and Organization* 11, no. 1 (2009): 1–18.

Grant, Robert M. "Toward a Knowledge-Based Theory of the Firm." *Strategic Management Journal* 17, (1996): 109–22.

Moore, James F. "Predators and Prey: A New Ecology of Competition." *Harvard Business Review* 71, no. 3 (1993): 75–86.

"Museum Definition." International Council of Museums. Accessed March 3, 2016. http://icom.museum/the-vision/museum-definition/.

Senge, Peter M. *The Fifth Discipline: The Art and Practice of the Learning Organization.* New York: Doubleday, 2006.

NOTES

1. This research was supported by a cooperative research grant from the Institute of Museum and Library Services, a federal agency.

2. Peter M. Senge, *The Fifth Discipline: The Art and Practice of the Learning Organization* (New York: Doubleday, 2006).

3. Kate Crawford, Helen Hasan, Leoni Warne, and Henry Linger, "From Traditional Knowledge Management in Hierarchical Organizations to a Network Centric Paradigm for a Changing World," *Emergence: Complexity and Organization* 11, no. 1 (2009): 1–18.

4. Robert M. Grant, "Toward a Knowledge-Based Theory of the Firm," *Strategic Management Journal* 17 (1996): 109–22.

5. James F. Moore, "Predators and Prey: A New Ecology of Competition," *Harvard Business Review* 71, no. 3 (1993): 75–86.

6. Museum and Library Services Act, S. 1972, 104th Congress, § 272 (1996).

7. "Museum Definition," International Council of Museums, accessed March 3, 2016. http://icom.museum/the-vision/museum-definition/.

8. The National Taxonomy of Exempt Entities (NTEE) is a definitive classification system for nonprofit organizations recognized as tax exempt under the Internal Revenue Code. It divides the universe of nonprofit organizations into twenty-six major groups under ten broad categories. NTEE Codes A50–A57 are used to identify the range of museums recognized by the Internal Revenue Service.

9. To access Museum Universe Data File, please go to http://data.imls.gov.

10. To access MuseumStat, please go to www.museumstat.org.

Part II

SYSTEMS THINKING AND MUSEUM FUNCTIONS

The chapters in this part present theoretical orientations regarding the changing paradigms that reinterpret the roles and functions of museums. Traditional museum structures divide museum functions into several different departments often with curatorial and collections departments at the top of the museum hierarchy.[1] In this disconnected environment, the work of the museum can be less about the people it is serving and become more about the collections and the vision of a few people who have traditional knowledge of the collections (e.g., curators and directors).

The Museum (the fictional museum based on a real museum first introduced in the Part I introduction) has this compartmentalized setup and hierarchy of management and leadership. The collaboration among different departments has been infrequent and often not successful. For instance, the curatorial and education departments do not work together to create cohesive exhibitions and programs that would appeal to local community members. The curator typically works on her own, researching collections and creating an exhibition while the education department comes up with the programs that accompany the exhibition separately. Sometimes the curator finds out what kind of programs are developed for her recent exhibition by flipping through the museum's program book rather than from her education staff colleagues. This illustrates that the two departments do not work together to create the museum's most important services and there is almost no communication between these two departments. The rigid and hierarchical museum structure and functional categorization of departments without collaboration caused them to be in their own silos. This in turn affected the museum's workplace culture to be one of hostility and competitiveness toward other departments. This hostile environment took time and energy away from paying attention to programming for the community. Rather, this museum focused on the compartmentalized components without seeing the interconnected networks of museum functions, departments, and people as well as its connection to the larger community.

This museum is not alone in adopting a highly compartmentalized organizational structure with museum-focused programs and exhibitions as opposed to visitor-centered ones. This is a traditional practice that has been perpetuated without thinking critically about the viability of structure. In addition, the fact that it works at some level does not mean that it is the best way or cannot be improved. When museums adopt systems thinking, traditional functions such as collecting, preserving, researching, exhibiting, and educating are collapsed, blurred, combined, and shifted as more emphasis is placed on visitors and engagement as the center of museum practice.

The two chapters included in Part II will further explain how the traditional paradigm can change. Victoria Eudy in chapter 3 uses open systems thinking, visitor-centered outlooks, and digital strategies to rethink museum functions and roles. Her approach to explaining systems thinking will be beneficial to readers, especially those who are not familiar with this theory; she uses popular cultural metaphors to describe her views on systems thinking as applied to museums. In chapter 4, Pat Villeneuve and Juyeon Song introduce the path leading to paradigm change in museum practices by applying Checkland's *soft systems methodology* based on soft systems thinking, thereby breaking the old ways of thinking and doing museum work and suggesting more systems-based ways of museum practices in a broad and theoretical manner.

NOTE

1. Theodore L. Low, *The Museum as a Social Instrument* (New York: Metropolitan Museum of Art, 1942).

3

Dr. Seuss, Systems, and Digital Strategies

Making Sense of Systems Theory as an Emerging Museum Professional

Victoria Eudy

To illustrate the value of systems thinking, I will call upon the work of *one* of my favorite doctors, *The Cat in the Hat Comes Back!* by Dr. Seuss. In case some of us are not familiar with this story, I will revisit the literature briefly: The story begins with two children at home alone while their mother is out of the house. The mischievous Cat in the Hat enters the house and eats a cake in the bathtub; the icing leaves a pink stain around the tub. This frustrates the children and they worry about their mother's reaction to the mess when she returns. So the Cat decides to solve the problem by using the mother's white dress to wipe off the stain. Although this solves the issue of the pink stain in the bathtub, another problem arises as the stain is now on the white dress. These antics continue—the Cat flings the stain on the dress onto the wall, onto shoes, onto the rug, and so forth until eventually the Cat removes the stain entirely using the magical power of *voom*.[1]

Had the Cat in the Hat applied systems thinking to resolve the issue of the stain, he would have known to use *voom* first. Instead, the cat first used a narrow, compartmentalized reasoning to solve the issue that only shifted the problem to other areas of the house instead of focusing on removing the stain entirely. In short, systems thinking allows us the benefit of taking a more holistic approach to seeking, defining, and solving problems. To lift from the old adage, it keeps us from not being able to see the forest for the trees.

Luckily, I discovered the benefits of systems thinking early in my graduate career. A forward-thinking professor introduced me to systems thinking during my master's work in art education and museums, and I felt as if I had struck gold. When the going got tough, as it often does in graduate school, systems thinking encouraged me to step back and take a look at the bigger picture. As a graduate student and emerging researcher, I often asked myself, was I only moving the stain to the curtain from the bathtub, or was I on the right track to get rid of it entirely? In other words, was I asking the correct questions about my research? If not, was I learning from my mistakes? Systems thinking challenged me to think differently about my work with museums. It challenged me to think holistically and flexibly and to avoid the rigidity of reductionist thinking. As a result, I found myself more able to synthesize and find meaning in seemingly disparate concepts. Now, as a doctoral student in museum education, I use systems thinking to provide the vantage point with which I understand the field, and the complex but exciting challenges museums face as we begin to settle firmly into the twenty-first century.

I began my doctoral program with a general interest in systems thinking and museum technology. I wanted to learn more about how technology assists in engaging and educating museum visitors through opportunities for personalized meaning making. As a result of conducting research with my advisor, I became intimately aware of the number of existing and emerging technological initiatives within art museums.[2] As I grew in my doctoral program, I became curious as to how museums went about planning for and integrating technology into their organizational and educational practices. My focus narrowed to an exploration of digital strategies, or roadmaps for the implementation of technology, in the visitor-centered museum.

By allowing my interest in systems thinking to drive my research focus, I was better able to understand and synthesize the interrelatedness of the philosophical and practical components behind the development of digital strategies in the visitor-centered museum. This chapter is an opportunity to share my development in thinking about systems, museums, and technology from a graduate student perspective. What follows is an exploration of and introduction to the different iterations and history behind systems thinking, how those different iterations intersect with the philosophical basis of the visitor-centered museum, and how they might be applied to better understand the role of digital strategies and technology in the museum.

INTRODUCTION TO CLOSED VERSUS OPEN SYSTEMS

Systems thinking as a philosophy emerged with Laszlo's *Introduction to Systems Philosophy*, which broadened the principles of cybernetics to the philosophical realm. In this work, Laszlo applied closed-systems principles as a lens with which to consider epistemological, technological, and ontological concerns. In doing so, Laszlo was one of the first to use the principles of systems as a philosophy, and argue for their standing as a reflection of reality. In other words, Laszlo's philosophy stemmed from a belief that the world is a conglomeration of interwoven systems, the manipulation of which results in practical and predictable solutions.[3]

However, sociological issues tend to challenge the set-fast boundaries of the closed systems envisioned by Laszlo. Unlike closed systems, open systems' boundaries are more flexible and unpredictable. As the situation or the context becomes more complex, interwoven, and subjective, it becomes increasingly difficult to draw hard and fast lines around which factors (or system elements) to include and which to omit. Likewise, problems arise when considering qualitative information in terms of closed systems.[4]

In terms of open systems, the behavior of the system may be seemingly erratic or chaotic, and take on a less predictive and more explanatory role. Elements of the system, as they become increasingly intangible and socially based, become less easy to control and more difficult to understand in the way a closed system may permit. Instead of dealing with absolutes, stocks, and flows, the nature of open systems takes on an almost rhizomatic form where systems boundaries become permeable. Like rhizomes, open systems focus on the ecological (rather than traditionally systemic) formation of primarily social systems.[5]

Bertalanffy's *general systems theory* introduced the idea of open, as opposed to closed, systems as a model for social and biological systems models and solutions. In a general sense, open systems are a means of applying a systems perspective to qualities as opposed to quantities, such as those found in the social sciences.[6] Likewise, both Capra's *The Turning Point* and Gregory Bateson's *Steps to an Ecology of Mind* made significant contributions to systems theory's application within the social and life sciences. Bateson pioneered the idea that humans and nature exist as interdependent systems, linked through communication networks.[7] Bateson's views on the interconnected and ecological nature of human existence within the natural world influenced a string of second-generation systems thinkers, including Capra, who also emphasized the ecological implications of systems thinking in *The Turning Point*.[8]

Despite the different angles with which Laszlo, von Bertalanffy, and Bateson approached systems thinking, each argued that at a philosophical level, understanding the world in terms of systems requires a paradigm shift. This shift entails a rejection of the world as a reductionist Cartesian machine, but rather as an interconnected, ecological system predicated on the principles of holism. Likewise the second generation of systems thinkers such as Senge, Meadows, and Capra saw systems less in terms of their cybernetic roots than for their abilities to incite a holistic form of learning and understanding.[9] Pertinent to our interests as museum educators is the connection between the vein of systems thinking proposed by these second-generation systems thinkers and constructivism, the underlying philosophy of the visitor-centered museum.

CONSTRUCTIVISM AND SYSTEMS THINKING

Instead of considering learning as the process of transmitting and receiving knowledge, constructivism acknowledges the learner's agency in the development of his or her learning. Therefore, learning becomes more than a response to a stimulus or the circuiting of information through the brain, such as the underlying assumptions of behaviorists and information processing theory.[10] Constructivism instead argues that the interactions between an individual and their environment serve as the nexus of understanding. In practice, constructivism promotes an embodied, holistic, and exploratory learning process navigated by the learner and facilitated by the instructor in educational settings such as museums. The theory, or paradigm, of constructivism likewise acknowledges the self-organizing and self-transcendent properties of human understanding and development aligning closely with the principles of systems thinking and the construction of worldviews associated with the process.

Likewise, the continuous nature of learning in a systems-informed, constructivist learning environment implies that learning takes on a nonlinear form.[11] Feedback, leverage, and delays all must be taken into account when considering the visitor's learning—as well as the idea of transcendence. Meadows referred to an individual's ability to self-transcend as a kind of wrench in the machine of a closed system. She argued that the human learning process (or system) tests the principles of a closed system.[12] To better explain the idea of transcendence, it may help to think about the Beatles.

Opinions aside, the solo careers of John, Paul, George, and Ringo gave us some critical songs and musical collaborations of the past century. Without them there would be no "Imagine," no Wings, no Traveling Wilburys, and we wouldn't have Ringo's All-Starr Band. Nevertheless, these solo careers never produced the magic of the Beatles whose sound, timing, and authorship created shockwaves around the world. Together, the Beatles *transcended* the abilities of its members. The whole became greater than the sum of its parts. Likewise, and to bring it back to the museum, the individual museum visitor may transcend the information placed in front of them to understand issues in a different way than expected.

You may be asking yourself, *how can I teach the visitor if he or she will arrive at any number of conclusions?* Meadows would argue that the answer lies not in control, but leverage, a ubiquitous but powerful form of systems regulation.[13] Leverage is another way of intervening in system elements to change the overall behavior of that system. Where the individual applies this intervention is a *leverage point*. Meadows outlines a number of leverage points to exemplify how one elemental change within a system can produce considerable results. One of the leverage points Meadows offered includes altering a system's goals. For example, if the learner does not experience success with the current method of instruction or engagement, it might be worth adjusting the desired educational outcomes. This encourages educators to ask whether they are asking the right questions about the goals of their instruction instead of continuing to push in an ineffective direction. Therefore, the question becomes not how can museum educators control the visitor's learning. Rather, the question becomes how to *leverage* the system (in this case, of the learning process) in order to facilitate changes that in turn allow the learner to continue to organize information in a way that is constructive and meaningful, rather than destructive or stagnating. Understanding learning as a matter of leverage as opposed to control helps promote deeper, embodied understandings that rote transmission of knowledge cannot.

What systems thinking and constructivism ultimately encourage is viewing the process of learning as an evolution rather than a series of objective destinations of understanding. In the museum this means providing differentiated learning opportunities for visitors and providing tools that can be used to make meaning from otherwise inaccessible objects. Currently technology offers itself as a critical and powerful tool for engagement and the provision of differentiated learning opportunities in the museum. The focus of my research concerns how technology might assist in the creation of meaning in the museum setting, and how organizations create sustainable plans for the future of technology in the museum using digital strategies.

SYSTEMS THINKING AND TECHNOLOGY IN THE MUSEUM

Visitor-centered museum practices reflect a shift in thinking about museums as being about some*body* instead of some*thing*.[14] Likewise, the visitor-centered paradigm emphasizes the importance of the construction of meaning making as an integral part of the museum experience.[15] Whereas in the past individuals were limited to the provisional text or lecture, with technological advents such as social media, handheld devices, and an increased digital museum presence, the visitor may choose from a number of different avenues and information sources to promote and assist with the meaning making process.[16] As is with the general technological landscape, the issue has evolved from finding information to how to navigate, or curate, that information to suit his or her individual taste and learning needs. Currently museums find themselves faced with the challenge of implementing sustainable technological practices to better serve their audiences. As I will argue, the communication encouraged through the development of these technologies supports a holistic and systems-based approach to museum management and organization, in addition to fostering the personalized and differentiated learning opportunities for visitors.

Museums with long-term technological visions are turning inward to find advanced solutions to the integration of mobile (and other) technologies into the museum's main framework. Museums such as the Royal Ontario Museum and the Indianapolis Museum of Art implemented creative efforts to involve a number of voices within the museum organization in developing a technological vision, or framework, for the museum's future.[17] As they continue to evolve, the idea of a digital strategy becomes an organizational concern and effort, as opposed to that of one singular department with a technological or media-based focus (such as IT). In doing so the fluidity of communication among departments begins to echo the principles of holistic, ecological systems.

Jung argued that the traditional, hierarchical model of the museum with the curator as the sole genius behind exhibition development becomes obsolete when the focus of the museum shifts from the collection to the visitor. Jung offered Bateson's work on open, ecologically structured social systems as a conceptual framework for a theoretical reorganization of the museum.[18] In this model, as she and others argue, education takes a central role, acting as a liaison between the collection, the visitor, and other peripheral museum departments.[19] This new model requires a renegotiation of the traditional boundaries and responsibilities of the position. This places demands upon the educator to become literate in a number of museum components including visitor studies, evaluation, education, and as I argue, museum technology and the creation of digital strategies.[20]

As the customization and proliferation of technology becomes more ingrained in the everyday activities of the public, it becomes an increasingly vital component to the creation of meaning making and personal relevance within the visitor-centered museum.[21] In this sense, if the educators see technology as a necessary interpretive tool, they must take an active role in its development and application, as an integral node in the new ecological model of museum organization.

MOVING FORWARD

Now is an exciting time for museums. We need systems thinkers in the museum field to think holistically and to take a historical perspective about the current problems cultural organizations face, technology included. The integration of personalized, sophisticated technologies into the visitor experience opens new opportunities for engagement and interpretation. These new opportunities, coupled with the advent of the visitor-centered shift in thinking about museum practices and the principles of systems thinking is a combination that has the potential to engage new audiences and allow museums to become better stewards of the arts and culture.

However, it is important to note that, in and of itself, systems thinking does not solve problems. Rather, systems thinking allows us the correct vantage point to define the problem, and in doing so, we can ask better questions. And when we can ask better questions about our problems, we allow ourselves to arrive at more appropriate and inventive solutions. As John Dewey once said, "a problem well put is half-solved."[22]

BIBLIOGRAPHY

Alexander, Jane. "Gallery One at the Cleveland Museum of Art." *Curator* 57, no. 3 (2014): 347–62. doi:10.1111/cura.12073.

Bateson, Gregory. *Steps to an Ecology of Mind: Collected Essays in Anthropology, Psychiatry, Evolution, and Epistemology.* Chicago: University of Chicago Press, 2000.

Burnham, Rika, and Elliott Kai-Kee. "Museum Education and the Project of Interpretation in the Twenty-First Century." *Journal of Aesthetic Education* 41, no. 2 (2007): 11–13. doi:10.1353/jae.2007.0010.

Capra, Fritjof. *The Turning Point: Science, Society, and the Rising Culture.* New York: Bantam, 1984.

Charitonos, Koula, Blake Canan, Eileen Scanlon, and Ann Jones. "Museum Learning via Social and Mobile Technologies: (How) Can Online Interactions Enhance the Visitor Experience?" *British Journal of Educational Technology* 43, no. 5 (2012): 802–19. doi:10.1111/j.1467-8535.2012.01360.x.

Dewey, John. *Logic—The Theory of Inquiry*. Worcestershire, UK: Read Books Ltd, 2013.

Falk, John H., and Lynn D. Dierking. *Learning from Museums: Visitor Experiences and the Making of Meaning*. Walnut Creek, CA: AltaMira, 2000.

———. *The Museum Experience Revisited*. Walnut Creek, CA: Left Coast, 2012.

Jung, Yuha. "The Art Museum Ecosystem: A New Alternative Model." *Museum Management and Curatorship* 26, no. 4 (2011): 321–38. doi:10.1080/09647775.2011.603927.

Laszlo, Ervin. *Introduction to Systems Philosophy: Toward a New Paradigm of Contemporary Thought*. New York: Gordon and Breach, 1972.

Liu, Chu Chih, and Ju Crissa Chen. "Evolution of Constructivism." *Contemporary Issues in Education Research* 3, no. 4 (2010): 63–66.

Love, Ann Rowson, Victoria Eudy, and Deborah Randolph. "Where Do We Go from Here? Research on Art Museum Mobile App Makers' Future Directions for Interactivity." Paper presented at the International Conference on the Arts in Society, London, July 22–24, 2015.

Meadows, Donella H. *Thinking in Systems: A Primer*. Edited by Diana Wright. White River Junction, VT: Chelsea Green, 2008.

Reich, Kersten. "Interactive Constructivism in Education." *Education and Culture* 23, no. 1 (2007): 7–26. doi:10.1353/eac.2007.0011.

Senge, Peter M. *The Fifth Discipline: The Art and Practice of the Learning Organization*. New York: Doubleday, 2006.

Seuss, Dr. *The Cat in the Hat Comes Back!* New York: Beginner, 1958.

Villeneuve, Pat, and Ann Rowson Love, eds. *Visitor-Centered Exhibitions and Edu-Curation in Art Museums*. New York: Rowman & Littlefield, 2017.

Weil, Stephen E. "From Being *about* Something to Being *for* Somebody: The Ongoing Transformation of the American Museum." *Daedalus* 128, no. 3 (1999): 229–58.

NOTES

1. Dr. Seuss, *The Cat in the Hat Comes Back!* (New York: Beginner, 1958).

2. Ann Rowson Love, Victoria Eudy, and Deborah Randolph, "Where Do We Go from Here? Research on Art Museum Mobile App Makers' Future Directions for Interactivity," Presentation at the International Conference on the Arts in Society, London, July 22–24, 2015.

3. Ervin Laszlo, *Introduction to Systems Philosophy: Toward a New Paradigm of Contemporary Thought* (New York: Gordon and Breach, 1972).

4. Donella H. Meadows, *Thinking in Systems: A Primer*, ed. Diana Wright (White River Junction, VT: Chelsea Green, 2008).

5. Gregory Bateson, *Steps to an Ecology of Mind: Collected Essays in Anthropology, Psychiatry, Evolution, and Epistemology* (Chicago: University of Chicago Press, 2000).

6. Meadows, *Thinking in Systems*.

7. Bateson, *Steps to an Ecology of Mind*.

8. Fritjof Capra, *The Turning Point: Science, Society, and the Rising Culture* (New York: Bantam, 1984).

9. Peter M. Senge, *The Fifth Discipline: The Art and Practice of the Learning Organization* (New York: Doubleday, 2006).

10. Chu Chih Liu and Chen Ju Crissa, "Evolution of Constructivism," *Contemporary Issues in Education Research* 3, no. 4 (2010): 63–66.

11. Kersten Reich, "Interactive Constructivism in Education," *Education and Culture* 23, no. 1 (2007): 7–26, doi:10.1353/eac.2007.0011.

12. Meadows, *Thinking in Systems*.

13. Ibid.

14. Stephen E. Weil, "From Being *about* Something to Being *for* Somebody: The Ongoing Transformation of the American Museum," *Daedalus* 128, no. 3 (1999): 229–58.

15. John H. Falk and Lynn D. Dierking, *Learning from Museums: Visitor Experiences and the Making of Meaning* (Walnut Creek, CA: Altamira, 2000).

16. Koula Charitonos, Blake Canan, Eileen Scanlon, and Ann Jones. "Museum Learning via Social and Mobile Technologies: (How) Can Online Interactions Enhance the Visitor Experience?" *British Journal of Educational Technology* 43, no. 5 (2012): 802–19, doi:10.1111/j.1467-8535.2012.01360.x.

17. Jane Alexander, "Gallery One at the Cleveland Museum of Art," *Curator* 57, no. 3 (2014): 347–62, doi:10.1111/cura.12073.

18. Yuha Jung, "The Art Museum Ecosystem: A New Alternative Model," *Museum Management and Curatorship* 26, no. 4 (2011): 321–38, doi:10.1080/09647775.2011.603927.

19. Rika Burnham and Elliott Kai-Kee, "Museum Education and the Project of Interpretation in the Twenty-First Century," *Journal of Aesthetic Education* 41, no. 2 (2007): 11–13, doi:10.1353/jae.2007.0010.

20. Pat Villeneuve and Ann Rowson Love, eds., *Visitor-Centered Exhibitions and Edu-Curation in Art Museums* (New York: Rowman & Littlefield, 2017).

21. John H. Falk and Lynn D. Dierking, *The Museum Experience Revisited* (Walnut Creek, CA: Left Coast, 2012).

22. John, I. Dewey, *Logic—The Theory of Inquiry* (Worcestershire, UK: Read Books Ltd, 2013), 112.

4

Paradigms, Visitor-Centered Museum Practices, and Systems Thinking

Pat Villeneuve and Juyeon Song

Writing this chapter makes me think back to one of my doctoral classes. The professor regularly set up elaborate organizational scenarios for us and then questioned why things were the way they were. It didn't take long to learn his one-size-fits-all answer: history and tradition. Although I found it rather flip at the time, I now realize the merit in Professor Larry Leslie's answer, and I'm going to invoke it here. In this chapter, cowritten with one of my doctoral students who has a strong interest in systems thinking, we consider what it will take for museums to embrace a systems approach, as advocated in this book, treating it as a case of paradigmatic change. We begin by juxtaposing a traditional conception of paradigms with the realities of museum practice. Then we argue that pending paradigmatic shifts to visitor-centered museum practices and systems approaches to organizational structures will occur hand in hand.

PARADIGMS 101

It is impossible to write about paradigmatic change without reference to Thomas S. Kuhn's classic work on scientific revolutions, first published decades ago.[1] Kuhn began by describing achievements that a specific scientific community acknowledges and uses to guide further work for a time (until replaced by a newly accepted achievement). He used the term *paradigm* to refer to certain types of achievements that were both: (1) new enough in their ideas to attract a group of followers from other competing scientific activities and (2) not yet resolved, leaving multiple problems for its new supporters to pursue.[2] Once accepted, paradigms serve as the basis of "particularly coherent traditions of scientific research" and what we would call a process of professional socialization as students study, accept, and perpetuate them as they move into the field.[3]

DIFFERENT WORLDS

Although Kuhn was able to clearly document paradigmatic changes in science, shifts can be harder to realize in unstructured or nonempirical fields such as museum practice.[4] The traditional training track for museum directors and curators has been through advanced degrees in their disciplines followed by curatorial work in the field.[5] In art museums, this usually is art historical training with little to no preparation in any aspect of museum work or administration except, perhaps, from experience gained through internships. On-the-job training—professional socialization into museum practice—occurs after placement, effectively perpetuating the history and tradition of the given museum, for lack of any scholarly knowledge base to work from. The inherited organizational structure of traditional museums is hierarchical with divisionalized functions that frequently work without much interaction, as if mired in individual silos.[6]

CONSIDERING PARADIGMATIC CHANGE
IN MUSEUM PRACTICE

In the absence of rigorously considered paradigms for museum administration or other museum functions, how does a field "disprove" its practice and call for a replacement paradigm?

The impetus, we think, lies in a twentieth-century principle from modernist architecture and industrial design: form follows function. This suggests that museums' inherited, hierarchical organizational structure will continue as long as it works for the way museums function. Traditional museum structure, for instance, has supported a curator-centric practice that has effectively eliminated educational and other input in the earlier stages of exhibition development, leaving the curator to function as a lone creative.[7] This paradigm has prevailed despite twenty-some years of publications and policy statements attempting to advance an alternate, visitor-centered paradigm for museum practices.

Dutch museologist Van Mensch set the stage for such a transformation with a 1990 publication.[8] In his methodological museology, he reconceived museum functions from the traditional five—collect, preserve, exhibit, study, educate—to three, preserve (which presumed collecting), study, and communicate.[9] His newly proposed communication function was a conflation of exhibit and educate, mandating a collaborative approach to exhibition making to the benefit of museum audiences.

In 1992, the American Association of Museums released a landmark policy publication, *Excellence and Equity: Education and the Public Dimension of Museums.*[10] The report implicitly challenged the priority on curatorial functions with the command: "Assert that museums place education—in the broadest sense of the word—at the center of their public service role. Assure that the commitment to serve the public is clearly stated in every museum's mission and central to every museum's activities."[11] Among its recommendations was, "Develop collaborative efforts with individuals, organizations, corporations, and other museums that extend the museum's public dimension and enhance its ability to fulfill its educational mission."[12]

The same year, Falk and Dierking published the museum experience model describing three contexts that collectively impact museum visits: personal (including previous experience, interest, and motivation), social (group interaction and mediation), and physical (space and design).[13] The varied factors addressed within the model presented the opportunity for diverse museum functions to influence visitor experience. Shortly thereafter, Hein, Hooper-Greenhill, and others began writing about the constructivist museum, a concept that shifts the responsibility for interpretation to visitors through an approach to exhibitions intended to support individual meaning making.[14]

At the end of the decade, Weil, then the most widely recognized US museum theorist, famously argued that museums must go from being *about* something (the object) to being *for* something (the visitor).[15] Despite what Villeneuve has referred to as these many invitations to change, museum practice has not yet fully converted to a visitor-centered paradigm.[16] However, in the absence of a scientific breakthrough, these publications could be viewed as establishing momentum for a paradigmatic shift.[17]

PARADIGMATIC CHANGE BEGETS PARADIGMATIC CHANGE

Thus far we have argued that traditional museum practices—those continued through history and tradition rather than rigorously defended scholarship—will not change until museums deem it necessary. Recent publications demonstrate that there are notable museums embracing change and suggest that the field may finally be poised to complete a paradigmatic shift to visitor-centered practices.[18] We contend that such changes in function will also affect organizational form, requiring organizational restructuring to renegotiate power arrangements and facilitate communication among newly configured work groups.[19] This will necessitate a concomitant shift to systems-informed museum practices, as exemplified by the visitor-centered, interdepartmental team approaches developed by the Detroit Institute of the Arts or the Minnesota History Center.[20] However, because of differences between museums and their communities, it is imperative that institutions not simply "borrow" a structure that works elsewhere. Instead, we offer an example below that uses soft systems methodology (SSM) to effect paradigmatic changes appropriate to local circumstances.

SOFT SYSTEMS METHODOLOGY

SSM is a process of inquiry into the world that is useful for investigating unstructured problem situations.[21] As introduced by Checkland, soft systems methodology transforms systems thinking, addressed throughout this book, to systems practice.[22] The SSM model, seen in figure 4.1, incorporates both real-world aspects and systems thinking *about* the real world. Its purpose is to diagnose complex problems in real situations and produce structured models to guide thinking about and to improve real-world problems.[23]

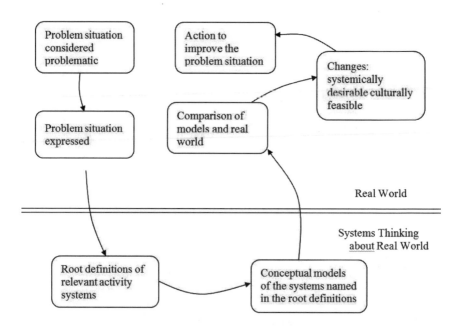

Figure 4.1. The Seven-Stage SSM Model. *Source*: **Adapted from Checkland and Scholes,** *Soft Systems Methodology in Action.* **Created by the author.**

SSM uses the seven stages defined in table 4.1 to diagnose problems by perceiving purposeful human activities in complex, real-world situations, leading to new knowledge and insights about problematic situations.[24]

Table 4.1. Soft Systems Methodology

Stage	Action	Stage Location in Model (See figure 4.1)	
		Real World	Systems Thinking
1. Consider the situation.	List all the symptoms of the observed situation.	√	
2. Express the problem situation.	Examine elements identified in stage 1 and the relationship among them to define the problem situation.	√	
3. Develop root definitions of relative systems.	Respond to CATWOE questions (see below).		√
4. Derive a conceptual model.	Build an ideal model to address CATWOE responses.		√
5. Compare the conceptual model with the real world.	Identify gaps between the ideal and the reality of the systems and analyze problems as components in terms of process and structure.	√	
6. Analyze feasible and desirable changes.	Consider possible changes based on feasibility and desirability.	√	
7. Take action.	Implement changes to improve the problematic situation.	√	

Source: Author.

WHAT IT COULD LOOK LIKE

To illustrate how a museum could use soft systems methodology to change its practices, we'll invoke a hypothetical "City Museum." The museum could be interested in visitor-centered practices, or it might simply be concerned about flagging attendance for its traditional exhibitions. The City Museum would begin the soft systems reflective inquiry process by listing what it has observed of its situation (stage 1). Perhaps it recognizes a 20 percent drop in exhibition attendance over the previous five years or notes that few families come to the museum. Those and other symptoms might lead it to label its problem situation as unexciting, static exhibitions (stage 2). Next, the museum would use CATWOE to formulate the root definitions required for stage 3.[25] The acronym asks the questions listed in table 4.2 to reflect the system that surrounds each transformation.[26]

Table 4.2. CATWOE Questions

Customers	Who is it for?
Actors	Who does the work?
Transformation	What is being changed?
Weltanschauung/Worldview	What is the view that drives the transformation?
Owners	Who holds power or authority?
Environmental constraints	What can limit the system from functioning?

Source: Author.

Its answers to CATWOE might show the City Museum that its *customers* are select older, educated visitors, and the *actor* and *owner* is the solitary curator who specializes in a relatively obscure area of scholarship. In contrast, in a visitor-centered exhibition paradigm, the customers extend to the general public and the actors are internal and external stakeholders, enlarging audiences while broadly distributing power and authority for exhibition making, as juxtaposed in table 4.3. If the City Museum finds it advantageous to adopt a *worldview* prioritizing inclusive, visitor-centered exhibitions—or is pressed to do so by *environmental constraints*—the curatorial process becomes its *transformation*, requiring a reconsideration of the traditional museum hierarchy to facilitate collaborative curation practices.

Informed by CATWOE, the City Museum could use SSM to develop a new, museum-specific conceptual model for a visitor-centered curatorial process incorporating additional actors, owners, and customers beyond the lone curator (stage 4). The museum would then compare the conceptual model with the real world (its community) to analyze feasibility and make any desired changes (stages 5 and 6). Its implementation (stage 7) would produce paradigmatic changes in both the exhibition-making process and organizational structure. Visitor-centered transformations initiated in other museum functions, from security to fundraising to conservation, could have similar results, extending systemically through the museum organization.

Table 4.3. CATWOE Comparison of Exhibition Paradigms

Elements	From Lone-Creative →	Visitor-Centered Paradigm
Customers	Visitors; educated (fewer)	Visitors; general public (many)
Actors	Curator	Internal and external stakeholders
Transformation	Exhibition curatorial process	
Weltanschauung	Inclusive, collaborative, visitor-centered exhibition	
Owners	Curator	Internal and external stakeholders
Environmental constraints	Resources, particularly financial	

Source: Author.

CONCLUSION

Because museum work is not scientific in nature, we cannot expect paradigm change to occur in predictable ways, as described by Kuhn.[27] Instead, we have argued that a paradigm and the museum organizational structures surrounding it will change when museums perceive change as necessary and desirable—or once there is enough momentum to foster change. In our example, soft systems methodology initiated the transformation of the curatorial process but necessarily impacted organizational structure, effecting a second paradigmatic shift toward systems-informed organizational structures.

BIBLIOGRAPHY

Alexander, Edward P. *Museums in Motion: An Introduction to the History and Functions of Museums*. Nashville, TN: American Association for State and Local History, 1979.

Blake, Kathryn E., Jerry N. Smith, and Christian Adame. "Aligning Authority with Responsibility for Interpretation." In *Visitor-Centered Exhibitions and Edu-Curation in Art Museums*, edited by Pat Villeneuve and Ann Rowson Love, 85–96. New York: Rowman & Littlefield, 2017.

Checkland, Peter. "The Development of Systems Thinking by Systems Practice: A Methodology from an Action Research Program." In *Progress in Cybernetics and Systems Research* vol. 2, edited by Robert Trappl, Franz R. Pichler, and Francis de Paula Hanika, 278–83. Washington, DC: Hemisphere, 1975.

———. "Soft System Methodology: A Thirty Year Retrospective." *System Research and Behavioral Science* 17, (2000): 11–58.

———. *Systems Thinking, Systems Practice: Soft Systems Methodology: A 30 Year Retrospective*. West Sussex, UK: John Wiley and Sons, 1999.

Checkland, Peter, and Jim Scholes. *Soft Systems Methodology in Action*. Chichester, UK: John Wiley and Sons, 1990.

Collins, Jim. *Good to Great: Why Some Companies Make the Leap . . . and Others Don't*. New York: Collins, 2001.

Czaijkowski, Jennifer Wild, and Salvador Salort-Pons. "Building a Workplace That Supports Educator-Curator Collaboration." In *Visitor-Centered Exhibitions and Edu-Curation in Art Museums*, edited by Pat Villeneuve and Ann Rowson Love, 237–48. New York: Rowman & Littlefield, 2017.

Ebitz, David. "Qualifications and the Professional Preparation and Development of Art Museum Educators." *Studies in Art Education* 46, no. 2 (2005): 150–69.

Falk, John H., and Lynn D. Dierking. *Learning from Museums: Visitor Experiences and the Making of Meaning*. Walnut Creek, CA: AltaMira, 2000.

———. *The Museum Experience*. Washington, DC: Whalesback, 1992.

Feldman, Kaywin. "Preface." In *Visitor-Centered Exhibitions and Edu-Curation in Art Museums*, edited by Pat Villeneuve and Ann Rowson Love, xiii. New York: Rowman & Littlefield, 2017.

Gasson, Susan. "The Purpose of Soft Systems Methodology." Accessed November 25, 2016. http://cci.drexel.edu/faculty/sgasson/SSM/Purpose.html

Hein, George E. "The Constructivist Museum." In *The Educational Role of the Art Museum*, edited by Eilean Hooper-Greenhill, 73–79. New York, Routledge, 1994.

Hirzy, Ellen Cochran, ed. *Excellence and Equity: Education and the Public Dimension of Museums*. Washington, DC: American Association of Museums, 1992.

Hooper-Greenhill, Eilean. "Museum Learners as Active Postmodernists: Contextualizing Constructivism." In *The Educational Role of the Art Museum*, edited by Eilean Hooper Greenhill, 67–72. New York: Routledge, 1994.

Kuhn, Thomas S. *The Structure of Scientific Revolutions*, 4th ed. Chicago: University of Chicago Press, 2012.

Love, Ann Rowson, and Pat Villeneuve. "Edu-Curation and the Edu-Curator." In *Visitor-Centered Exhibitions and Edu-Curation in Art Museums*, edited by Pat Villeneuve and Ann Rowson Love, 9–20. New York: Rowman & Littlefield, 2017.

———. "Edu-Curator: The New Leader in Art Museums." Paper presented at the National Convention of the National Art Education Association, Chicago, March 2016.

Samis, Peter, and Mimi Michaelson, eds. *Creating the Visitor-Centered Museum*. New York: Routledge, 2017.

Smyth, D. S., and Peter Checkland. "Using a Systems Approach: The Structure of Root Definitions." *Journal of Applied Systems Analysis* 5, no. 1 (1976): 75–83.

Van Mensch, Peter. "Methodological Museology, or Towards a Theory of Museum Practice." In *Objects of Knowledge*, edited by Sue Pearce, 141–57. London: Athlone, 1990.

Villeneuve, Pat, and Ann Rowson Love, eds. *Visitor-Centered Exhibitions and Edu-Curation in Art Museums*. New York: Rowman & Littlefield, 2017.

Weil, Stephen. "From Being *about* Something to Being *for* Somebody: The Ongoing Transformation of the American Museum." *Daedelus* 128, no. 3 (1999): 229–58.

NOTES

1. Thomas S. Kuhn, *The Structure of Scientific Revolutions*, 4th ed. (Chicago: University of Chicago Press, 2012).

2. Kuhn, *Structure of Scientific Revolutions*, 10.

3. Ibid.

4. Ibid.

5. Many museum educators have followed the same training path. David Ebitz, "Qualifications and the Professional Preparation and Development of Art Museum Educators," *Studies in Art Education* 46, no. 2 (2005): 150–69.

6. Kathryn E. Blake, Jerry N. Smith, and Christian Adame, "Aligning Authority with Responsibility for Interpretation," in *Visitor-Centered Exhibitions and Edu-Curation in Art Museums*, ed. Pat Villeneuve and Ann Rowson Love (New York: Rowman & Littlefield, 2017), 85–96; Kaywin Feldman, preface to *Visitor-Centered Exhibitions and Edu-Curation in Art Museums*, ed. Pat Villeneuve and Ann Rowson Love (New York: Rowman & Littlefield, 2017), xiii.

7. Ann Rowson Love and Pat Villeneuve, "Edu-Curation and the Edu-Curator," in *Visitor-Centered Exhibitions and Edu-Curation in Art Museums*, ed. Pat Villeneuve and Ann Rowson Love (New York: Rowman & Littlefield, 2017), 9–20.

8. Peter Van Mensch, "Methodological Museology, or Towards a Theory of Museum Practice," in *Objects of Knowledge*, ed. Sue Pearce (London: Athlone, 1990), 141–57.

9. Ibid.; Edward P. Alexander, *Museums in Motion: An Introduction to the History and Functions of Museums* (Nashville, TN: American Association for State and Local History, 1979).

10. Ellen Cochran Hirzy, ed., *Excellence and Equity: Education and the Public Dimension of Museums* (Washington, DC: American Association of Museums, 1992).

11. Ibid., 7.

12. Ibid., 20.

13. John H. Falk and Lynn D. Dierking, *The Museum Experience* (Washington, DC: Whalesback, 1992); John H. Falk and Lynn D. Dierking, *Learning from Museums: Visitor Experiences and the Making of Meaning* (Walnut Creek, CA: AltaMira, 2000). In the latter publication, the authors used the term *sociocultural context*.

14. George E. Hein, "The Constructivist Museum," in *The Educational Role of the Art Museum*, ed. Eilean Hooper-Greenhill (New York, Routledge, 1994), 73–79; Eilean Hooper-Greenhill, "Museum Learners as Active Postmodernists: Contextualizing Constructivism," in *The Educational Role of the Art Museum*, ed. Eilean Hooper Greenhill (New York: Routledge, 1994), 67–72.

15. Stephen Weil, "From Being *about* Something to Being *for* Somebody: The Ongoing Transformation of the American Museum," *Daedelus* 128, no. 3 (1999): 229–58.

16. Ann Rowson Love and Pat Villeneuve, "Edu-Curator: The New Leader in Art Museums," paper presented at National Convention of the National Art Education Association, Chicago, March 2016.

17. Collins used the metaphor of a flywheel when describing how organizations go from good to great. Although it's difficult to start a flywheel spinning, a series of small pushes eventually establishes the rotation. Jim Collins, *Good to Great: Why Some Companies Make the Leap . . . and Others Don't* (New York: Collins, 2001).

18. Peter Samis and Mimi Michaelson, eds., *Creating the Visitor-Centered Museum* (New York: Routledge, 2017); Pat Villeneuve and Ann Rowson Love, eds., *Visitor-Centered Exhibitions and Edu-Curation in Art Museums* (New York: Rowman & Littlefield, 2017).

19. Blake, Smith, and Adame, "Aligning Authority with Responsibility."

20. Jennifer Wild Czaijkowski and Salvador Salort-Pons, "Building a Workplace That Supports Educator-Curator Collaboration," in *Visitor-Centered Exhibitions and Edu-Curation in Art Museums*, ed. Pat Villeneuve and Ann Rowson Love (New York: Rowman & Littlefield, 2017), 237–48; Samis and Michaelson, *Creating the Visitor-Centered Museum*.

21. Peter Checkland and Jim Scholes, *Soft Systems Methodology in Action* (Chichester, UK: John Wiley and Sons, 1990); Susan Gasson, "The Purpose of Soft Systems Methodology," accessed November 25, 2016. http://cci.drexel.edu/faculty/sgasson/SSM/Purpose.html.

22. Peter Checkland, "The Development of Systems Thinking by Systems Practice: A Methodology from an Action Research Program," in *Progress in Cybernetics and Systems Research*, vol. 2, ed. Robert Trappl, Franz R. Pichler, and Francis de Paula Hanika (Washington, DC: Hemisphere), 278–83; Peter Checkland, "Soft System Methodology: A Thirty Year Retrospective," *System Research and Behavioral Science* 17, (2000): 11–58.

23. Peter Checkland, *Systems Thinking, Systems Practice: Soft Systems Methodology: A 30 Year Retrospective* (West Sussex, UK: John Wiley and Sons, 1999); Checkland, "Soft System Methodology."

24. Checkland, *Systems Thinking, Systems Practice.*

25. D. S. Smyth and Peter Checkland, "Using a Systems Approach: The Structure of Root Definitions," *Journal of Applied Systems Analysis* 5, no. 1 (1976): 75–83.

26. Unlike the stages of soft systems methodology, CATWOE questions need not be answered in the presented order.

27. Kuhn, *Structure of Scientific Revolutions.*

Part II

Take Action

1. After reading Eudy's overview of systems thinking and her grappling with how the theories apply to her work as an emerging museum professional, how do you define systems thinking? Is there a particular systems thinking theory that you're drawn to in your work? How would you apply it? Eudy used metaphors—Dr. Seuss and the Beatles—as a way of framing how systems thinking works. What metaphor could you use as an illustrative example?

2. Try applying Checkland's CATWOE as suggested by Villeneuve and Song during your next team-based museum task or project. What are your overall project goals? Who should work with you on your team? What kinds of roles or expertise does each team member bring to the work? Use the following CATWOE parameters to structure your project planning process:

   - Customers: Who is it for? (Who is the audience or beneficiary of this project?)
   - Actors: Who does the work? (How will this project be carried out and how will you measure success?)
   - Transformation: What is being changed? (How will this project bring about change for the targeted audience and your museum?)
   - Worldview: What is the view that drives the transformation? (What does your team value about this project and its potential transformation? Write out the values and share them.)
   - Owners: Who holds the power or authority? (Who is the gatekeeper? How can you promote shared or cooperative authority?)
   - Environmental Constraints: What can limit the system from functioning? (If there are limits, how do you move beyond them?)

3. After using Checkland's CATWOE questions to guide your project process, how do you see this approach working across your organization?

Part III

SYSTEMS THINKING IN MANAGEMENT AND LEADERSHIP

This part focuses on how systems thinking is applied to reshaping management and governing structures, leadership, and organizational culture. Hierarchical management systems and single leadership may lead to ineffective communication systems and non-collaborative workplace cultures, therefore contributing to a stagnant organization that is not reflective of its own practice and does not grow and learn to create an impact. At *The Museum* (the fictional museum based on a real museum first introduced in the Part I introduction), its management structure is hierarchical, its leadership is not collective or inclusive, and staff members do not see the continuous and interconnected nature of their work—therefore, completing work without a clear intention and expected impact. Rather, one director oversees making most decisions and unit heads report to him, seeing museum work as a linear and separate process.

Janes states that museums have used a hierarchical and top-down management approach from early models of business administration with a lone director in charge of major decision making.[1] This practice does not critically reflect the changing museum practice and rather conditions museum leaders to repeat the same work every year.[2] It also does not support a networked communication system that helps generate genuine conversations and synergized ideas among involved individuals; the top-down model prevents feedback and diverse perspectives from being reflected in museum practices.[3] While this structure is one that is found in most museums, there are different ways to management and leadership.

Management is not just the work of museum administration or upper-level museum staff members. Rather it is for *all* museum workers who are involved in achieving the museum's positive and intentional impact on its audiences. Chapter 5, written by Randi Korn, highlights intentional and reflective practice of museum management. Intentional practice urges museum professionals to plan and evaluate their work intentionally, reflect on it critically and honestly, and as a result align their future work to be relevant to the strengths of the museum and needs of its community.

Patrick Greene, Paul Bowers, and Kathy Fox, in chapter 6, share a collective leadership and team-based approach at Museums Victoria in Melbourne, Australia. The networked museum is a best practice for managing a large-scale complex of museums, including the Melbourne Museum, Immigration Museum, and Scienceworks Museum, creating shared goals and outcomes, implementing rotating and delegated leadership, and empowering a team of museum staff to take charge of what they are passionate about and good at. The networked museum practice influences and is influenced by the learning organizational culture of continuous improvement based on collective vision and trust. The goals of these two alternative models presented in the two chapters in this part are to transform museums into learning organizations[4] that collectively learn to be better and relevant.

NOTES

1. Robert R. Janes, *Museums in a Troubled World: Renewal, Irrelevance or Collapse?* (Abingdon, UK: Routledge, 2009).

2. Robert R. Janes, "The Mindful Museum," *Curator* 53, no. 3 (2010): 325–38.

3. Janes, *Museums in a Troubled World*.

4. Peter Senge, *The Fifth Discipline: The Art and Practice of the Learning Organization* (New York: Doubleday, 2006).

5

Intentional Practice

A Way of Thinking, A Way of Working

Randi Korn

Intentional practice—first as a concept and then as a way of working—emerged from reflecting on observations of individual museums' organizational practices, my experiences as a staff member at numerous museums, and nearly three decades of working as an evaluation consultant in all types of museums—from art museums to zoos.[1] Intentional practice became an idea of necessity in response to three primary observations: (1) seeing that staff conceived of evaluation as a linear, episodic event; (2) seeing that staff also conceived of their project work as linear events, usually disconnected from past projects; and (3) seeing that individuals tended to work independently or within their departmental boundaries rather than collaboratively or across departments. These three linear and disconnected organizational behaviors intersect. Even for museums that conducted evaluations repeatedly, evaluation results were neither discussed, nor shared, nor applied to future projects. Learning from one's work was of little interest, almost as if there was not anything to be learned, and even though people work for the same organization, staff may view the work that happens in one department as unrelated to work in other departments.

Operating as if one's work—evaluation *and* projects—is disconnected, and not working collaboratively with colleagues who are in the same organization leads to a stagnant learning environment and a broken system that tends to foster an organization that hobbles along from one project to the next without a unified purpose. What if a museum were to adopt a systems thinking approach—a holistic mindset in which its projects were viewed along a continuum and part of a network of projects all serving a particular end? And, what if departments across the organization were operating as an organic system, unified in their common cause? And finally, what if staff collectively took time to reflect on and discuss their practice and evaluation results? Such a museum would be working collaboratively, learning continuously,

49

moving forward with momentum, and possibly achieving desired results. This portrayal well describes an organization that is pursuing intentional practice; it also describes a highly functioning system comprised of interconnected and interdependent parts.

Intentional practice is a holistic way of thinking[2] and an approach to work focused on achieving intentions. It is one strategy of several that a museum can apply to achieve impact in its community. Intentional practice, like systems thinking, is a whole-organization approach to doing the work of a museum (or any other nonprofit). As with any approach to work, there are basic principles that collectively constitute intentional practice:

1. The organization wants to achieve something greater than itself (e.g., impact) for the benefit of the audiences it serves;
2. Staff articulate and know the impact the museum hopes to achieve on audiences;
3. Staff align work to achieve the museum's intended impact;
4. Staff regularly evaluate the effect the museum is having against what they hope to achieve, in order to learn and improve;
5. Staff reflect on their museum practice and evaluation data, and apply learnings to future work;
6. Staff work collaboratively across and up and down the organization; and
7. Staff use inquiry and active listening to understand and appreciate varying viewpoints and to learn.

INTENTIONAL PRACTICE IS
AN EVOLVING WAY OF WORKING

Intentional practice has changed a great deal over the course of a decade, and it will continue to change because I will always be applying what I learn to refine the concept and how I practice it. In its current state, intentional practice includes four action quadrants (plan, align, evaluate, and reflect) situated around a nucleus—impact (see figure 5.1). These five elements connect to and are dependent on each other, and together they comprise an idealized system of work.

Intentional practice means that a highly functioning system—the organization—is working around the nucleus and across the quadrants as staff focus on the intended impact and outcomes the museum wants to achieve among target audiences. Working from the nucleus and through the quadrants of intentional practice should not be considered add-on work for staff; it is the *only* work for staff. Such focus and intensity are necessary because without an unwavering focus from the organization's leadership and staff, intended impact is not likely to happen.

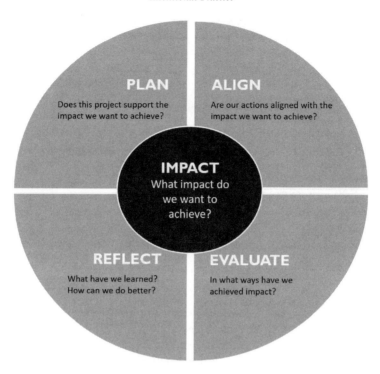

Figure 5.1. Cycle of Intentional Practice. *Source*: Author.

Having a unified purpose or impact statement is a prerequisite for a museum pursuing intentional practice. Museums that do not have an impact statement with supporting outcomes to serve as guideposts for their work run the risk of becoming lost and rudderless. (Figure 5.2, the Impact Pyramid, illustrates the relationship among the impact statement, outcomes, and indicators.) Stephen Weil[3] wrote about and was a proponent of museums clarifying their purpose, and he suggested that museums adopt as their own the United Way of America's cornerstone "to make a positive difference in the quality of people's lives."[4] He asked, "Will any difference do, or is it only intended differences with which we are concerned?" He concluded,

> In terms of accountability, it must surely be the latter. A museum's program . . . may produce a range of outcomes, both intended and unintended. Nevertheless, the core question of positive accountability—in carrying out its program, has this organization made effective use of its resources?—can only be answered in terms of the program's *intended* consequences. . . . The good museum is one that is operated with a clearly formulated purpose, described in terms of these particular and positive outcomes that it hopes and expects to achieve.[5]

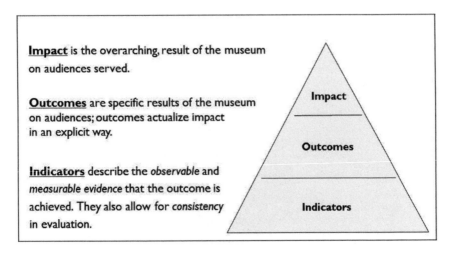

Impact is the overarching, result of the museum on audiences served.

Outcomes are specific results of the museum on audiences; outcomes actualize impact in an explicit way.

Indicators describe the *observable* and *measurable evidence* that the outcome is achieved. They also allow for *consistency* in evaluation.

Impact

Outcomes

Indicators

Figure 5.2. Impact Pyramid. *Source:* **Author.**

Without an impact statement and associated outcomes that describe what the organization wants to achieve among audiences, the organization cannot move forward with purposeful work. An impact statement is a one-sentence statement that melds three vital concepts: (1) the collective passion of staff—why they do what they do; (2) distinctive qualities of the museum—what the museum is best at; and (3) what is relevant to its public (which may require conducting evaluation and research), so the museum can make a positive difference in people's lives. To generate an impact statement and outcomes, leadership and staff collectively explore and discuss the above three ideas in facilitated exercises. Though this work is challenging (because it requires consensus building and negotiation), it is also highly invigorating and inspiring for leadership and staff to be operating as one.

Below is an impact statement shown with the museum's mission statement. Mission statements describe what a museum does, and impact statements describe the result of what the museum does on audiences served. Mission and impact statements are complementary, companion statements. Mission statements usually begin with the name of the museum and are about the work of the museum; impact statements usually begin with "visitors" or "audiences," and they are about the recipients of the museum's work.

Mission statement:

The mission of the Morgan Library & Museum is to preserve, build, study, present, and interpret a collection of extraordinary quality, in order to stimulate enjoyment, excite the imagination, advance learning, and nurture creativity.

Impact statement:

Visitors feel intimately engaged with creative expression and the history of ideas.

NAVIGATING THROUGH THE
INTENTIONAL PRACTICE SYSTEM

With an impact statement in hand, organizations will be able to make decisions about future projects, remembering that all projects should connect to the impact and outcomes the museum wants to achieve. An organization can start with any of the intentional practice quadrants and it can move between quadrants in any order; however, most museums start with the plan quadrant or evaluate quadrant out of need because they do not know their audience beyond demographics, and sometimes a museum will address both quadrants simultaneously. While there are four distinct parts or processes around the nucleus that comprise intentional practice, these parts are not mutually exclusive; staff can align while planning, evaluate while planning, and can and should regularly reflect on their practice and evaluation data. When a museum internalizes intentional practice, leadership and staff are working simultaneously toward one end and they are using the impact statement that they have collectively articulated to guide their work and decisions.

Plan

In the plan quadrant, staff use the impact statement to analyze, vet, and scrutinize existing and new project ideas. An impact statement can also guide decision making during difficult times; for example, the Reynolda House and Museum of American Art in North Carolina used its impact statement to guide budget planning during a recent recession. An obvious question is: "Does this project/program support the impact we want to achieve?" Finer questions are about who the target audience is and whether the project accentuates the organization's distinct qualities (see the list of vetting questions below). Staff should be able to demonstrate effortlessly how a project is directly related to some of the intended outcomes that staff identified during the development of the impact statement, and staff should also recognize the courage it takes to turn projects away; museums excel at saying "yes" and do poorly at saying "no." The vetting questions invite staff to thoughtfully and honestly discuss traditional and new projects in the context of the impact statement, the museum's distinct qualities, target audiences, and intended outcomes for those targeted audiences so staff can determine what new work the museum should accept and what work the museum should decline (or stop doing). An impact statement can provide executive directors, for example, with the courage to say "no" to requests that fall outside the museum's intended impact. For example, the then director at the Baltimore Museum of Art, who also used an impact statement to guide her decisions, looked at the impact statement above her desk and knew she had a strong rationale for her decision!

Vetting Questions

1. Audience: Who is the target audience? Which aspects of the project strongly align with the target audience? Which do not?

2. Mission/Impact/Outcomes: Does the project support mission *and* impact? How so? Which specific outcomes does the project support?
3. Distinct Qualities: Does the project accentuate three or more of the museum's distinct qualities? Which ones and in what ways?
4. Resources: Does the funding environment accommodate resource needs? Does it require new resources or resource realignment? If there is a gap, how will you address it?
5. Staff: Does the project require additional staff or staff realignment? Which staff need to be directly involved?

Evaluate

A museum might start with the evaluate quadrant because it needs to learn about its visitors; knowing about visitors can suggest how to best engage visitors. Sometimes visitors are studied without framing it as an evaluation (e.g., basic audience research); other times studies are conducted to determine the ways in which an exhibition or program is achieving what it sets out to achieve (e.g., impact and outcomes). Traditionally, evaluation systematically collects information from users and examines users' program experiences against what staff wanted to achieve. For intentional practice, evaluation is raised from the program level to the institutional level, whereby the evaluation would be designed to study the ways in which the *whole museum* is achieving what it set out to achieve. Thinking about the whole museum is akin to applying a systems thinking approach to work. The gauge for success is the outcomes and impact evaluation. Impact evaluation uses more complex data collection tools and analysis strategies than those used to evaluate stand-alone programs or exhibitions. For example, impact evaluation, by necessity, might include collecting data from a range of populations such as members, onsite visitors, educators, community leaders, etc., using qualitative and quantitative methods to enable data triangulation.

Reflect

Reflection is about personal and organizational learning,[6] and such learning is not likely to happen unless people take dedicated time to think about their work, their museum, and what evaluation data say about both. And a museum doesn't necessarily need data to reflect; it is possible and even advisable to reflect on your museum's practice with colleagues. While internal collaboration is expected for any museum that pursues intentional practice, convening staff from up, down, and across the museum is vital for reflection because of the power of group sharing and learning, given the different perspectives that comprise the whole museum. Because the most significant barrier to organizational reflection is lack of time, the trick is to build new habits that will force the issue—like repurposing one weekly staff meeting a month to facilitate reflection rather than review who is doing what.

Or once a month hold a brown bag gathering during lunch for the sole purpose of reflecting on a recently completed project or program. Any effort that promotes staff learning from each other about their work will begin to build a culture of learning where asking questions and exploring options becomes welcome and commonplace.

Align

So that leaves the align quadrant, the most difficult quadrant for a museum to tackle. Once the museum has an impact statement and supporting outcomes, it then makes sense to ask, how can we align our work so visitors have the kinds of experiences we envision? Only the most courageous museums do this part of intentional practice work. So why is the "Align" quadrant so difficult? There are a few reasons:

1. The alignment questions listed below ask staff to look at their actions and resources in relationship to the impact they would like to achieve. If a museum has gone through the hard work of clarifying impact and specifying outcomes for particular audiences, then it should look at all its programs and projects to determine those that achieve their intended impact and those that do not. A museum could stop ineffective programs, thereby freeing resources to either change existing programs or create new ones that more strongly align with the impact the museum wants to achieve.[7] Herein lies the problem: changing personal and organizational behavior is hard because people really do not want to change; they like things just the way they are. When I ask a museum why it does things in the way it does them, the answer is usually, "because we have always done them that way."

Alignment Questions

a. Target Audiences: Which target audiences do current exhibitions, programs, and initiatives accommodate? Which target audiences are overlooked? Which exhibitions, programs, and initiatives may need to be changed to better accommodate target audiences?

b. Impact and Outcomes: Does X exhibition/program/initiative support achieving the museum's impact and outcomes? Specifically, which exhibition/program/initiative elements support achieving impact and outcomes? Which program elements do not support achieving the museum's impact and outcomes? Which elements can be strengthened, and in what ways, to support achieving museum's impact and outcomes?

c. Distinct Qualities: Does X program accentuate three or more of the museum's distinct qualities? Which ones and in what ways? Are there ways to strengthen how the distinct qualities are accentuated in X program? Are there other distinct qualities that X program could accentuate?

    d. Resources: How is program X funded? Does it require extra resources or resource realignment? Are resources expended worth the level of impact potentially achieved?

    e. Staff: Does program X require extra staffing? Is staff time worth the level of impact potentially achieved?

2. Even though people avoid change, accepting change becomes okay when a museum chooses to take on a new initiative. For some reason it is easier to continue adding more and more onto people's workloads while never taking anything away—as if every new initiative supports the impact the museum wants to achieve. This idea of always adding more work is not sustainable—in terms of staff capacity—but I think I know why it is easier for museums to add more work than take away work. Workload is associated with how museums measure success; traditionally, success is tangled up with how big and how many. For example, when programming staff are reviewed, one metric is the number of programs that were produced; another is the number of people who attended. Numbers have always been the markers of success; however, one can reasonably argue that numbers no longer suffice as the key success metric because attendance figures, for example, only mean that people came—they offer no indication of meaningfulness. The same holds true for the quantity of programs a museum produces—the quality of a program may not be discussed because quantity often trumps quality. At some point someone will ask, "So what difference has the museum made in the quality of life in your community?" In this chapter, achievement of impact is more about measuring quality than quantity. That is not to say that quantity is unimportant, and that there haven't been quality programs that also attracted high quantities of people. Numbers have a purpose, but they may become more meaningful once the qualitative value of an organization is articulated by those who are affected, which can happen through research and evaluation.

3. When staff are asked to plot their work on a resource-impact grid where there is high and low impact on one axis and high and low resources on another, staff invariably plot their programs as having high impact and using low resources. If all museum programs used as few resources and had as high impact as staff led themselves and others to believe, then there would be nothing more to learn about museum practice—because the field has already reached nirvana. Weil noticed and wrote about this phenomenon, too: "To some extent, our almost congenital avoidance of open references to bad museums may simply rest on an understandably collegial and even sympathetic desire to protect one another."[8]

Because the align quadrant is intertwined with the evaluate quadrant and traditional metrics of success, and the align quadrant requires that staff accurately and honestly represent the quality of their work, the align quadrant receives little attention. If a museum wants to pursue intentional practice, organizational change is inevitable. So how can a museum address alignment or break illogical work habits? Because it is always easy for the human mind to rationalize, honesty is needed to pursue intentional practice, and alignment in particular. Staff will need to examine which projects might have high impact and which might have low impact so they can determine which exhibitions, programs, and initiatives need revising and which should be discarded.

IMPLEMENTING INTENTIONAL PRACTICE

How a museum pursues intentional practice is central to the success of intentional practice. First, collaboration across and up and down the organization (leadership and staff) is essential. Inclusivity and collaboration are vital; organizational intentions are far more difficult to attain when staff operate independently toward disparate ends. Collaboration may need to be cultivated if the culture of the organization does not have a congenial networking infrastructure in place. Leadership, openness, courage, and trust are just a few organizational characteristics needed to begin building a museum-wide collaborative infrastructure. All staff will need to become knowledgeable about the work of their colleagues across the museum so they can begin constructing and strengthening pathways toward achieving impact. Leadership, too, will need to become knowledgeable about the museum's work. If the museum is building a collaborative infrastructure from the ground up and top down, it will need to use an effective communication strategy.

Communication is associated with how information and ideas are exchanged, and in the case of collaborative work, expert facilitation is needed to bring people together toward a common goal. Inquiry, or asking questions, is a highly effective facilitation strategy for all intentional practice work; asking questions serves to neutralize and democratize situations. It is through asking questions that an individual gains awareness, clarity, and deeper levels of appreciation and understanding of others' points of view. Inquiry also leads to dialogue, and dialogue is the primary way that people learn.[9] Some believe that "not asking questions leads to action without thought,"[10] and as museums pursue intentional practice, thoughtful actions are central. Preskill and Torres also note: "consistent and ongoing questioning about the practices, processes, and outcomes of our work stimulates continuous learning, a sense of connectedness, and improved individual, team, and organizational performance."[11]

As museums struggle to be viewed as important and relevant institutions, they may need to engage in two seemingly divergent actions—searching within their institutional selves and exploring what might be relevant to their communities. Once they find the commonalities, they can then realign their work to accommodate both. If a museum chooses to do such work, its efforts will be rewarded by becoming an organization that values and practices a continuous cycle of learning; it will also become an organization that is functioning with passion and integrity—two attributes visitors and museum professionals are apt to recognize and respect.

BIBLIOGRAPHY

Gutwill, Joshua P., and Sue Allen. *Group Inquiry at Science Museum Exhibits*. San Francisco: Exploratorium, 2010.

Korn, Randi. "The Case for Holistic Intentionality." *Curator: The Museum Journal* 50, no. 2 (2007): 255–63.

———. "Creating Public Value through Intentional Practice." In *Museums and Public Value: Creating Sustainable Futures*, edited by Carol A. Scott. Surrey, UK: Ashgate, 2013.

Leinhardt, Gaea, Kevin Crowley, and Karen Knutson. *Learning Conversations in Museums*. Mahwah, NJ: Lawrence Erlbaum, 2002.

Preskill, Hallie, and Rosalie T. Torres. *Evaluative Inquiry for Learning in Organizations*. Thousand Oaks, CA: Sage, 1999.

Senge, Peter M. *The Fifth Discipline: The Art and Practice of the Learning Organization*. New York: Doubleday, 2006.

Weil, Stephen. "From Being *about* Something to Being *for* Somebody: The Ongoing Transformation of the American Museum." *Daedalus* 128, no. 3 (1999): 229–58.

———. *Making Museums Matter*. Washington, DC: Smithsonian Institution Press, 2002.

———. "A Success/Failure Matrix for Museums." *Museum News* 84, no. 1 (2002): 36–40.

NOTES

1. Randi Korn, "The Case for Holistic Intentionality," *Curator: The Museum Journal* 50, no. 2 (2007): 255–63.

2. Randi Korn, "Creating Public Value through Intentional Practice," in *Museums and Public Value: Creating Sustainable Futures*, ed. Carol A. Scott (Surrey, UK: Ashgate, 2013), 31–44.

3. Stephen Weil, "From Being *about* Something to Being *for* Somebody: The Ongoing Transformation of the American Museum," *Daedalus* 128, no. 3 (1999): 229–58.

4. Stephen Weil, *Making Museums Matter* (Washington, DC: Smithsonian Institution Press, 2002), 60.

5. Ibid., 61–62.

6. Peter Senge, *The Fifth Discipline: The Art and Practice of the Learning Organization* (New York: Doubleday, 2006).

7. Stephen Weil, "A Success/Failure Matrix for Museums," *Museum News* 84, no. 1 (2002): 36–40.

8. Ibid., 58.

9. Joshua Gutwill and Sue Allen, *Group Inquiry at Science Museum Exhibits* (San Francisco: Exploratorium, 2010); Gaea Leinhardt, Kevin Crowley, and Karen Knutson, *Learning Conversations in Museums* (Mahwah, NJ: Lawrence Erlbaum, 2002).

10. Hallie Preskill and Rosalie T. Torres, *Evaluative Inquiry for Learning in Organizations* (Thousand Oaks, CA: Sage, 1999), 61.

11. Ibid., 65–66.

6

Leadership in the Networked Museum

Systems Thinking at Museums Victoria

Patrick Greene, Paul Bowers, and Kathy Fox

Museums Victoria, Australia's largest museum group, operates as a *networked organization*, in which "independent people and groups act as independent nodes, link across boundaries, to work together for a common purpose; it has multiple leaders, lots of voluntary links and interacting levels."[1] This approach is the antithesis of the hierarchical, command-and-control, compartmentalized, top-down management practice that is still widespread in the museum sector. In this chapter, we will describe how the principles of the networked organization have been applied to Museums Victoria to demonstrate their practical application using the development of the Pauline Gandel Children's Gallery as a case study.

Museums Victoria is the state museum established under statute of the Parliament of Victoria, with encyclopedic collections numbering some seventeen million items and covering a broad range of sciences, indigenous cultures, and social and technological history. It operates from multiple sites, including the Melbourne Museum (including the Bunjilaka Aboriginal Cultural Centre and IMAX Melbourne cinema), the Immigration Museum, and Scienceworks Museum (including the Melbourne Planetarium). It is also steward of the Royal Exhibition Building, built in 1880 as the Great Hall of the Melbourne International Exhibition, now inscribed as a UNESCO World Heritage Site. There are also two off-site collection storage facilities. There are 500 full-time employees, organized into three divisions, each managed by a director under the leadership of the Chief Executive Officer (CEO). This group of four (three division directors and the CEO) forms the museum's executive team, and acts under the board to run the museum. When one of the authors (Greene) was appointed CEO of Museums Victoria in 2002, he sought to adopt an approach to create a more robust and agile organization by strengthening its interconnectedness.[2] In consultation with staff, the organization defined its preferred working culture: teams and individuals working in different places and spaces to achieve shared goals and a shared outcome.

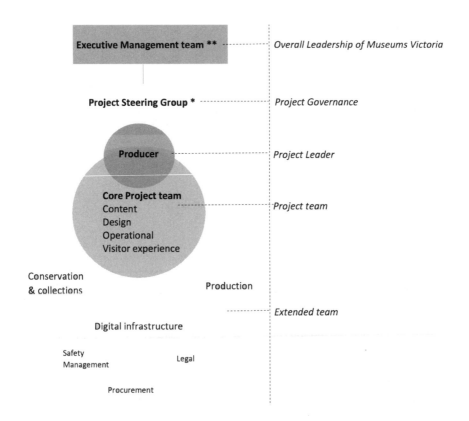

Executive Management team ** ---------- *Overall Leadership of Museums Victoria*

Project Steering Group * ---------- *Project Governance*

Producer ---------- *Project Leader*

Core Project team ---------- *Project team*
Content
Design
Operational
Visitor experience

Conservation
& collections

Production

---------- *Extended team*

Digital infrastructure

Safety
Management

Legal

Procurement

* **Executive Management team:** this is made up of the
Chief Executive Officer;
Director – Collections, Research & Exhibitions;
Director - Public Engagement;
Director – Corporate Services

** **Project Steering Group: for the Children's Gallery project this was made up of**
Manager, Exhibitions;
Manager, Melbourne Museum;
Manager, Education & Public programs;
Manager, Production & Technical Services

Figure 6.1. Organizational Structure at Museums Victoria. *Source*: Author.

Although Greene was not aware of the theory of systems thinking in his consideration of a new structure for Museums Victoria, there are underlying similarities in his efforts to create a more holistic and effective organization. Systems thinking encourages all involved members of the team to understand interconnection and interdependence among different departments, roles, constituents, and perspectives in moving toward common goals and vision benefiting both the museum and its community, seeing an organization as a networked entity within a larger societal system.[3] This is embodied in the structure and culture of Museums Victoria's networked system as demonstrated below.

This working culture has been consciously maintained for over a decade and is the foundation for the museum's operation. The development of the Children's Gallery was a project that reworked Museums Victoria's offer for its youngest audience, babies to five-year-old children. The project began in July 2014 and opened to the public in December 2016. Installed in an existing part of the Melbourne Museum, it is a physically large project at 22,000 square feet including large inside and outside spaces joined by a glass wall and doors. The project draws on Museums Victoria's internal expertise across areas of education, community partnerships, audience engagement, design, production services, and the full spectrum of curatorial areas (natural sciences, indigenous cultures and history, and technology). The practical application of the networked museum culture, and its benefits, can be seen clearly through this project.

PROJECT TEAMS: AN EXTENSION OF TRUST, EMPOWERMENT, AND CONFIDENCE

The networked model is centered on the concept of sapiential authority—the authority that an individual possesses based on their knowledge and wisdom, not upon their position in a hierarchy. The working culture of the networked museum is to enable, empower, and guide its staff, based on a foundation of trust and confidence. This trust and confidence, both between team members and between managers and delegates, are at the core of this model's success. The project team has the authority to shape how resources and spending are prioritized within the project. The vision making and decision making also sit with the project team. On a project as large in scale and as complex as the Children's Gallery, there is a constant need to balance priorities with resources. A hierarchical decision-making process would mean opportunities would be missed, with the project's measure of success skewed toward more quantitative project management measures such as budget and schedule.

This traditional hierarchy corresponds with many project management systems that are highly structured with many rules, but such an approach would run against the grain of our organizational culture. There are a small number of fixed requirements in our methodologies (e.g., a project plan and a steering group), but the process is considered more as a suite of tools for a skilled team with a *producer* at the helm. It is assumed that the team will adapt and customize its approach to the needs of the project, team, and context. Templates and method guides are centrally updated and accessible to all. They are live documents and reflect the networked museum's learning culture of continuous improvement.

Open-ended thinking and processes allow for greater project integrity, where subtler qualitative judgments made by the project team prioritize the best outcomes for the audience. As such, systems thinking as expressed through a networked museum does more than just encourage ideas—it enables the realization of ideas by empowering small teams with the authority to both articulate a vision and then follow through its realization.

CHARACTERISTICS OF THE NETWORKED MUSEUM

The museum adheres to three key characteristics of a networked organization: an emphasis on a culture of shared values; clear leadership and delegated authority; and projects delivered by empowered teams with members drawn from different work groups who share responsibility for a project's success. The application of these characteristics, coupled with our networked museum culture, benefits Museums Victoria, enabling continual innovation and fostering and expanding constructive relationships both within and external to the museum.

A Culture of Shared Values

Ensuring the alignment of staff requires orientation toward common shared goals—the strategic plan. A key ingredient in formulating the plan is to involve staff from across the organization at all levels and functions. Our current plan began with an environmental scan carried out by a group of staff that looked at many factors impacting the museum. These included technological, financial, political, demographic, and professional. The process continued with workshops (including members of our board and organizational leaders) and *open-door* sessions for any interested staff. The strategic plan recognizes the changing external environment in which museums operate and the necessity of an agile and adaptive organization.

Bringing such a large range of staff into the planning process ensures that the completed strategic plan has buy-in and support from all staff. It is deployed into practical projects and staff members work plans through organizational policies, annual business plans, and departmental plans. This in turn leads to more successful implementation as staff members can see how it relates to their area of work and how they can contribute to the outcomes. With shared vision and values, clear goals, timelines, and processes, staff members can be freely creative because they can identify opportunities while understanding where the boundaries lie.

The Children's Gallery project exemplifies the extension of the shared values of an organization. It began with a team of two (a producer and the manager of Melbourne Museum's education and community partnerships) and extensive internal and external discussion. Initially there was no brief or plan beyond the gallery space, a general understanding of the goals of the project, a budget, and a deadline. Formal documentation would come much later.

This sharing of ideas internally created an inclusive environment, and the positive attitude at the conception of this project was essential. The networked museum is reliant on effective communication and shared understanding and values that inspire creativity and collaboration. It can be derailed by political or hierarchical positioning, territory grabs, or the privileging of specific knowledge and expertise. The Children's Gallery project was clearly valuable from the preliminary discussion sessions used to engage a wide range of staff and stakeholders in the project, including those who would later become part of the *core project team*. Through this, we established a culture reflecting our values of open and transparent communication.

We spent several months gathering this diversity of materials—including opinions, audience research, existing documentation, and building plans—and allowed the objectives and constraints for the project to emerge. The skill of the producer in this phase was to integrate this consultation into a *project brief* (i.e., what shall we do?) and a *project plan* (i.e., how shall we do it?). By unifying these activities under one person's leadership, we ensured that the brief and plan match each other; the budget is driven by purpose, team members are selected based on need, and the schedule is built around requirements.

This phase concluded with an approval of the brief and plan by Museums Victoria's executive team. This also sets up the project's *steering group*—who oversee the project's delivery and hold the producer accountable. Membership was based on relevance, expertise, and influence rather than structure, authority, or history.

Clear Leadership and Delegated Authority

Leadership does not occur by chance; it needs to be fostered and individuals must be trained to be effective managers and leaders. We have invested heavily in the development of the leadership team and in emerging leaders, and recognize that many people in the organization will play a leadership role at some point, even if they do not occupy a managerial position. Our project-team approach, involving small groups drawn from relevant parts of the museum, necessitates high competence in leadership and project management. We recruit for these abilities, and have an extensive training process in place for staff development. Formal training includes interpersonal skills, project management, mentoring, and coaching in addition to specialist technical training. In addition, managers are expected to mentor staff in using our networked museum principles.

Delegation is key, which requires trust and confidence. Encouraging people to take responsibility requires that they have the support of the managers and colleagues and that they have a clear understanding of what is expected of them. The result is that the four-person *executive management team* concentrates on the strategically critical areas of culture, policies, decisions, and governance; it delegates to the teams selected for their ability to deliver projects.

Museums Victoria's exhibition development methodologies are products of this organizational culture. Centered on the notion of highly skilled practitioners acting with autonomy, our custom processes seek to enable collaborative teams working with just enough rules and tools for effective governance. The role of producer— which combines the traditional roles of the project manager and creative director— envisions, develops, and delivers a project through a team drawn from across the organization. The producer must be collaborative and consultative while recognizing distinct skills and accountabilities. It is the producer's responsibility to embrace the project team's multiple cultures and channel them into creating a cohesive project vision. Therefore, it is crucial that the producer is tolerant of uncertainty, for themselves and for the team, and can hold the energy of the team through failures and difficulties. The role has proved challenging to recruit, but when occupied by the right person it is extremely effective.

To ensure the full empowerment of the project team, the steering group and executive management team maintain appropriate distance. Each project's steering group is explicitly in the service of the producer, not the other way around. Monthly reporting via a simple dashboard template allows the producer to report progress against the plan, ask for assistance, or request decisions. But the structure of the documentation mitigates against the steering group becoming bogged down in minutiae. For the Children's Gallery, three senior managers (museum manager, head of education and community programs, and head of exhibitions) formed the steering group for the design phase, with the head of production joining the group once fabrication commenced. At the top of the organization, the executive management team is updated using a monthly dashboard on all exhibition projects; this simply indicates a status for budget, delivery, and people, and highlights major early warnings or issues. This active distancing of governance from the project is unusual in museums, and would not work without the networked museum culture. This level of trust creates an empowered and trusted team.

All projects share a need for some form of approvals at the end of a stage of work. It is common in museums for this to be managed by silo structures: for example, a CEO to judge the design or a chief financial officer to review the budget. The inevitable misalignment caused by this system then falls on the team to manage; implementing design changes for which there is insufficient budget, for example. To avoid this, and ensure the embedding of the project within our overall museum culture, we have an explicitly transparent *stage boundary* process.

At the end of a stage of work, the team presents everything and invites open comments. In a networked museum, this means that staff from a huge diversity of areas are considered as genuine stakeholders with meaningful input into specific aspects of the project. The steering group can accept or reject the producer's recommendations or escalate issues to the executive management team. A large exhibition project may have approximately five of these stages (brief and plan; concept design; developed design; construction; and readiness for service) through a three-year delivery. The investment of time from the organization is significant, but the structured engagement of a range of skilled staff ensures a coherent project far better than a frequent scrutiny by a small clique of senior staff.

There is always a need for formal controls on expenditure, risk management, and legal compliance. The skills of networked museum staff are to accept and incorporate these into planning and day-to-day activities. It is easy for a team motivated by design and audience to cohere around demonizing those chiefly concerned with policy and rules, but this is unhelpful in the long term. Rather, we take time to discuss apparent contradictions openly. There is always a way to ensure a good creative outcome if time is taken to appreciate the contextual framework in which the project is being delivered and create the systems and processes to manage these assurances.

These organization-wide reviews of the emerging Children's Gallery designs enabled the team to check and refine its approach, and contributed to a sense of momentum for the project's delivery.

Empowered Teams

Our approach presupposes that exhibition development activities are interdependent. In addition to delivering an exhibition that delights audiences, a successful project must operate within the parameters defined by the organization, for example the realities of the number of floor staff available to assist visitors or the cleaning resources. This interdependence is expressed through the roles of the team members, in which, for example, the needs of the maintenance team are as much a part of the designers' considerations as audience needs.

As a project's plan and brief are put into effect, a small core team is drawn from within the networked museum, and the conditions created for them to function well. Along with the producer, the core team includes five clearly defined roles—experience developer, curator, designer, project support, and lead operator—which are then further supported by a network of specialists, such as audience research or procurement, or those required for specific tasks at defined project stages, such as carpentry. We develop and maintain this team coherence through co-location, social activities, and a workshop approach to development. When there are team changes, we make sure we farewell and welcome in a thankful and celebratory manner.

For the Children's Gallery, deep affinity with audience-focused practice was the common feature of team members. All staff supported the notion that creative ideas would be tested rather than directed, and design and fabrication staff accepted the need for prototyping and refinement rather than simply building and installing. After the design was developed, the core team expanded to a team of eight key staff, drawn from education, curatorial, design, and operational areas, later growing to be supported by a larger group of production and technical staff in the development and delivery stages. This team-based approach transcended departmental divisions and ensured that the project was considered in a multifaceted way, including activities such as staff training and post-opening operational planning alongside the development of the exhibition and education programs.

The open working culture of the Children's Gallery project team exemplifies a responsive attitude. Starting with extensive open-ended discussion with a diversity of groups—children, families, museum members, educators, academics, community groups, creative professionals, and specialists who work across areas of children's health, disability, and access—the project team members were open about what they knew and what they did not know. For the project team these sessions were about listening rather than prescribing, with the team undertaking rigorous non-hierarchical critique of developing ideas.

Subsequent external working sessions, review sessions, and evaluation and critique sessions have been undertaken with these groups throughout the project. One of the important groups to come out of these early discussion sessions was a group described generally by the project team as the health professionals. This was a group of individuals with expertise in early childhood health such as occupational therapists, physiotherapists, early intervention/children at risk teachers, autism spectrum specialists, and more. The engagement with this informal working group was organized to best support the developing project, rather than as a governance task checklist required by others external to the project team. These sessions were set up to allow listening and equal participation. They featured designers discussing built form ideas with physiotherapists; technical staff talking directly with experts in hearing impairment; graphic designers critiquing concepts with speech pathologists; operational staff evaluating construction activities with occupational therapists, and so on. Genuine insights emerged from these conversations. While seemingly simple to implement, these insights have a profound benefit for a child with additional needs and would not have been developed without these open and trusting conversations.

THE BENEFITS OF NETWORKED THINKING WITHIN AND BEYOND THE MUSEUM

The success of the Children's Gallery project is reliant on a strong project-team approach, involving a small group of people drawn from relevant parts of the museum who shared a unity of purpose. This in turn relies on managers to empower this team to collectively create a deep understanding of audience needs, aspirations, and mission, which will later feed back into their specific area of expertise. Underpinning all is a culture of open and transparent communication, with the result being both an improved project outcome and a broader understanding for all museum staff about the project and its audiences. This was achieved throughout the developing project, rather than post opening. The resulting holistic project outcomes exceeded simply delivering an exhibition gallery beyond the museum.

In the case of the Children's Gallery project, the team established connections with creative leaders working outside the museum sector. For example, the creative director of a children's theater group was introduced to the team and this resulted in an ongoing relationship that established child-led evaluation practices. Similarly, introductions to an early learning academic resulted in one of the best-practice child-care centers participating in several evaluation sessions with their children, staff, and parents. Ultimately the project connected these external groups to each other and to the museum, acknowledging necessary interconnection between the museum and its community and resulting in mutually beneficial relationships.

In a networked environment these external relationships are a logical extension of the ethos existing internally. Enthusiasm, commitment, and confidence in the project's objectives and value, and confidence in the museum's support for the project's realization all contribute to a team culture that sees benefit in sharing openly with a broader professional community. The methods we employ at Museums Victoria, including exhibition development, work because they are interdependent with the cultural context in which they are situated—the Networked Museum—in which the inherent benefits of systems thinking or thinking in networks are expressed.

BIBLIOGRAPHY

Greene, J. Patrick. "Creating a Culture of Change in Museums." In *Museum 2000: Confirmation or Challenge*, edited by Per-Uno Ågren and Sophie Nyman, 187–90. Stockholm: Riksutställniinga, 2002.

———. "Museum Victoria: Building the Networked Museum." *reCollections: Journal of the National Museum of Australia* 1, no. 2 (2006).

Lipnack, Jessica, and Jeffrey Stamps. *The TeamNet Factor: Bringing the Power of Boundary Crossing into the Heart of Your Business*. Essex Junction, VT: Oliver Wight, 1993.

Senge, Peter M. *The Fifth Discipline: The Art and Practice of the Learning Organization*. New York: Doubleday, 2006.

NOTES

1. Jessica Lipnack and Jeffrey Stamps, *The TeamNet Factor: Bringing the Power of Boundary Crossing into the Heart of Your Business* (Essex Junction, VT: Oliver Wight, 1993).

2. J. Patrick Greene, "Creating a Culture of Change in Museums," in *Museum 2000: Confirmation or Challenge*, ed. Per-Uno Ågren and Sophie Nyman (Stockholm: Riksutställniinga, 2002), 187–90; J. Patrick Greene, "Museum Victoria: Building the Networked Museum," *reCollections: Journal of the National Museum of Australia* 1, no. 2 (2006).

3. Peter M. Senge, *The Fifth Discipline: The Art and Practice of the Learning Organization* (New York: Doubleday, 2006).

Part III

Take Action

1. How would you describe your museum's organizational structure right now? Does it look like a top-down model? What visually best describes your organizational chart or framework? On a day-to-day basis, does the leadership model in your museum seem hierarchical and compartmentalized in terms of staff interaction or does the model invite collaboration and shared authority? Where do community partnerships fit into your organizational structure?

2. In Part II, you applied Checkland's CATWOE to a collaborative project. Similarly, in this section, you can apply Korn's approach of intentionality during a project planning and implementation process. Using the impact pyramid (figure 5.2) as a guide, what is the result or impact you aim to accomplish during this project? What are the outcomes for audiences? What specific indicators will measure success or achieving the outcomes? All team members should agree upon the answers to these questions and write them down to share with colleagues and audiences. When developing the impact your team wishes to achieve, consider the cycle of intentional practice (figure 5.1) through the following questions:

   - What impact do we want to achieve? (impact)
   - Does this project support the impact we want to achieve? (plan)
   - Do our actions align with the impact we want to achieve? (align)
   - In what ways have we achieved the impact? (evaluate)
   - What did we learn and how can we do better? (reflect)

3. After reading about Museums Victoria's approaches to team-based leadership, how would you characterize the potential for shared leadership in your museum? What could it look like in your museum? How would you convince your director, board, or colleagues to move toward more collaborative leadership?

Part IV

SYSTEMS THINKING IN PERSONNEL MANAGEMENT

Museum professionals are important assets of museums; they are the ones who run museums, interpret artifacts and histories, and communicate with the audiences through exhibitions and programs. Yet many museums do not invest their time and financial resources in creating workplace cultures that encourage them to be prepared to deal with any unexpected challenges, prepare them for new positions in the future, and train them to learn how they can systemically connect with the museum's communities in a more meaningful and relevant manner. The chapters in this part discuss these issues.

At *The Museum* (the fictional museum based on a real museum first introduced in the Part I introduction), anticipating challenges and training staff to be ready for them are not things the museum devotes its time or money to doing. It is not part of the museum's day-to-day conversation and people in each department tend to worry about what would have to be done for that specific department, although challenges like flood—the museum resides right next to a big river—would affect the museum in a holistic way. In fact, the museum eliminated its HR director many years ago and there is no regular staff training of any kind. There are also risks in succession planning at *The Museum*; there is high turnover in many positions, such as the development director and the executive director. For example, although the development director position has frequent turnover, there is no training for the development staff to learn the work and potentially move into the director position. Rather they hire a new development director every year. In addition, because of the compartmentalized and non-collaborative workplace culture, the museum rarely has an opportunity to reflect on its work in relation to the community's needs and interests.

This is not peculiar to *The Museum* but common in many museums. Rather than just focusing on what is on each person's or department's current priorities list, museums need to anticipate future challenges and prepare to deal with them. This includes training staff to be in the mindset of reflecting on what the community wants and needs through professional development opportunities rather than creating what the museum thinks the community needs, so they can respond to shifting demographics, economics, and so forth that influence their visitors. This requires a systems thinking paradigm, looking at the complicated, big, and long-term picture as well as day-to-day operational problems and challenges, based on long-term strategic planning and integrated processes to deal with challenges.

The Toledo Museum of Art in chapter 7, written by Amy Gilman and Lynn Miller, implemented museum-wide enterprise risk management (ERM) and talent management (TM) systems that include all levels of staff and departments of the organization, which helped the museum to have more engaged staff and be a sustainable organization. ERM expects the unexpected and trains all staff to be ready for many possible challenges that can affect the entire museum and TM helps the museum to identify personnel risks by identifying positions that are in risk of retirement or vacancy so the museum proactively trains its junior staff to be ready for more senior-level positions and strengthens its internship programs to educate future museum professionals who are more diverse than its current staff. This museum identified lack of diversity as a risk and created a system to prevent it for its future, to help create staff that are representative of the community they serve.

Douglas Worts in chapter 8 describes the process of sustainability workshop at the Georgia O'Keeffe Museum, using sustainability tools developed by Alan AtKisson, president and CEO of a global sustainability consulting firm. The goals of the workshop were to identify emerging needs of local communities and to apply local cultural relevance to the museum's work. Planning for cultural relevance creates an environment where all staff can participate in discussing pressing issues in the community through open communication and come up with a program or activity idea for implementation. While this was a one-time workshop, this is a great gateway for the museum professionals to holistically think about the museum's role and interconnected place in the community.

7

Enterprise Risk Management and Talent Management as Vehicles for a Sustainable Museum

Amy Gilman and Lynn Miller

Museums talk a great deal about cross-institutional thinking and breaking down silos, but implementing and sustaining the process is significantly harder in practice than in theory. At the Toledo Museum of Art (TMA) we have taken a particular approach to systems thinking and how it applies across the museum. We have begun a rigorous *enterprise risk management* (ERM) and *talent management* practice that has had concrete results in the form of better integrated processes, more engaged staff, and an increasingly sustainable organization. A sustainable organization begins with people (hence the focus on talent management as a key component of the risk management assessment), but it is only realized through process implementation across all departments and within all levels of the organization. This chapter will first provide an overview of the ERM process and emphasize practical aspects of ERM that may be implemented at any size institution. The second part of this chapter will focus on risk management specifically within the human resources arm of the museum.

Risk at the TMA has historically been assessed at a departmental level, and primarily through the lens of finances or security. But risk as a concept crosses all boundaries and assessing risk is not really about preparing for large-scale disasters—although that is certainly one component. It is, in fact, the interweaving of large and small issues that make up the full web of institutional risks within any given museum. As eminent systems theorist Russell Ackoff put it, "Managers are not confronted with problems that are independent of each other, but with dynamic situations that consist of complex systems of changing problems that interact with each other. I call such situations messes. Problems are extracted from messes by analysis. Managers do not solve problems, they manage messes."[1] Museums are complex organizations and issues of various types will arise, often in areas that are unexpected. What pragmatic tools can we give to the staff to best equip them to handle those inevitable events (messes) calmly and with purpose?

ERM AT THE TMA

First, it is important to know what exactly constitutes a risk, and then, in a very clear-sighted way, methodically evaluate risk across all levels of the organization. Risk here is defined as anything that constitutes an exposure (large or small) to a potential injury or loss. Enterprise risk management defines those risks across the whole institution. Often this kind of analysis produces an initial list that is as complex and overwhelming as the organization itself. That is why, as ERM becomes increasingly embedded within the organization, it is important to regularly toggle between micro-focus on individual risks, and macro-focus on where we stand as an organization. The only way to do this effectively is to take a systems-thinking approach to the initiative. You must focus on the details in order to embed risk management culture throughout all staff levels, but you also have to drive it from the top so that there is also a holistic view of the overall risk portfolio. Every day employees, volunteers, visitors, and boards of museums make decisions that affect overall exposure to risk. For example, it may seem expeditious to put off a full-scale roof repair and focus on patching and dealing with small problems as they arise. That decision should not be made solely at the ground level. It could be that a decision to wait on deferred maintenance could be fine (i.e., no significant events and eventually the situation is fully resolved) or it could be that there is a dramatic weather event (a particularly heavy snow winter, or a windstorm) and suddenly the small maintenance issue is a crisis and the outlay of money is large and unplanned.

The point of an ERM process is *not* to advocate that everything is equally risky, or to scare staff or leadership by raising the specter of catastrophic events that are indeed out of the institution's control. Instead it is designed to help all levels of the organization look holistically at risk and make informed decisions. This systematic process of simultaneously looking globally across the whole organization to assess risk while also working with the frontline staff to understand how those risks can be mitigated at the individual level creates a prioritization and a culture of awareness. You will never be able to fully anticipate what issues will arise; you can only better prepare to handle them when they appear.

The TMA has now undertaken an identification of organizational risks, prioritized the list, and then established concrete steps to mitigate as far as possible or reasonable, understanding that not all risks can be completely mitigated. Sometimes the best mitigation is to simply be prepared in the event that something happens. Since initiating ERM, we developed a heat map that places each risk category in a matrix that identifies the likelihood and then potential impact of an event around that risk category (see figure 7.1).

This heat map is a useful strategic overview of risk categories across the museum. We then established a working group of executive-level staff and key department heads and developed an easy-to-follow template for how to approach any unexpected event. By doing this, we have empowered employees at the departmental level to be invested in understanding how their work fits into the broader risk matrix. We are now systematically identifying more department-specific risks and updating standard

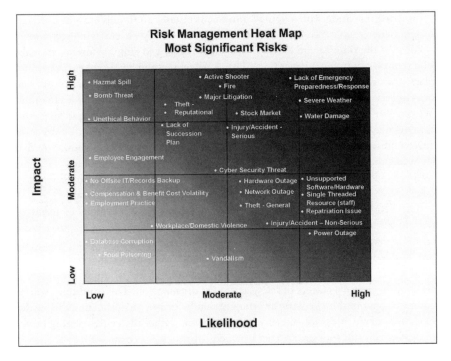

Figure 7.1. Risk Management Heat Map. *Source*: Author.

operation procedures (SOP) within each museum working group. This close examination of SOP helps individual employees understand the relationship between their daily activities and institutional risk.

One of the key issues surrounding risk management is that you will never know from where the issue you will deal with on a given day will emerge. Is it a staff issue? Weather? Outside event? So it is important to actually practice. Periodically get together an appropriate group and walk through a potential scenario that explores an actual risk from the heat map. What the TMA discovered immediately is that these exercises, while they can be anxiety producing in the moment, often result in immediately actionable items to mitigate risk. It can feel quite odd to talk through a crisis such as a tanker fire on a nearby highway, or an internal theft issue, but practicing will help you keep calm in an actual emergent situation. Remember that the reason flight attendants go through the emergency procedures at the beginning of every single flight is *not* because they think there are people who are unfamiliar with the material, but because time and again studies have demonstrated that rehearsing information (even in your mind), just taking a few moments to visually identify where the nearest exit is, will help establish muscle memory that will aid you in responding best in an unexpected and emergent situation. Nicola Davies, in an article addressing the importance of muscle memory and training on crisis response states that "by habituating repetition with a desired movement or task, our minds are able to recognize the desired task and react more effectively and swiftly" in emerging scenarios.[2]

Most of the time we are dealing with small issues, and simply working to make sure they do not become larger ones. That is where the human resources component plays a central role. We cannot control weather or *acts of God* but we can ensure that our employees are informed, trained, and proactive about approaching risk situations. We can also be pragmatic about succession planning and team-building to guarantee that the museum does not have areas where a great deal of resources or information are centralized with a single staff member. These are also risks to the organization that are sometimes difficult or sensitive to discuss, and hence are often avoided. The next section is included here to give some insight into the pragmatic approach we have taken internally. Its structure can be easily adapted to museums of any scale.

The ERM team is comprised of three key teams—these overlap in terms of personnel, but the two teams are designed to have distinctly different purviews: a senior management group responsible for policy decisions, and an operations group responsible for taking actions to mitigate the incident or emergency response. The third team (the safety team) is specifically focused on daily operations of the museum and how to embed a culture of safety across the organization. This third team will be addressed later in this chapter; the group generally focuses on optimizing the regular operations of the museum (thereby mitigating risk) rather than either setting policy or dealing directly with unexpected or emergent issues (see figure 7.2).

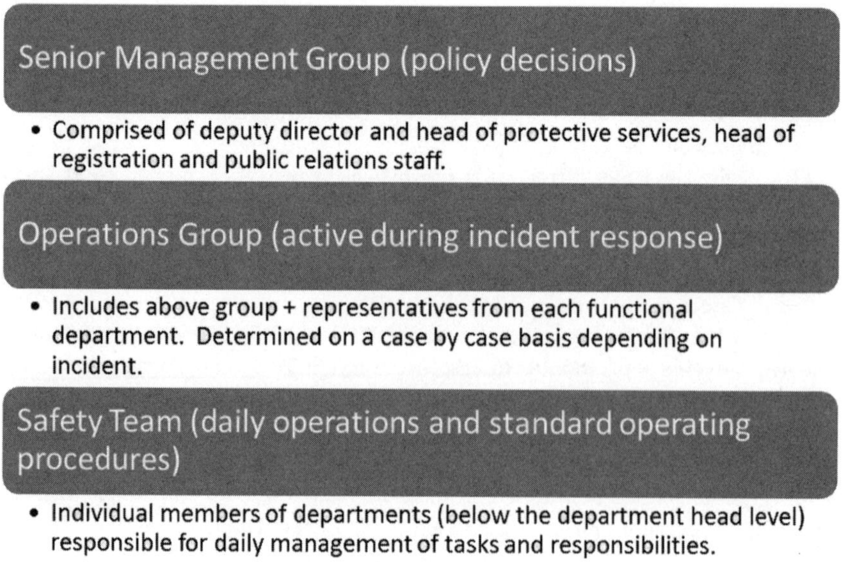

Senior Management Group (policy decisions)

- Comprised of deputy director and head of protective services, head of registration and public relations staff.

Operations Group (active during incident response)

- Includes above group + representatives from each functional department. Determined on a case by case basis depending on incident.

Safety Team (daily operations and standard operating procedures)

- Individual members of departments (below the department head level) responsible for daily management of tasks and responsibilities.

Figure 7.2. ERM Team Structure. *Source:* Author.

Members of the ERM operations group are the leaders and designated alternates who represent key functional areas of the museum. The deputy director of the museum acts as the liaison with the operations group and keeps the director fully informed of the group's work resolving issues and emergencies. The ERM operations group includes representatives from the following areas: collections, finance, development, information technology, facilities, marketing/communications, human resources, security, education, registrar, and outside consultants (legal counsel or others, as appropriate). In its initial work the group determined that the emergency plan, in order to maximize potential usefulness, would be as short as possible and would focus on giving guidance in determining the level of an emerging situation. These emergency levels require different kinds of communication and engagement with departmental or senior staff. Each level is briefly defined in the following paragraphs, to best demonstrate the escalation of seriousness of event, as well as the scope of response required.

A level one emergency is a short-term incident that usually can be resolved by the responding service area. The event is not likely to adversely affect life, health, property, or the overall operation of the museum. Notification of the incident is limited to those directly involved in the event, as well as the director of communications. Examples of a level one incident might include a computer-related hoax or virus, a localized water-pipe break, or a short-term power outage.

A level two emergency may adversely affect museum operations, threaten life or health of staff, volunteers, and visitors, the art collection, or other property. It is usually a relatively minor event that has a predictable duration and little impact beyond those using the part of the building in which it occurred. Senior management is notified and kept informed of progress made resolving the issue. Examples of level two emergencies might include a gas leak at the hot shop of the glass studio, a small fire in the café kitchen, or weather-related incidents. Because of their limited, or focused nature, a museum-wide response is not required for a level one or level two emergency. Standard operating procedures are used to address the situation.

A level three emergency has an unpredictable duration and likely disrupts some or all museum operations. Some emergencies can become quite complex because various areas become involved in responding—sometimes alongside outside fire, medical, or police personnel—and must be coordinated. In these situations, the senior management liaison determines whether to activate the ERM operations team because of the many complex decisions and actions that are required. Examples of a level three emergency may include a blizzard, tornado, explosion, criminal or terrorist threats, a shooting, civil unrest in or near the museum, hostage situation, major theft, or significant computer security breach. Management must respond quickly and effectively in the event of a level three emergency. The ERM team senior management liaison determines when a situation is a level three emergency, assembles the operations group, and manages a response.

A comprehensive approach to risk management relies on having the right people in the right positions within the organization, and being sure you can trust them to both follow the ERM plans as we have outlined for the institution and exercise good judgment when faced with the real-world situations that do not conform to what was presented in training or subsequent discussions. In the remainder of this chapter, we will focus on highlighting the TMA's approach to human resources, and how to both evaluate and mitigate risk in this vital area.

HUMAN RESOURCES AND ERM

Human Resources and the museum's approach to talent is a source of the museum's greatest strength (its people) and one of its most significant risk areas. Hence the need for a comprehensive approach to talent management. In *Being the Boss*, one of the key concepts Linda Hill and Kent Lineback address is the need to balance strategic thinking with practical and tactical actions on a daily basis.[3] A focus on talent development at all organizational levels helps significantly with both arenas: you can proactively identify areas of conflict, under-performance, or retention risk that may affect your strategic thinking, but the ways in which you approach solving those issues are tactical and the focus of everyday activities. It is important to emphasize that this is equally true of the director of the museum as it is of the supervisor of the visitor services staff. With the hiring of a director of human resources in 2013, the museum made a commitment to a more holistic focus on the entire staff and volunteer corps that work at the museum. This has had an impact at all levels of the organization. The organization has now begun to address succession planning for key leadership staff and has a talent acquisition process that ensures the museum has the talent required to appropriately mitigate risks at the individual level, and a pipeline of early career professionals to diversify the institution.

MAPPING TALENT NEEDS TO RISK NEEDS

At the senior leadership level, the museum began to link enterprise risk to departmental and individual roles. When opportunities presented, the HR staff collaborated with hiring managers to conduct work inventories and role evaluations. By doing so, the museum was able to align risk at the individual level to drive a higher degree of accountability from frontline staff. Overall, this has created greater transparency regarding risk ownership, allowed the organization to identify needed redundancies, and helped draw out skill and competency gaps. Through this and a comprehensive talent acquisition process, the museum was able to make structure and staffing changes that allow for a greater distribution of risk management accountability and capabilities.

As an example, the structure of the security department has made incremental changes over three years to transition from traditional foot patrol security to a comprehensive safety and protective services department. This represents a shift in thinking from security as purely a tactical endeavor to one that is both strategic (i.e., proactively identifying issues that may affect the museum in the future) and pragmatic (e.g., number of ground staff and kinds of patrols) in nature. Or to put it succinctly, a shift from a narrow definition that just sees the security department from within its own bubble to a systems thinking approach focused on how security issues and personnel both affect and are affected by other parts of the organization. This fundamental change began by mapping talent needs with a more comprehensive security risk assessment, beginning with leadership then filtering down to the organizational structure, standard operating procedures, and finally the core skills and competencies required at the staff level of the department. With the structure of security now being safety and protective services, it is more encompassing of risk assessment and response.

Additionally, various department leaders and staff came together to formulate the safety team (the third team mentioned above in the ERM section) to address health and safety issues across the museum, a key component of enterprise risk management. As this team formed, it became increasingly evident that to create a true culture of safety, the team would require broad representation and accountability at the individual level to identify and mitigate safety risks. The team continues to work across departments and through various communications channels for engagement at all levels to recognize and address health and safety risks.

SUCCESSION PLANNING

The Toledo Museum of Art believes that the development and recognition of talent improves both individual and organizational performance, differentiating the museum from other organizations in the community. As the employment market and demographics shift, the acquisition and retention of engaged talent will continue to constrain. When considering enterprise risk management and sustainability, another key talent component that the museum considers is succession planning.

In 2013, the museum created a succession planning matrix that allowed senior leadership to look across the entire organization and categorize talent departure risks from the top down. This succession planning matrix was organized by department and assessed on a scale of 1–3 the criticality of the role, retirement risk, and retention risk. To assist with the visualization, the three areas were coded by red, yellow, and green. Red indicates significant retention risk, yellow equals medium risk, and green is low risk. Additional data was gathered to quantify the number of staff ready for succession and prioritize planning needs. (Figure 7.3 is an example of the chart with sample data filled in for several departments.)

This was the first step toward utilizing a systematic approach to identifying long-term talent risks and allowed the museum to establish plans to address any inadequacies. From here, the museum identified significant risks within various senior-level knowledge and technical roles. To address these risks, the talent acquisition function

Department	Position Title	Incumbent	Hire Date	Critical Role?	Retirement Risk	Retention Risk	Number of Staff Ready Now	Number of Staff Ready in 1-2 Years	Succession Planning Priorities
Directors Office	Director	Green	09/01/2010				1	1	
Directors Office	COO	Holiday	01/28/1991				1	2	
Directors Office	Associate Director	Miller	05/10/2005				1	1	
Directors Office	Coordinator, Office of Special Projects	Silverman	08/06/2010						
Directors Office	Executive Asst	Kreptt	06/16/2010						
Finance	CFO	Fitzpatrick	05/05/2014						In role development; Look for EIC strategy
Finance	Purchasing Administrator	Sullivan	09/15/1981				1	1	
Finance	Asst.Controller	Miller	09/18/1975					1	In role development
Curatorial	Director of Collections	Williams	06/19/1978						External
Curatorial	Senior Curator	Open	09/11/1989					1	External
Conservation	Head of Conservation	Caremore	02/21/2003					1	
Conservation	Conservation Technician	Smith	11/19/1929					1	
Human Resources	Director of Human Resources	Miller	06/10/2013					1	
Human Resources	MGR of Human Resources	Boyd	07/14/2014						
Information Systems	Chief Information Officer	Jobs	07/21/2014						In role development; Look for EIC strategy
Information Systems	Asst Systems Officer/Registrar	Mill	07/10/2006					2	In role development; Look for EIC strategy
Information Systems	Tech/AV Equipment Technician	Open	06/05/2013						
Information Systems	Head Librarian	Stanbrock	06/16/2008					1	
Protective Services	Director, of Protective Services	Manning	07/13/2014						In role development; Look for EIC strategy
Protective Services	Manager, Protective Services	Joyce	02/19/2001					1	
Communications	Director of Communications	Fitzgerald	03/04/2009					1	
Communications	MGR of Social Media & Digital Communications	Samson	05/28/2013				1		
Communications	MGR of Press and PR	Bittman	05/27/2009				1		
Development	Director of Development	Opencheck	10/04/2013						In role development; Look for EIC strategy
Development	Development Officer	Clinton	12/01/2009						
Development	MGR of Development Services	Leonard	07/14/2014					1	In role development; Look for EIC strategy
Development	Head of Membership	McGee	10/28/2010						
Education	Director of Education	Cross	08/29/2011					1	In role development
Education	Manager, Family Center	McDonald	09/01/2001						
Education	Manager, Curriculum	Murphy	07/15/2013					1	
Facilities	Director, Facilities	Burgess	06/29/1992						In role development; Look for EIC strategy
Facilities	Night Supervisor, Facilities	Milner	07/11/1987						
Retail - Store	Manager, Retail Operations	Stork	08/14/1928						
Retail - Store	Assistant Manager, Retail Operations	May	09/01/2009						

Figure 7.3. TMA Succession Plan. *Source: Author.*

shifted to focus on the development of various early-in-career roles and positions that would act as a pipeline for future leadership. By moving to a more proactive talent management organization, various promotional opportunities were successfully filled internally and a number of talent-related risks were mitigated.

The museum has since grown the internship and youth work programs exponentially to meet various talent needs. A core museum principle that we must demonstrate diversity and inclusion in what we do is also a long-term ERM concern. In this instance, risk can be seen as the possibility of becoming increasingly irrelevant because as an organization we do not adequately reflect, through our personnel, the communities we serve. The early in career program also worked to address the museum's desire to drive more toward a significantly diverse workforce. Most recently, the museum was able to improve diversity recruitment to 40 percent for the summer internship program (all TMA internships are paid). A systems thinking approach provides the framework for moving these goals from aspirational and strategic to tactical and pragmatic. Working toward that goal can feel incremental, but as demonstrated with the shift in the summer internship program, significant changes can happen when clear goals align with senior leadership sponsorship and advocacy. You cannot simply *say* that you want to be more diverse. You must take specific actions in order to impact the bottom line number. Those actions may involve changing the *how* you recruit, for example, but you will only realize the larger institutional changes by accumulating steps forward.

The Toledo Museum of Art's journey through a broad-spectrum ERM examination has been one of discovery. While many involved in the process have been at the institution for years, this close consideration has allowed all involved to see even the most familiar aspects of the museum anew, and has given us a template for examining not only *what* we are doing, but *how* we are doing it. We have worked to marry the institutional strategic goals with practical and tactical actions that accumulatively result in getting closer to the broader objectives, and also help frontline staff prioritize this way of thinking as they execute their work. The next steps involve delving even more deeply into goals such as the one outlined here focused on talent management. Already, in the short time since we began in earnest, we have empowered staff to bring forward issues, enabled difficult discussions, and created a structure for approaching the unexpected events that are part and parcel of managing a complex public-facing institution, resulting in a stronger, more resilient, and more effective community resource.

BIBLIOGRAPHY

Ackoff, Russel L. "The Future of Operational Research is Past." *Journal of the Operational Research Society* 30 (1979): 93–104.
Davies, Nicola. "Muscle Memory and Visualization." *Frontline Security* 9, no. 3 (2014): 20–22.
Hill, Linda, and Kent Lineback. *Being the Boss: The 3 Imperatives for Becoming a Great Leader.* Boston: Harvard Business Review Press, 2011, 16.

NOTES

1. Russell L. Ackoff, "The Future of Operational Research is Past," *Journal of the Operational Research Society* 30 (1979): 93–104.

2. Nicola Davies, "Muscle Memory and Visualization," *Frontline Security* 9, no. 3 (2014): 20–22.

3. Linda Hill and Kent Lineback, *Being the Boss: The 3 Imperatives for Becoming a Great Leader* (Boston: Harvard Business Review Press, 2011), 16.

8

Planning for Cultural Relevance

A Systems Workshop at the Georgia O'Keeffe Museum

Douglas Worts

"When people who are actually creating a system start to see themselves as the source of their problems, they invariably discover a new capacity to create results they truly desire."[1]

"Human endeavors are part of larger systems . . . bound by invisible fabrics of interrelated actions, which often take years to fully play out their effects on each other. . . . Systems thinking is a conceptual framework, a body of knowledge and tools that has been developed over the past fifty years, to make the full patterns clearer, and to help us see how to change them effectively."[2] Within a cultural context, the purpose of using a systems thinking approach is to shed light on interconnections between and within societal and natural spheres. Museums are part of large social, economic, and environmental systems and have the potential to create cultural impacts that go well beyond the museum itself. Among the biggest challenges for museums is the planning for and measurement of cultural outcomes within the larger world as opposed to being focused on internal museum functions and public outputs. It is through systems thinking that museums can best realize their full value and relevance, for individuals, groups, and communities that all must exist within the constraints of the biosphere.

C. S. Holling is one of the many architects of systems thinking. Holling examined complex forest ecosystems[3] to better understand relationships among the smallest levels (cellular) to the largest levels (the large forest as a whole). The book he coedited, *Panarchy: Understanding Transformations in Human and Natural Systems*, offers a compelling lens for understanding how systems dynamics (methodology to study nonlinear and complex systems and phenomena) apply to culture as well as natural settings.[4]

Culture is a word that means different things, depending on the context.[5] In the broad sense, culture refers to how individuals and groups live their lives, over time. In

81

a Western context, our living culture is linked to a complex set of forces and factors that currently result in our pluralistic, urbanized, and globalized reality—which happen to include the systematic degradation of the biosphere (e.g., climate change and loss of species), as well as significant social and economic inequality across certain groups of people. Values, attitudes, beliefs, traditions, knowledge, goals, and measures of success, which together help to form the cultural foundation of humanity, drive existing human systems.

Museums are widely thought to be cultural organizations. While they collect historical, symbolic, and artistic materials that come from both earlier and contemporary periods, they also have cultural focuses. In the book *Mastering Civic Engagement: A Challenge to Museums*, the authors encouraged museums to think about culture as an organic and adaptive process—one that is marked by significant material culture, but not itself equal to the living culture.[6] Edgar Schein is quoted in this volume saying that culture is "a basic pattern of assumptions invented, discovered or developed by a given group as it learns to cope with its problems of external adaptation and internal integration."[7]

Museums aim to improve quality of life within society, through a focus on culture (or at least a subset of culture). As museums strive to be as culturally relevant as they can be to their local constituencies, systems thinking approaches offer powerful and holistic ways forward. It is possible for museums to engage with individuals, communities, and organizations to help create a culture that is adaptive to the changing realities of our world. The trick is that museums are generally more focused on carrying out traditional museum activities (e.g., collection building and exhibit development), rather than crafting new outcomes that impact the broader culture that underpins society. As such, generating socially impactful museum outcomes may take staff members outside their comfort zones. That museums have historically favored internal authority structures to drive expert-to-novice approaches to public engagement suggests that using a larger, systems-based approach to planning will challenge and potentially upset existing power hierarchies. Also, a systems thinking approach requires the adoption of an attitude of humility in the face of great complexity. Humility can be a challenge in environments that have historically relied on expertise and an authoritative voice.

This chapter outlines a workshop methodology designed to help museum staff plan for community cultural engagement in ways that are seen as relevant to the public through asking the following set of questions:

- What are the trends that currently are shaping the lives of citizens?
- What are the social, environmental, economic, and cultural forces that are creating these trends?
- Where are leverage points within the larger cultural system that could help enable desirable, cascading change across the system?
- What types of innovations related to history, art, and creativity are best able to create meaningful change?

- What types of feedback mechanisms will help guide the development of these innovations and have impact on the larger community, not simply museum visitors?

BACKGROUND ON THE GOKM AND SANTA FE

In 2014, the Georgia O'Keeffe Museum Research Center invited me to become its research center's first research fellow (museum studies). The residency required that I work for a month at the museum in Santa Fe, New Mexico. I focused on working with staff to identify ways to build new and stronger relationships among the museum, Santa Fe citizens, organizations, and local communities.

Santa Fe attracts a large number of tourists each year and museums are both drivers and recipients of this tourism. The Georgia O'Keeffe Museum (GOKM) has a healthy attendance (about 158,000 in 2015).[8] Based on a review of visitor comments, visitors (primarily tourists) seem happy with their experiences at the museum. However, serving tourists was not the focus of my workshop.

An important reference point for my project came from the director of the Georgia O'Keeffe Museum, Robert Kret, who told me that 85 percent of visitors to the museum came from outside New Mexico and that he wanted to find new ways to build meaningful connections to local populations. This statistic is not unique to the O'Keeffe Museum. It is a common phenomenon in many places where tourism is a principal driver of local economies. My goal was to introduce some tools, skills, and motivations to support the O'Keeffe Museum in thinking and planning differently to better connect with local communities while having positive impacts on the living culture by facilitating a two-day workshop with the museum staff.

The culture of Santa Fe is complex, vibrant, diverse, and challenged in numerous ways. Its 70,000 permanent residents spread out across the desert primarily in one- and two-story buildings, many of which are made of adobe that blends into the landscape. The city is home to a large population of artists with the arts contributing significantly to its economy. Yet conversely, large income gaps, undernourishment, low graduation rates, and underemployment are also ongoing.[9] With the focus of this project on the GOKM seeking to strengthen its connections with the local communities, it seemed essential to clearly identify what is important to those various local constituencies as a starting point for building bridges and relationships.

Historically, the focus of the museum has been to use the artworks of Georgia O'Keeffe to engage those who want to see and learn more about the paintings and the artist. However, local inhabitants have demonstrated over the years that relatively few visit the museum. For this workshop, I suggested the staff broadly consider the *spirit* of Georgia O'Keeffe in relation to the needs and interests of the local community. Although O'Keeffe's artworks could be useful in this work, the expansive creative spirit of O'Keeffe could provide many more options for innovation and public engagement than the narrower focus on her legacy in painting. A critical question for embarking on this path was "who will be framing the nature of the relationships that the museum wants to build with the local community?" It became clear that both the museum and community need to collaborate on and negotiate such relationships, which will be destined to change over time.

FRAMING THE WORKSHOP

The purpose of this workshop was to generate discussions and ideas of how the museum might better connect to the living culture within Santa Fe. Georgia O'Keeffe was tremendously attuned to the complex dynamics of nature, as well as to the human dimension of her community. Although her artworks are famous around the world, the artist's legacy goes beyond the material products of her creativity. Researchers investigating O'Keeffe continue to generate tremendous insights into how she inspired people in many other ways besides her art.[10]

The stated workshop goal was: "to generate meaningful discussion, identify useful relationships, and develop good ideas for how this museum could best build vital connections that are relevant to local communities." Twenty of the seventy-nine museum staff attended the workshop, including most senior managers, educators, and curators, as well as information technology and marketing specialists. The participants were asked to temporarily set aside their ordinary way of thinking about the museum in order to think outside the box over the course of the two days. If they could see the museum as one actor in a much larger system of interconnected parts (social, environmental, economic, and cultural), joined by a wide range of dynamics and variables, then new opportunities could be identified. If the museum hoped to build new relationships with locals, then it would need to address the following: (1) develop a new understanding of the forces shaping the local culture; (2) generate innovative strategies for cultivating new relationships with the public; and (3) develop an appreciation of how to build appropriate feedback loops (e.g., front-end, formative, and summative evaluation strategies) to help guide the evolving relationships.

TOOLS FOR SYSTEMS THINKING
AND SUSTAINABILITY PLANNING

The workshop revolved around a couple of sustainability planning tools (the compass of sustainability and pyramid explained below) developed by Alan AtKisson, an American sustainability educator and consultant.[11] Over two days, the group would work through five basic steps that guide and help manage the systems thinking process:

1. Identify the major *trends and indicators* that shape the local community;
2. Identify the *systems* forces (e.g., economic, social, environmental, and historical values and forces) that shape the trends along with potential leverage points to introduce new innovations;

3. Generate potential *innovations* that can be implemented at the leverage points to create shifts in the cultural trends along with cultural indicators that will help guide the innovation;
4. Identify the *strategies* to implement the innovations effectively; and
5. Take *action*.

The Compass of Sustainability

One of the tools provided in this workshop is called the *compass of sustainability*, developed to help individuals, organizations, and groups integrate multiple perspectives into their planning processes.[12] In this workshop context, participants were divided into four small groups and assigned one of the compass points to aid in fleshing out different perspectives on the task at hand—nature, economy, society, and well-being (see figure 8.1). *Sustainability* is a term that refers to the health and resilience of a complex system. It is not a term that is focused on an environmental perspective, nor is it linked only to social justice. Rather sustainability is a systems-thinking–based approach to understanding and planning for dynamic balance within the interwoven realms of nature, society, and economy. Culture is the foundational layer of human values, practices, and systems that link people to the vast world in which we live.

To help concretize the processes that the groups were exploring, a four-sided, multi-layered pyramid would be produced, with each side being dedicated to one of the four lenses of the compass (figure 8.1). The goal was to combine the focused insights produced by the four different perspectives into a holistic understanding of the complex interdependent systems.

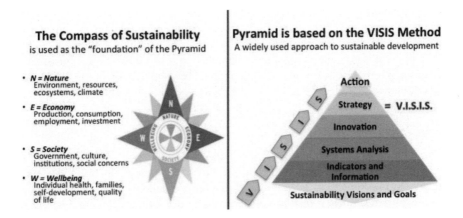

The Compass of Sustainability
is used as the "foundation" of the Pyramid

- **N = Nature**
  Environment, resources, ecosystems, climate
- **E = Economy**
  Production, consumption, employment, investment
- **S = Society**
  Government, culture, institutions, social concerns
- **W = Wellbeing**
  Individual health, families, self-development, quality of life

Pyramid is based on the VISIS Method
A widely used approach to sustainable development

Action
Strategy = V.I.S.I.S.
Innovation
Systems Analysis
Indicators and Information
Sustainability Visions and Goals

Figure 8.1. The Compass of Sustainability and Pyramid. *Source*: Alan AtKisson.

Pyramid

The building of a pyramid is a relatively simple way to add a playful, physical dimension to what is otherwise a rather complex thinking exercise. In short, it is easier for participants to make sense of the information generated through the different stages of the planning process. The pyramid helps weave together four perspectives with five different steps (levels 1-5 below) that can help bring insight and clarity to the problem at hand. In exercises like this, it is essential to build the pyramid upon a clear goal.

The groups developed lists of trends and indicators that they felt were meaningful as they thought about the overarching needs and realities of local communities. These trends were based on the perceptions within the groups. In some instances, there was data from reports, such as *Santa Fe Trends—2014*,[13] whereas others were consensus-based understanding of trends, based on their experiences of living in the community. Ultimately, it is useful to become as clear as possible on these trends. However, it can also be useful to reflect on trends that may be happening, which may not have actual measurements associated with them. In an actual planning exercise, all efforts would be made to verify actual trend data.

Level 1: Trends and Indicators

The following is a sampling of trends that participants identified as being important within local communities. Through the four lenses of the compass, participants shifted their focus from being museum-centric (collections, exhibits, etc.) to one of being community-centric (local needs, opportunities, etc.). Groups identified the trends and the direction in which each was heading (table 8.1).

As part of building the first layer of the pyramid—*indicators* and *information*—participants reviewed the work of all four groups as it was added to the base level of the pyramid structure (see figure 8.1). It became clear to all that there was much overlap between the perspectives. For example, employment rates are an element of economics, but they also have large social and well-being implications. The benefit of this approach is not only to reflect on the local context within which the museum is attempting to be relevant, but it also encourages the group to look at the issues and trends that are actively shaping the local culture.

Level 2: Systems Mapping

Having identified a wide range of trends and indicators, each of the four groups selected one or two of their most significant trends and issues to create a systems map of causes and effects. Indicators and trends often point to how well a system is working. Trends, such as increasing income disparities, the loss of natural habitats, cross-cultural tensions, or increasing interest in food and health help identify where shifts need to occur. Sometimes there is a need to reinforce some trends or reverse

Table 8.1. Trends and Directions Important in Communities

SOCIETY	ECONOMY *(Group made two Economy lists— museum-based & state-based)*	NATURE	WELL-BEING
Racism—tolerance is increasing	*Museum*: Number memberships (local)—increasing	Water supply (rain, precipitation)— declining	Opportunities for seeking spirituality— increasing
Hunger— increasing	*Museum*: Number of major donors— increasing	Average temperature—rising	Effectiveness of education in preparing youth for life—declining
Quality of Public Education— declining	*Museum*: Number of tourists by air— increasing	Forest loss (and risk of loss)—rising	Wealth gap— increasing
Wage Gap between haves/have-nots— increasing	*State*: Number of young professionals— declining	Public interest in local food (farm to table)—rising	Rewarding jobs (i.e., meaningful)— declining
Youth population— declining (leaving the state)	*State*: Real wages— declining		
	State: Employment rate—increasing		
	State: Poverty rate—rising		

Source: Author.

others. By examining causes of the trends, such as how increasing carbon dioxide emissions leads to rising temperatures, as well as the causes of the causes, such as how increasing tourism increases carbon dioxide emissions from travel, it is possible to identify potential leverage points in the larger system. It is at these leverage points where, given the right kind of innovation, cascading impacts can be generated across the system.

Every group that goes through this planning process produces a systems map as a working document for the group. They may look like a plate of spaghetti (figure 8.2) because there are many factors identified, as well as a number of cause and effect connections.

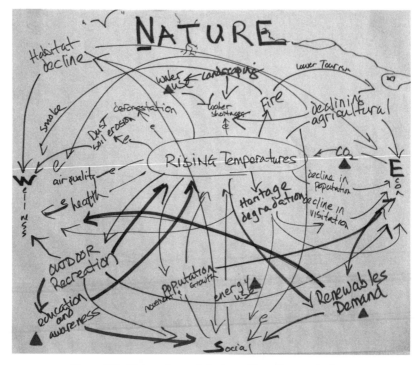

Figure 8.2. Nature Group's Systems Map. *Source*: Author.

Figure 8.3. Georgia O'Keeffe Museum Staff with Finished Pyramid. *Source*: Author.

The four main trends selected as centers for the mapping exercises (one per group) were: economy—lack of city and state funding for museums; nature—rising temperatures; society—effectiveness of public education; and well-being—lack of good jobs. The teams asked themselves questions such as:

- What causes shifts in this trend and issue?
- What are the effects of this trend and issue?
- What connections can be seen in the various effects and causes?
- Are there leverage points in the systems that, if the right intervention could be initiated, the system would shift in significant ways?

I am illuminating one of the teams' approaches here, for illustrative purposes.

In Figure 8.2, the nature group selected rising temperatures as its major trend to map. Small triangles mark the spots where group members identified potential leverage points, at which the right innovation could create meaningful change in the system, thereby helping to address the troubling trend of rising temperatures and its implications. At this point, the group had not generated innovations but was simply examining the systems environment for good places to intervene.[14]

The following possible leverage points were identified and added to the nature side of the pyramid: carbon emissions; managing energy use; education and awareness; water usage; and increasing demand for renewable energy.

Level 3: Innovations

Innovations are interventions in systems. There are many types of innovations, and they include new products, novel processes, and mindset changes. For a museum, thinking outside the box involves considering options for programming that may go well beyond traditional public engagement strategies, like exhibits, and that may occur outside leisure time. Innovations could occur in the community; involve partnerships with other organizations; potentially focus less on teaching about Georgia O'Keeffe; and focus more on using O'Keeffe as an inspiration for community-based creativity that addresses current trends and needs. Pursuing innovations generated through this type of process may strongly encourage an organization to expand its existing stated mission and vision. Leaders in organizations may feel quite uncomfortable exploring such territory. However, this is simply part of how a learning organization stretches itself to better fit in a world that is changing.[15]

Part of the museum's challenge was to find ways in which the organization, with or without partners, could carry out the innovations. Participants also needed to think about the feedback loops that would let the museum know if the initiative was having the imagined positive impacts on individuals, groups, neighborhoods, businesses, government, and so on. Each group generated a set of ideas for innovations they felt could be implemented, considering the leverage points previously identified. After brainstorming the innovations, along with accompanying goals, impacts, and strategies, the groups then selected their top three ideas and these were then put on the pyramid as each group presented their ideas to the other groups.

Once all the innovations were presented to the full group by the four compass subgroups, each participant voted to select one innovation from each side of the pyramid. The result of the voting was as follows:

1. *Create a community garden (and potentially many)*: drawing on the inspired creativity of the artist as a gardener and observer of the natural world. The garden would be a place to foster community dialogue, creativity, awareness of issues, and skill development in relation to food, eating habits, and natural systems.
2. *Staff volunteering initiative*: developing a program to support museum staff in volunteering at a range of organizations across the city, to both better understand the diverse needs of communities within the city and build relationships with other potential partner organizations.
3. *Become a learning-living museum*: involving the creativity of both art and science (likely through partnerships) to explore alternative energy, sustainable cultures, and green architecture.
4. *Create museum apprenticeships for locals*: establishing at the museum a way of proactively engaging local young people from diverse backgrounds to develop skills related to the operation of museums.

At this stage in the workshop, it was agreed that these ideas must be fleshed out in significant detail, because they need to be fully assessed before a commitment of resources for prototype development is made. Ideally, a project brief would be developed for each idea, including clear statement of goals; the needs being addressed; the detailed strategies to be used; and feedback loops that would guide how the impacts of these initiatives would be assessed.

Level 4: Strategies

The fourth level of the pyramid is reserved for the strategies that will be necessary to move the selected innovations to the next stage. Each group spent time preparing a list of appropriate actions for moving their selected initiative toward realization and identifying individuals who will lead these processes. Beyond this, the groups generated many practical ideas for laying a solid foundation for the projects, building internal and external support and exploring financial considerations. One example is from the group that advanced the staff volunteering innovation, which came to be known as the *community compass*. This project involves museum staff being paid to volunteer in the community as a way of building relationships and better understanding the needs of local populations. The group suggested the following strategies:

- Create partnerships with various community organizations where GOKM staff could actively participate in targeted volunteer projects.
- Develop a pilot project to test the idea.

- Review how well volunteers gather insights into community needs and opportunities.
- Assess potential to generate community-based partnerships in which the GOKM could help bring the spirit of Georgia O'Keeffe to bear in a productive way.
- Increase visibility for GOKM through collaborative initiatives.

Of all the project innovations generated through this workshop, the community compass was the one that was carried forward and now has been implemented.[16]

Level 5: Actions

The capstone activity for the workshop, including the moment when the very top section of the pyramid is put in place, involves having individuals make commitments to take next steps. In this case, members of museum staff made commitments to taking next steps to formulate their ideas fully so that prototypes can be created, tested, and then implemented formally.

POTENTIAL FOR PROFESSIONAL DEVELOPMENT IN HUMAN RESOURCES

As a result of this professional development workshop, the O'Keeffe museum is poised for next steps to make its work more embedded in community issues. Human resources may provide an important entry point for helping staff members become acquainted with systems approaches, which can be a challenging process. Those who put a great deal of effort into building specialized expertise may have to put it aside in order to build relationships of mutual trust, common vision, and methods for working together with our staff and community. This process may take time. Initiatives may move forward incrementally with shorter- and longer-term goals. By embracing a systems thinking approach, it is possible for museums to expand their traditional sphere of influence and step into the role of a facilitator of cultural dynamics. New skills, goals, and measures of success will be necessary, but there are many tools to help museums realize this vision of fostering cultures of resilience, flourishing, and sustainability.

BIBLIOGRAPHY

American Association of Museums. *Mastering Civic Engagement: A Challenge to Museums.* Washington, DC: American Association of Museums, 2002.
AtKisson, Alan. *The Sustainability Transformation: How to Accelerate Positive Change in Challenging Times.* New York: Routledge, 2010.

Georgia O'Keeffe Museum. "2015: The Story in Numbers." Accessed December 2016. https://www.okeeffemuseum.org/about-the-museum/annual-reports/.

Gunderson, Lance, and Crawford S. Holling, eds. *Panarchy: Understanding Transformations in Human and Natural Systems*. Washington, DC: Island Press, 2002.

Holling, Crawford S. "Resilience and Stability of Ecological Systems." *Annual Review of Ecology and Systematics* 4, no. 1 (1973): 1–23.

Imm-Stroukoff, Eumie, Director of GOKM Research Center, correspondence with author, August 25, 2016.

Janes, Robert R. *Museums in a Troubled World: Renewal, Irrelevance or Collapse?* New York: Routledge, 2009.

Liming, Reed, ed. *Santa Fe Trends—2014*. Santa Fe, NM: City of Santa Fe, 2014. www.santa fenm.gov/document_center/document/1528.

Meadows, Donella. *Places to Intervene in a System*. Hartland, VT: The Sustainability Institute, 1999. http://donellameadows.org/archives/leverage-points-places-to-intervene-in -a-system/.

———. *Thinking in Systems*. White River Junction, VT: Chelsea Green, 2008.

Museums Association (UK). *Museums Change Lives*. London: Museums Association, 2013.

Senge, Peter. "Does Your Organization Have a Learning Disability?" In *The Fifth Discipline: The Art and Practice of the Learning Organization*, 17–26. New York: Doubleday, 1990.

———. *The Fifth Discipline: The Art and Practice of the Learning Organization*. New York: Doubleday, 1990.

Senge, Peter, C. Otto Scharmer, Joseph Jaworski, and Betty Sue Flowers. *Presence: An Exploration of Profound Change in People, Organizations, and Society*. New York: Doubleday, 2004.

Stein, Edgar H. *Organizational Culture and Leadership: A Dynamic View*. San Francisco: Jossey-Bass, 1985. Quoted in Kertzner, Daniel. "The Lens of Organizational Culture." In *Mastering Civic Engagement: A Challenge to Museums*, 40. Washington, DC: American Association of Museums, 2002.

Sutter, Glenn. "Thinking Like a System: Are Museums Up to the Challenge?" *Museums & Social Issues* 1, no. 2 (2006): 203–18.

Worts, Douglas. "On Museums, Culture and Sustainable Development." In *Museums and Sustainable Communities: Canadian Perspectives*, edited by Lisette Ferera, 21–27. Quebec City: International Council of Museums–Canada, 1998.

NOTES

1. Peter Senge, Otto Scharmer, Joseph Jaworski, and Betty Sue Flowers, *Presence: An Exploration of Profound Change in People, Organizations, and Society* (New York: Doubleday, 2004), 45.

2. Peter Senge, *The Fifth Discipline: The Art and Practice of the Learning Organization* (New York: Doubleday, 1990), 7.

3. Crawford S. Holling, "Resilience and Stability of Ecological Systems," *Annual Review of Ecology and Systematics* 4, no. 1 (1973): 1–23.

4. Lance Gunderson and Crawford S. Holling, eds., *Panarchy: Understanding Transformations in Human and Natural Systems* (Washington, DC: Island Press, 2002).

5. For example: Robert R. Janes, *Museums in a Troubled World. Renewal, Irrelevance or Collapse?* (New York: Routledge, 2009); Glenn Sutter, "Thinking Like a System: Are Museums

Up for the Challenge?" *Museums and Social Issues* 1, no. 2 (2006): 203–18; Douglas Worts, "On Museums, Culture and Sustainable Development," in *Museums and Sustainable Communities: Canadian Perspectives*, ed. Lisette Ferera (Quebec City: International Council of Museums–Canada, 1998), 21–27.

6. American Association of Museums, *Mastering Civic Engagement: A Challenge to Museums* (Washington, DC: American Association of Museums, 2002).

7. Edgar H. Stein, *Organizational Culture and Leadership: A Dynamic View* (San Francisco: Jossey-Bass, 1985), quoted in Daniel Kertzner, "The Lens of Organizational Culture," in *Mastering Civic Engagement: A Challenge to Museums* (Washington, DC: American Association of Museums, 2002), 40.

8. "2015: The Story in Numbers," Georgia O'Keeffe Museum, accessed December 2016, https://www.okeeffemuseum.org/about-the-museum/annual-reports/.

9. Reed Liming, ed., *Santa Fe Trends—2014* (Santa Fe, NM: City of Santa Fe, 2014), www.santafenm.gov/document_center/document/1528.

10. See the museum's research files on O'Keeffe and her relationship to the community of Abiquiu, New Mexico.

11. Alan AtKisson is president and CEO of the global sustainability consulting firm AtKisson Inc.

12. Alan AtKisson, *The Sustainability Transformation: How to Accelerate Positive Change in Challenging Times* (London: Routledge, 2010).

13. Liming, *Santa Fe Trends—2014.*

14. For further discussion on this topic, see Donella Meadows, *Places to Intervene in a System* (Hartland, VT: The Sustainability Institute, 1999), http://donellameadows.org/archives/leverage-points-places-to-intervene-in-a-system/.

15. Peter Senge, "Does Your Organization Have a Learning Disability?" in *The Fifth Discipline: The Art and Practice of the Learning Organization* (New York: Doubleday, 1990), 17–26.

16. Eumie Imm-Stroukoff, Director of GOKM Research Center, correspondence with author, August 25, 2016.

Part IV

Take Action

1. Often the first step to invite change in organizational structure involves professional development (testing the waters, so to speak) followed by team-oriented organizational planning. Worts's chapter shared one museum's attempt to think about community needs and how the museum can become more relevant to and embedded in its community. The Georgia O'Keeffe Museum, with Worts's facilitation, used Alan AtKisson's sustainability steps. How would your museum address the following steps?

    - Identify the trends and indicators that shape the local community.
    - Identify the systems forces that shape the trends along with potential leverage points to introduce new innovations.
    - Generate potential innovations that can be implemented at the leverage points to create shifts in the cultural trends along with cultural indicators that will help guide the innovation.
    - Identify the strategies to implement the innovations effectively.
    - Take action.

2. Both chapters offer approaches that illustrate how human resources can initiate and offer continuing support for collaborative teamwork across departments at the Toledo Museum of Art and the Georgia O'Keeffe Museum. In what ways are your museum's human resources supporting cross-department planning for retaining staff, promoting sustainability, addressing risk management, and fostering diversity and community engagement? What are potential new directions?

Part V

SYSTEMS THINKING IN EXHIBITIONS AND PROGRAMS

In systems-based museum practices, museum work is visitor-centered and exhibitions and programs are interconnected to provide well-rounded museum experiences to visitors. In addition, the process of creating exhibitions and programs are organic, fluid, and sometimes unexpected. In order to create impactful museum exhibitions and programs, museums must think about multiple stakeholders (both internal and external) and long-term planning; these are part of an ongoing and complicated learning process that can create the most enjoyable and educational experience for diverse audiences.

The Museum (the fictional museum based on a real museum first introduced in the Part I introduction) plans exhibitions and programs separately often without various constituents in mind. Exhibitions are created by few people, often by one curator, without any input from other functions of the museum, visitors, or external stakeholders and their needs, and programs are created by the education department after the exhibition is developed. In addition, although other functions such as development and marketing play an important role in raising funding for and promoting exhibitions and programs, they are never part of the exhibition team and they do not know what the museum is planning. This creates a difficult disconnect where development staff are trying to raise funding for the programs and exhibitions that they do not have in-depth knowledge of and marketing staff are trying to promote the services without knowing how they can be beneficial to general audiences. Additionally, the exhibition itself, created by one or two people, is not about how it can have impact on visitors; visitor input was rarely included in the planning process. Rather it is more about one person's vision and scholarship, which may not matter to most community members. This is an extreme example of a non-collaborative and isolated museum exhibition and program development. The chapters in this part will provide examples that are quite different from *The Museum*'s approach.

These chapters present exhibition and program development processes that adopt a more collective approach. In them, a team of various museum professionals, partners, and other external constituents plan and execute museum services from the outset, working together for the benefit of the whole museum and its community. Caroline Angel Burke and Monica Parker-James in chapter 9 use complexity theory to explain the exhibition itself as a complicated and organic system as well as articulating the process of developing exhibitions as involving various internal and external subsystems, using large-scale exhibition development examples at the Museum of Science and the Edward M. Kennedy Institute for the Senate in Boston. This chapter also explains how exhibition development outcomes are based on visitor experience and expectations by involving visitors in getting feedback and testing prototypes.

Chapter 10, written by Deborah Randolph and Cora Fisher, highlights a collective exhibition development process co-facilitated by a curator (Randolph) and educator (Fisher) in partnership with local organizations in not only creating exhibitions but also developing programs encouraging collective actions that are creative, socially inclusive, and sustainable. The exhibition, *Collective Actions*, at the Southeastern Center for Contemporary Art in Winston-Salem, North Carolina, featured in this chapter not only uses the systems approach in developing the exhibition that is characterized as anti-hierarchical, communal, and inclusive but also embeds systems thinkers and artists in creating systems thinking knowledge as content of the exhibition.

9

Managing Exhibit Development in a Fluid Environment

Caroline Angel Burke and Monica Parker-James

Creating a relevant, unique, and meaningful museum visitor experience is both exhilarating and challenging. Museum experiences are not created in a vacuum. Exhibits are complex projects created in a fluid environment by teams of people with diverse expertise and experiences. The process calls upon a broad range of internal and external stakeholders with varying levels of input, influence, and involvement. Every exhibit is the result of an idea that undergoes a process particular to an organization. In this chapter, we will explore how a systems thinking approach to the exhibit development process can help to ensure a positive experience for the development team and a final product that achieves project goals and supports the museum's mission.

Systems thinking is a natural fit for exhibit development; it is a creative process involving a wide variety of parts or subsystems working together in service of a whole. In our experience, the concepts most relevant to the exhibit development process fall in the realm of complexity theory. As summarized by Jackson, complexity theory focuses on the relationships between the parts of the system, which is viewed as a constantly changing process. The system may only be understood in the context of these relationship patterns.[1]

In this context, the *system* refers to two interrelated ecologies: the exhibition itself, with its many interrelated parts, and the dynamic process by which exhibitions are developed. The former arguably is one complex product of the latter, but the key elements of a system are present: dynamic relationships between interconnected people, parts, and resources that act according to rules and norms and in reaction to internal and external forces. By acknowledging that a system is a dynamic environment, systems thinkers employ expectations for change and complexity, model those expectations, and change accordingly in ways that match a successful exhibit development process.

For the purposes of this chapter, we will focus on one model of exhibit development in which a project manager guides an idea through a process involving a team of exhibit development experts. In our experience as creative project managers, our roles were to manage that creative process, striking a careful balance between responding to changes and staying focused on project goals.

The exhibit development model we follow evolves through progressively more interconnected phases. The description may seem linear, but in fact the exhibit development process is complex, iterative, and responsive to a constantly shifting development environment. The project manager's role is to recognize this complexity and, with an understanding of the roles of all members of the exhibit project team and an appreciation for the nuances of the exhibit development environment, guide the creative effort to the successful completion of the project.

Exhibit project teams vary in size and makeup. Our experience is in the development of both permanent and traveling exhibits that ranged in size from 500 square feet to 13,000 square feet, including the 10,000-square-foot permanent exhibition the *Hall of Human Life* at the Museum of Science, Boston, *The Science Behind Pixar*, a 13,000-square-foot traveling exhibition developed by the Museum of Science, Boston, in collaboration with Pixar Animation Studios, and smaller collections-based installations at the Museum of Science, Boston, and the Edward M. Kennedy Institute for the Senate.

These exhibits involved core teams that included a project manager and one or more professionals in the roles of exhibit developer (also called a content developer or exhibit planner, among other titles), graphic designer, exhibit designer, technical designer, software designer, and curatorial staff. Additional team members include marketing representatives, development or advancement officers, education staff, facilities representatives, traveling exhibit staff who will be responsible for touring the exhibit if it will travel to other museums, and access advisors who ensure that the exhibit is meeting goals for visitors who may be visually or hearing impaired or have other barriers to accessing content.

In order to provide context for how a systems thinking approach benefits the exhibit development process, we will give an overview of the process model we use, beginning with *idea initiation and development* (see Figure 9.1). One practice is to hold large brainstorming sessions with numerous museum professionals and additional stakeholders to gather a broad range of ideas and perspectives on the exhibit concept. This not only serves to generate energy, enthusiasm, and buy-in for the project in the larger organizational system; it also arms the project team with baseline ideas, assumptions, and connections to the mission of the museum. Initially the project team may include a full core team as described above, or simply a project manager, exhibit developer or curator, and exhibit designer. The project team will determine the scope and direction for the exhibit, and build foundational understandings around a project. The team will identify must-haves, nice-to-haves, and must-not-haves; create a funding plan, initial timeline, and budget; and secure input and approval from project champions, who may be trustees, senior leadership representatives, board members, key collaborators, or other invested individuals. The end product is the

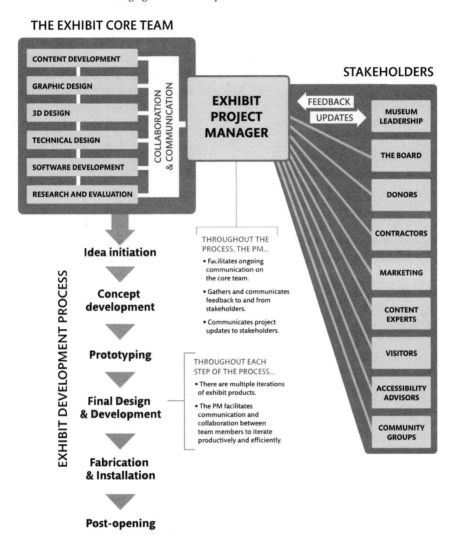

Figure 9.1. Exhibit Development Process Model Graphic. *Source:* **Emily Marsh.**

museum's version of the design brief and will set the course of phases to follow. One might imagine that these phase deliverables will need to be iterated as the team secures consensus from stakeholders, but it is the job of the project manager to balance this collaborative participation from other subsystems with the rules of project management. Somewhere among the dynamism, there are rules and resource parameters that are firm, and one of the project team's jobs is to meet these firm parameters.

During *concept development*, the team drafts a comprehensive plan for content, design, and learning objectives for the project. The team may expand to include additional members with varying skill sets, including content and education; physical, graphic, software, and technical design; evaluation; marketing; and development. This is a great time to undertake team research, conduct front-end evaluation, begin preliminary market testing, review existing benchmarks, discuss universal design considerations, and identify relevant educational standards. Collaborative development of the look and feel in combination with expectations of visitor flow and throughput will be important to pin down, with the team identifying and describing key visitor experiences. The final deliverable for this, as with all phases, is consent to move to the next phase by museum management.

Prototyping happens throughout the exhibit development process and involves testing concepts and experiences with potential users (visitors), ideally in progressive levels of complexity resulting in testing the experience in as close to the final environment as possible, and iterating design and content as needed. While prototyping could theoretically go on forever, eventually an exhibit will need to be built and opened, so the project team should decide upon ground rules for testing prior to initiating prototyping. In *final design and development*, all necessary elements, from refined label copy or media scripts to interactive wireframes and fabrication drawings, are put into place so that fabrication and installation may begin. The *fabrication and installation* phase seems—but rarely is—straightforward, with iterative course corrections occasionally required when as designed becomes as built.

Post opening is a crucial period in an exhibit development process to complete all technical and support documentation in situ, reflect on the project, and recommend modifications to the running of the next exhibition project. The work doesn't stop when the exhibit opens. If the project has been sufficiently funded and planned, there will be financial and staff resources available to conduct summative and remedial evaluation, and when possible, make improvements to the exhibit based on early visitor feedback. Analyzing how successfully exhibit components contribute to larger exhibition goals and experiences not only acknowledges the model of exhibition as a system of subsystems (exhibits and gallery programs); it reminds the organization that the system continues to be dynamic after it is opened, with programmatic needs still to be addressed. For example, part of the *Hall of Human Life*'s project budget also included an endowment to make sure that content, interactive, and graphic label components could be updated on an annual basis to reflect the advances in researchers' knowledge of human health and biology.

THE ROLE OF SUBSYSTEMS

Systems thinking in exhibit development relies on operating from the perspective that each system in the process is an element in a larger system. J. Alex Sherrer, who writes about systems thinking for project management, underscores this concept as the "realization that separates systems thinking from ordinary linear thought."[2]

This willingness to see the project as a whole system, rather than just the siloed parts as defined by the roles of individuals, is what enables a successful exhibition. A museum may have the best graphic designer in the country on the team, but if she views her work only in terms of her own aesthetic, the exhibition will fail. Instead, she must be able to see how her work can support the exhibition's educational goals, accessibility requirements, physical design, technical usability standards, and more.

PROTOTYPING: AN INTERNAL SUBSYSTEM EXAMPLE

We can use prototyping as an example of an internal subsystem. The majority of exhibit projects we have managed have involved multiple interactive, hands-on visitor activities and experiences (components) designed to support informal education goals. As each component is essentially a brand-new product or unknown subsystem, prototyping developing solutions is crucial to eventual component success. Prototyping is a form of modeling in which the exhibit team creates mock-ups, or beta versions, of visitor experiences. The prototypes are designed to test a variety of factors: Can visitors figure out how to use the component? Does the experience support the learning goals that the museum set for that component? Is it fun or enjoyable?

While final prototyping typically happens toward the end of the exhibit development process, iterative testing may take place throughout the process. Early prototyping may be very rough and simple, using pencil and paper and lots of conversations with visitors, while later prototyping may include fairly sophisticated and robust approximations of exhibit components. The outputs, or results, of prototyping become inputs that impact other subsystems in the process. Physical design will be tested for usability, its ability to reinforce intended activities, and its physical accessibility to all visitors. If prototyping reveals that visitors have difficulty operating a particular lever or handle, for example, the exhibit designers will investigate alternative physical designs.

Prototyping also helps content developers affirm that label copy supports learning objectives or identify copy that is confusing. Based on these inputs, graphic designers will take that copy and design a label that is readable, attractive, and accessible. For example, on *The Science Behind Pixar* exhibit, prototyping revealed that visitors were very focused on the images from Pixar movies used in the design of the exhibit. The graphic designer capitalized on this focus and created a novel approach that used callouts on large Pixar images to emphasize key content concepts. This enabled the exhibit team to convey math and science content in a way that was engaging, appealing, and accessible.

Material selection will also be influenced by the outcomes of prototyping; testing reveals whether certain materials are robust enough to support usage. If the team is anticipating welcoming 20,000 visitors a year to a particular exhibit, they may be able to make different technology and physical design choices than if the museum is anticipating welcoming two million guests annually. Each decision the team makes about the technology and materials for the exhibit is informed by inputs from other subsystems including prototyping, fundraising, technical design, and more, and also serves as an input into other subsystems, for example financing and exhibit maintenance. For example, durability was a significant factor in deciding on what material to use for component parts in the *Hall of Human Life*. These parts are expensive to manufacture, so testing with less expensive versions first was key. In addition, prototyping with the public helped the team to choose materials that encouraged visitors to participate but discouraged them from bringing parts home.

Figure 9.2. Photo of child interacting with museum activity. *Source*: Author.

THE EDUCATION ECOSYSTEM:
AN EXTERNAL SUBSYSTEM EXAMPLE

The exhibitions we have been involved with have been designed to meet specific informal educational objectives. If museum professionals operating in the informal education space hope to create valuable and relevant learning experiences for our audiences, we must understand the educational ecosystems of our visitors. This ecosystem is made up of informal elements including museums and other cultural experiences, libraries, educational programming, online offerings, and more. This ecosystem also includes formal education, and museum professionals must consider this subsystem throughout the exhibit development process.

For many museums, a good portion of current or potential visitation comes in the form of school groups. The American Alliance of Museums reports that museums receive approximately fifty-five million school group visits each year.[3] The exhibit development team must therefore think about how the exhibit they are creating relates to the formal education systems of their visitors.

For example, it is likely that the home state of an institution has adopted a set of kindergarten through twelfth grade learning and achievement standards that strongly shape how teachers approach the topics the museum explores. These state-specific formal education frameworks define skills that students are expected to master at each grade level. Teachers choose which museums and exhibits to visit and evaluate their visit experiences based on how well these standards are met. The exhibit development team's responsibility is to understand these standards as inputs into the system that will impact content choices, activity design, exhibit marketing, and scheduling.

For example, program popularity for various historical eras varies throughout the school year. At the Edward M. Kennedy Institute in Boston, a program devoted to the Compromise of 1850 is incredibly popular for a month or so in the spring, because that is when many school districts are teaching about that historical event.

COMMUNICATION AND FEEDBACK

At all phases of the exhibit development process, communication is key to ensuring that the many subsystems involved in the exhibit development process work in concert. The project manager is the conduit between the exhibit development team and museum leadership, the board, donors, outside contractors, the marketing department, external collaborators, visitors, the community, and more. The project manager must gather feedback for the exhibit team from all relevant stakeholders and also must ensure that the team's feedback for stakeholders is accurately and adequately communicated. In this way, communication serves as both an input and an output of the many subsystems involved in the larger system of the exhibit development process. The project manager must never lose sight of the interconnectedness of these subsystems and the impact that the flow of communication between them will have on the project as a whole. The project manager must convey the exhibit team's vision—the tone, approach, content, and *personality* of the exhibit.

For example, *The Science Behind Pixar* aimed to help visitors understand the math and computer science behind their favorite Pixar films. Part of the project manager's role was to communicate this focus to trustees, potential funders, and other supporters in order to promote investment from those interested in supporting this type of educational effort. Communicating this focus to the marketing department was equally important in order to promote the exhibit accurately and set visitor expectations appropriately. Systems thinking ensures that all of the subsystems are considered, with a focus on what communication outputs are necessary, what impact those outputs are likely to have, and how those impacts will serve as inputs back into the system. At the same time, the project manager must take feedback about what museum leadership, funders, and other stakeholders consider important and communicate it back to the exhibit development team. This feedback serves as an input that will affect decisions the team makes about how best to do their jobs.

The example of the *Hall of Human Life* exhibit at the Museum of Science, Boston, illustrates the impact that good communication can have on a project. This 10,000-square-foot permanent exhibit, which opened in late 2013, was created over a period of five years and involved hundreds of stakeholders, including the exhibit development team and other museum staff tasked with its creation, various funders, museum leadership, community members, content advisors, government agencies, external collaborative organizations, and of course, museum visitors. An essential function of good project management was to ensure regular, ongoing, comprehensive, and clear communication between these groups, with a focus on the relationships between all of these subsystems and their relationship to the project as a whole.

CONCLUSION

The exhibit development process is a complex system involving many phases and an even greater number of subsystems, both internal and external. All of these subsystems impact and are impacted by one another, and these relationships operate in an ever-changing environment. Understanding this interconnectedness and managing the relationships among the various subsystems is critical to good exhibit development as a physical manifestation of those systems. The project manager's role is to guide the exhibit development process in the context of a framework of goals, resources, and desired outcomes within the museum environment.

The beauty of systems-based thinking in exhibit development is that the outcomes of any given project can, will, and should grow as part of this fluid and organic process. Some factors will be controllable, or at least predictable, by a project team, and some factors will not. Some team members will be more comfortable with the fluid nature of the exhibit development process and will more readily accept inputs from other subsystems that affect his or her work. A skilled project manager anticipates what levels of change are likely or possible, and works to prepare the team to adapt to those changes as the exhibition project progresses.

Ultimately, exhibit project teams must recognize that there are almost infinite numbers of possible good, great, excellent, and phenomenal outcomes to any set of goals. Embracing a model of systems thinking in exhibition development allows team members to view change as a state of being, filled with opportunities for further exploration and creative problem solving.

BIBLIOGRAPHY

The American Alliance of Museums. "Museum Facts." Accessed August 2, 2016. http://aam-us
.org/about-museums/museum-facts.
Jackson, Michael C. *Systems Thinking: Creative Holism for Managers.* West Sussex, UK: Wiley,
2003.
Sherrer, J. Alex. "A Project Manager's Guide to Systems Thinking: Part I." July 18, 2010.
Accessed July 6, 2016. https://www.projectsmart.co.uk/project-managers-guide-to-systems
-thinking-part-1.php.

NOTES

1. Michael C. Jackson, *Systems Thinking: Creative Holism for Managers* (West Sussex, UK: Wiley, 2003), 113–33.

2. J. Alex Sherrer, "A Project Manager's Guide to Systems Thinking: Part I," July 18, 2010, accessed July 6, 2016. https://www.projectsmart.co.uk/project-managers-guide-to-systems -thinking-part-1.php.

3. "Museum Facts," The American Alliance of Museums, accessed August 2, 2016, http:// aam-us.org/about-museums/museum-facts.

10

We Built an Island

Deborah Randolph and Cora Fisher

The exhibition *Collective Actions*, which opened at the Southeastern Center of Contemporary Art (SECCA) in Winston-Salem, North Carolina, in January 2015, was jointly curated by the authors—a curator of contemporary art and a curator of education. In its three-month duration, *Collective Actions* imagined and activated new forms of collectivity, firmly based in historical examples, through arts and community action. A contemporary arts center is a relational system, defined by its links to its local and broader communities; thus SECCA is driven by its partnerships. The culture of the arts center supports and encourages relationships with community organizations by sustaining them for the long term, relying on them to build networks, and engaging them to provide multiple perspectives and angles in the interpretation of contemporary art. In other words, fostering these partnerships created a foundation from which the exhibition's collaborations were drawn and *collective actions* were naturally formed.

Through the telling of the story of the exhibition in this chapter, we will highlight the many ways *Collective Actions* echoed systems thinking generally within the arts center, in the diverse exhibited works, and specifically through the collaborative process of *actions*—creative interventions among artists, visitors, and community. The *actions* not only created a more dynamic participatory experience with socially engaged art, but they also visualized and strengthened human bonds.

Both the form and the content of the exhibition are systems thinking in action. The form of the exhibition *Collective Actions* is a community-engaged system. It acknowledges social and community relations that are often present in museums. The community-driven artistic practices of the artists featured in *Collective Actions* addressed questions of ecology and sustainability, work and play, accessibility for those differently abled, the consequences of the shift from industrial to post-Fordist labor, and most of all, how we form collective experiences. The community actions prompted us to ask, what does collectivity look like today? How can we further reimagine and shape collectivity through social action and trans-generational conversation? In this collaborative model of exhibition making and art engagement, one must rethink the exhibition itself as a dynamic system of actors and experiencing art as necessarily active.

SYSTEMS THINKING AS A MODEL FOR COLLECTIVITY AND ACTION

The work of systems theorist, architect, and designer Buckminster Fuller and feminist artist Nicola L. provided historical and social foundations for the exhibition. Fuller's work with Black Mountain College students in North Carolina not only provided a physical representation of systems thinking in the geodesic dome structure;[1] the process of designing and building the geodesic dome with students embodied the relational and organizational context of systems thinking. Through archival images depicting Fuller and his architecture students at Black Mountain College in the summer of 1949, we witness a creative and exploratory period in which Fuller and students test tensile structures, such as the geodesic dome, make models, and carry out the early stages of systems thinking Fuller would later formalize. Fuller theorized that synergy "is the behavior of whole systems unpredicated by the behavior of their parts taken separately."[2] Synergetics, the study of this spatial complexity based on nature's energy-efficient coordinating system, encourages problem solving, sustainability, and creativity.[3]

As remarked by Alfred Loeb in the preface to Fuller's theoretical book, *Synergetics*, "Fuller's hope for the future lies in doing more with less."[4] This principle hinges on the idea of formal structures with incredible strength due to their distributive weight-bearing capacity. In the historic photographs included in the *Collective Actions* exhibition, Black Mountain College students use the expansive lawns of the mountain college to drape strips of material to create a prototype of the geodesic dome, in the midst of the buildings of this storied summer residency program and Bauhaus-influenced institution, Black Mountain College. Figure 10.1 is a photo of these adult students dangling from the aluminum struts of a more advanced prototype of the geodesic dome, demonstrating the principles of distributed weight and tensegrity of this faceted dome structure as though hanging from a jungle gym. Such structures as the geodesic dome are a perfect realization of evenly distributed form and an inspiration for thinking collectivity in the form of a community-activated, participatory art exhibition. These domes became Fuller's signature contribution to systems thinking and the built environment that undergirds the notions of collectivity and action so central to this project.

Figure 10.1. Masato Nakagawa, "Buckminster Fuller's 'Autonomous Dwelling Facility' Dome at Black Mountain College." 1949. *Source*: State Archives of North Carolina.

If Buckminster Fuller's theories of structure were based in geometry and notions of future sustainability of living and built systems, the work of septuagenarian artist Nicola L. reflects notions of collectivity that are decidedly social and carry *feminist possibilities*. The performance art of Nicola L. is another foundational and histori-cal presence in the exhibition, captured through documentations of and sculptural costumes used in performances that she staged with passersby on the public streets of Europe in the 1960s and 1970s. Her *Red Coat for Eleven People* (1969) and *Blue Cape* (2004–2014) contour a group of individual bodies with one continuous piece of fabric. After approaching strangers and assembling a group of participants to col-lectively wear this sculptural costume, Nicola L. would then encourage them to walk in unison while wearing the form. With its impromptu and playful spirit, the pieces eventually were steered from their pop-aesthetic toward a function of social action and even political protest, by situating these group walking performances in sites with landmark historical or political significance such as the town square of Havana, Cuba (where slaves were auctioned in colonial days), the Great Wall of China, and the Parliament housing the European Union in Brussels, Belgium. In each setting, the cape reflects the local context and culture and the energy of the people wearing it. The pedestrian experience of walking is transformed into a ritual of discovery and social reorganization.

On December 16, 2014, the inaugural action of *Collective Actions* was a perfor-mance of the *Blue Cape* at SECCA. Twelve female community leaders inhabited a blue cape with accompaniment by jazz saxophone. The experience of wearing the blue cape is described by one participant who said,

> It was an extraordinary experience to be under that cape, which was all connected with so many of us trying to walk as a group. We cautiously tugged and pulled, gently of course, to try to walk as smoothly and coordinated as possible. We did it; but not before we felt each other's moves, cooperated with each other and became aware of each other. The result was very gratifying. I felt accomplished and with a little more patience than when I started. As it is with any living organism, every part of the corpus, or body, has its function . . . one part always needs the other and leads the other to be the best it can be.[5]

Another participant said, "I loved the collection of powerful women from our community that came together to take part in a living art exhibition. It was a real honor to take part in a project that had spanned the globe and was resting in the arms of a local museum."[6] The purpose of Nicola L.'s social sculptures and objects for performance such as the *Blue Cape* is to ask how art can memorably inspire and catalyze social action and collectivity.

It was a deliberate decision on the part of curators and artist Nicola L. to have women inhabit the Blue Cape for this debut performance, offering an empowered image of female leadership in the local community. Furthermore, the exhibition extends Buckminster Fuller's notions of systems thinking, rooted in the distribu-tive forms and powers of structures, to ask if less vertical models of power and participation might also be understood as feminist: anti-hierarchical, communal, socially conscious, and multigenerational. This was reflected not only in the theoretical possibilities of Buckminster Fuller's dome structure and Nicola L.'s living sculptures, but in the fact that all of the artists in the exhibition were multigenerational women, working inclusively with community and audience members of all ages, genders, races, and backgrounds. Here, we would distinguish between a feminist politics of collectivity and an effacement of the pluralism of gender and sexuality. It was primarily for their socially minded art work that the artists selected were all women, not only because they were women. *Collective Actions* proposed that, indeed, systems thinking could be reoriented toward a feminist sensibility of inclusion, lateral social relations, acceptance, and nurture.

THE ARTISTS FEATURED IN *COLLECTIVE ACTIONS*

The participating artists, whose art works were featured in *Collective Actions* and who will be discussed in this chapter, were Mary Mattingly, Martha Whittington, and Adelita Husni-Bey, as well as Buckminster Fuller and Nicola L., who set a historical foundation of systems thinking, collective action, and social activism. Mattingly, Whittington, and Husni-Bey were paired with community organizations to further enhance the participation in and interpretation of the exhibition. These groupings were imagined and realized through a collaborative process involving the curator of contemporary art and the curator of education.

Mary Mattingly is an artist whose work imagines sustainable futures. She invites us to consider how we inhabit our planet to co-create living systems. For example, in 2014 she launched *WetLand*, a floating ecosystem and living space on the Delaware River, and in 2012 she began the *Flock House Project*: three spherical living-systems that were choreographed through New York City's five boroughs. Her work is deeply influenced by Buckminster Fuller and other forward-looking thinkers grappling with ecological change and its effect on biological, human, and social systems. Martha Whittington's art objects evoke a time when the connection of the factory laborer to their work was invested and highly charged with craft and manual intelligence, in contrast to our own time, where work is made increasingly immaterial, virtual, and flexible. Her workerist installation presented in the exhibition, *Deus Ex Machina*, was inspired by early factory environments. Whittington argues for the importance of the hand and making as a response to automation in contemporary culture, as do maker movements taking shape across the country. Adelita Husni-Bey is an artist and researcher whose practice involves the analysis and counter-representation of hegemonic ideologies in contemporary Western societies. Recent projects have focused on rethinking radical pedagogical models. Her work explores social and political dimensions of equality, clustered around such issues as the privatization of space, gentrification, citizenship, progressive education, and the law.

COLLECTIVITY IN ACTION

Evoking the historical systems thinking practices of designer and architect Buckminster Fuller at Black Mountain College, North Carolina, in the 1940s and 1950s and the feminist social and political activism of artist Nicola L. in the 1960s and 1970s, the curators of *Collective Actions* invited the public to complete actions together with the artists, who were in residence in the galleries for periods of time. Actions included: (1) imagining a sustainable future with students from Authoring Action, an organization that empowers youth through writing and spoken word performances; (2) making healing bundles (groups of personal objects) with children and families facing illness in collaboration with Arts for Life, an organization that makes art with children in hospitals; (3) exchanging ideas with an artist and workers who were blind or had low vision from Winston-Salem Industries for the Blind; and (4) making a living biosphere with an artist working with Beta Verde and other activists who promote community engagement through local food. However, for these actions to happen, systems of collaboration had to be cultivated. The relational work of the exhibition began long before its conception.

The Partners for the Exhibition

Our partnership with Authoring Action spans fourteen years and stems from a desire to recognize and celebrate emerging artists, such as the young men and women of this organization, and give them a forum for presenting their raw, autobiographical spoken word pieces. This group was particularly suited for *Collective Actions* because their artistic practice involves individual writing, combined to create a single collective expression. Its mission of creating authors and advocates of social change also aligns with the goals of the exhibition.

Arts for Life teaches and exposes hospitalized children to the arts and provides support to their families. SECCA began its relationship with this organization by offering space for volunteer art making workshops and children's art exhibitions. One of the most memorable collaborations was the pairing of children's art with local musicians' compositions. These were exhibited and performed at SECCA. We believe in the service provided by Arts for Life and want to support the work and the staff and volunteers, whom we consider heroes.

Our partnership with Winston-Salem Industries for the Blind (IFB) began with a chicken dinner with the Blind Boys of Alabama following a concert in 2012. The concert became a way to highlight the remarkable work of IFB, an organization that employs over 700 individuals, making it the largest employer of people who are blind or have low vision in the United States. Our relationship with the organization continues. During one of our focus groups at IFB, one of the participants said, "I remember art"—an affecting statement that helped cement our commitment to this population. We create tours and interpretive materials specifically for people who are visually impaired to help them experience art.

Beta Verde is a local food project that includes farmers' markets, garden-to-table suppers, seed swaps, and local food advocacy. The owners, Margaret and Salem Neff, have worked with us on many projects including a Swamp Sista LaLa ("la la" is creole meaning party with a purpose). This concert raised funds that matched Supplemental Nutrition Assistance Program (SNAP) benefits at farmers' markets and provided awareness about hunger. These two dynamic women have changed how people think about food in this area.

The Actions in the Exhibition

Mary Mattingly + Beta Verde: Floating World

Nothing enacts ideas of sustainability like growing a plant. The artist Mary Mattingly, in collaboration with Beta Verde founder Margaret Norfleet Neff, invited visitors to plant a seed or nurture a plant in SECCA's gallery and to place it on a geodesic dome armature. Together, as a community, we covered the dome with plants and, over time, the dome became a growing biosphere. The biodome in the gallery, titled *Floating World,* echoed Buckminster Fuller's notion of sustainable systems and adapted his design for the geodesic dome toward the questions of biodiversity and climate change that plague our present. The project asked, "How can a human intervention support a self-sustaining living system?" The community creation of a living dome provided an example of a self-sustaining living system. Transforming visibly over time, *Floating World,* surrounded by floating wetlands, created by middle school students with Mattingly, had a destiny beyond the walls of the museum.

Mary Mattingly + Arts for Life: Bundling Sacred Objects

In several versions of her bundling project, Mary Mattingly creates, pulls, moves, buries, or disperses a gargantuan bundle made of personal objects contributed by public participants. She gathers stories about why these things we keep matter, exploring how and why we hold on to them, and allowing us the chance to reflect, share, and symbolically release them into a larger collective whole that is greater than the sum of its parts. As a collective action, Mattingly partnered with Arts for Life, whose leaders are from across the state of North Carolina. They gathered objects of significance from the young people they support, who are hospitalized and battling disease, and from bereaved families in their network. Guided by Mattingly, personal objects and the stories attached to them were collected, bundled, and exhibited at SECCA. A constellation of personal bundles hung throughout the space, manifesting the power of creativity and connection binding us.

Martha Whittington + Winston Salem Industries for the Blind: Artist Talk—Working with Hands

In thinking about collectivity, we think about work, the mainstay of daily life. Artists wrestle with ideas of productivity that structure economic production in their own studio. How do they surmount the expectations of functionality and usefulness in their own production? How do they provoke us in turn to think about labor and usefulness? As part of the programming during the exhibition, Whittington joined a panel of Industries for the Blind factory workers, who were blind or had low vision, to discuss the role of the hand in their work. Industries for the Blind employees are factory workers who work with their hands using their senses beyond sight to make dorm mattresses, glasses, office supplies, and armed services uniforms. The artist and workers offered objects (artistic and functional) as catalysts for a lively discussion about making by using all of the senses.

Adelita Husni-Bey + Authoring Action: Stargazing

Husni-Bey and teens from Authoring Action immersed themselves in the task of imagining the future of life on earth and in the galaxies beyond in light of the prospect of the privatization of space travel. The installation *Stargazing* in the exhibition was the artistic manifestation of the intense collaboration with the artist and teens to collectively propel the voices of the next generation forward through this written and spoken performance. These students, who usually wrote autobiographical pieces, were challenged by Husni-Bey during writing sessions to think beyond themselves. The students developed a stronger sense of the connectedness between personal and societal actions. Their individual imaginings about life in the future were combined to create a collective poem, which was performed as a group on the opening night of *Collective Actions.* The lines below are excerpted from the thirty-minute spoken-word cautionary poem collectively created by Authoring Action.

> She's never seen a bruised banana.
> Fruit doesn't go bad anymore
> Now that it grows inside.
> They stay highlighter yellow
> How convenient, huh?
> To never have anything wither.

> The only thing left of that little town, are a few buildings
> and a statue of this burly lady pointing at the sun.
> It's like she's pointing at the fireball to say,
> "Hey! Remember when we could actually
> See that thing? Feel it?
> Remember using sunscreen not smog repellent?"
> I know that stone-faced woman misses having the sun beam on her cheeks.

> They're watching.
> The surveillance of a species,
> of another kind.
> They call themselves "The privileged."

Guilt-ridden souls, rusted lies
Linger on their lips, their very existence is concealed in the mind.
Black silhouettes, distinct features.
No race to categorize,
better known as social creatures.
The guilt is only real if you want it to be.[7]

The diverse, community-engaged experiences of *Collective Actions* covered a range of issues at the intersection of social justice and ecology, offering a politics of active cooperation as its most important outlet for systems thinking. The various partnerships, sustained over years and activated with the input of guest artists, were only fully realized with the public involved. *Collective Actions* supplied a series of models and images of collectivity, and held these up as antidotes to an overwhelming individualism and paralysis in facing real social, environmental, and political challenges. *Collective Actions* held out the image of continuity and positive intervention. Even after the exhibition ended, there was a sendoff; Mary Mattingly's *Floating World*, made together with so many other hands, covered now with flowers and edible plants in bloom, set adrift on a lake on the museum's grounds (see figure 10.2). Set on a wooden raft, the living biodome was reflected in the water in perfect symmetry. Surrounding it was a web of individual floating wetlands. They floated there for several months, and we all watched to see how those hanging plants and tall cord grasses would thrive.

Figure 10.2.
Cliff Dossel, "Mary Mattingly's Floating World at SECCA." 2015. *Source*: Southeastern Center for Contemporary Art.

BIBLIOGRAPHY

Edmondson, Amy C. *A Fuller Explanation*. Cambridge, MA: Birkhauser Boston, 1986.

Fuller, R. Buckminster, and E. J. Applewhite. *Synergetics: Explorations in the Geometry of Thinking*. New York: Macmillan, 1975.

Loab, A. J. Preface to *Synergetics: Explorations in the Geometry of Thinking*, by R. Buckminster Fuller and E. J. Applewhite, xv-xvii. New York: Macmillan, 1975.

NOTES

1. A geodesic dome is a lightweight structure combining the properties of a tetrahedron and a sphere. Fuller received a US patent for the geodesic dome in 1954.

2. R. Buckminster Fuller and E. J. Applewhite, *Synergetics: Explorations in the Geometry of Thinking* (New York: Macmillan, 1975), section 101.01.

3. Amy C. Edmondson, *A Fuller Explanation* (Cambridge, MA: Birkhauser Boston, 1986).

4. A. L. Loeb, preface to *Synergetics: Explorations in the Geometry of Thinking*, by R. Buckminster Fuller and E. J. Applewhite (New York: Macmillan, 1975), xv.

5. Silvia Rodriguez in discussion with the author, August 2016.

6. Katherine Bowman in discussion with the author, August 2016.

7. Authoring Action, *Stargazing*, 2015.

Part V

Take Action

1. The two chapters in this section offer team-based approaches to exhibition development in two areas—science and contemporary art. When starting a new exhibition planning process at your museum, it is important to consider the appropriate team members from across departments and to work together throughout the entire process. Each project offers the opportunity to put different teams together—unique to the exhibition. For an upcoming exhibition, which staff members' perspectives would provide meaningful contributions? How will you propose this idea in your museum? If team-based exhibition planning is new to your museum, for the first experience it may be helpful to ask for staff volunteers to join the team and try it out.

2. In addition to staff members, how will you invite community participation into the exhibition teamwork? What community partners or agencies would provide essential resources or access to community expertise related to the exhibition? How would community participation change from the planning stage to the implementation phase to the evaluation phase?

Part VI

SYSTEMS THINKING IN EXTERNAL COMMUNICATIONS

This part focuses on how museums communicate with their external constituencies. When there is a communication disconnect between the museum and its wider audiences, the museum is listening and catering to only a small part of its community, one that is already supporting the museum while the majority of the community's perspectives are ignored. For example, *The Museum* (the fictional museum based on a real museum first introduced in the Part I introduction) is considered by many an elitist museum or a club where rich people go and enjoy art. This is due to lack of communication with its community and therefore the community's perspectives are not considered in museum practices. On a deeper level, the museum is not seeing itself as an integrated part of its community. While *The Museum* could have created a more favorable and inclusive image of itself through various marketing approaches to help change the community's perception of it from elitist to a more inclusive place, it tends to market toward existing visitors and donors and does not think creatively to reach out to people who are not currently coming to the museum. Rather it operates based on the assumption of what the community may want or what it thinks the community should learn and be exposed to. This can continue to perpetuate the perception that the museum is elitist and irrelevant. *The Museum* also lacks sufficient evaluation of exhibitions and programs and does not conduct regular visitor and non-visitor studies to find out why some people do not come to the museum while others do and what the museum can do better to attract non-visitors. The occasional member and donor surveys at the museum do not provide diverse community perspectives; rather this practice confirms that the museum is for a small elitist group; only their perspectives are asked for and included in museum structure and programming.

The chapters in this part will discuss innovative and effective ways to communicate with broader museum audiences. In chapter 11, Jonathan Paquette and Robin

Nelson discuss how museums use social media to communicate with their audiences when they close their spaces temporarily for remodeling or new construction. They use the concept of an open system and connect it to Deleuze and Guattari's idea of de-territorialization to examine seven museums from different parts of the world that utilized social media to create their environment. These case museums not only use social media to tell of the temporary closure of their spaces but to transform their images and identities, to create communities who may shape different perspectives about the updated and transformed museums, and to invite them back to their new spaces. This strategy demonstrates that museums are open systems and therefore they can not only be influenced by their external environments but also can influence their environment—therefore transforming what people think about them.

Chapter 12, written by Ana Flávia Machado, Diomira M. C. P. Faria, Sibelle C. Diniz, Bárbara F. Paglioto, Rodrigo C. Michel, and Gabriel Vaz de Melo, discusses how visitor and non-visitor studies can help evaluate a public cultural good or cultural complex, Circuito Liberdade (CL) in Minas Gerais, Brazil, and how this feedback can be used to help manage CL, making it a learning organization. The authors of this chapter conducted an evaluation study involving visitors and non-visitors to this cultural complex using an alternative to measure the quantitative value of a non-market good. They also examined cultural habits of visitors and non-visitors, drawing some distinctive characteristics among them. Constantly seeking feedback from visitors and non-visitors and incorporating them to cultural management is a strategy of systems thinking; it views the cultural organization as part of the community and therefore a museum must incorporate local perspectives to its management.

11

Behind Closed Doors

The Uses of Social Media in Museum Transformation and Development Projects

Jonathan Paquette and Robin Nelson

In recent years, many prestigious institutions have undergone significant transformations that necessitated closing their spaces to the public. As the 1990s ended, a vast number of museums expressed growing concerns about their spaces. Collections housed in buildings dating back to the end of nineteenth or the beginning of the twentieth century were facing important challenges maintaining contemporary standards for preserving collections. Moreover, some museums were struggling with buildings designed in an era where galleries and museums accommodated a different kind of public. These institutions were simply unprepared and not designed to accommodate a growing flow of museum visitors increased by mass global tourism. In countries where there is a strong public sector tradition and where museums are understood as a state public service, the rapid development of new national institutions after World War II gave rise to hasty projects and architectural endeavors that provided spaces that may no longer be adequate. In particular, some spaces challenge the ways in which museum professionals can engage with the public, compelling significant transformations. In their long histories, most museums will be significantly inconvenienced by transformation projects at some stage.

Museum spaces are never neutral. Instead, they are political and social spaces. In addition to a reputation based on their collections, museum spaces have an important symbolic value for professionals, their identification with the institution, and their own work.[1] Despite the fact that most museum professionals work backstage[2] (e.g., collections management, conservation, and facility management), they ultimately work for and with the front stage. They work with and for the exhibit space. Museum spaces are where most of the relationship between museums and the public is performed;[3] they are where the population and the *source communities* are transformed as the audience. Museum spaces are important in the construction of the museum's symbolic order. What happens when there is loss or absence of space?

This chapter documents some of these recent major transformation and long-term development projects. In particular, it raises questions regarding how social media is used in museum transformation strategies as a tool for public relations and community development. In other words, this chapter is concerned with temporary closures of museum spaces. Unlike a permanent closure, a temporary closure involves a series of backstage operations to maintain the museum in absence of its main symbolic and transaction good: its space. Building on a systemic approach to museums and their social environments, this chapter focuses on seven cases from a broader study of twenty-eight museum transformation strategies. After further discussing the theoretical dimension of this important issue, this chapter outlines how these different institutions have mobilized a variety of social media strategies to keep their activities opened to the public and to maintain their presence in their communities. The outcome of this study is a typology of the activities put in place by museums during the time their main exhibit spaces were unavailable to the public, which in general was two to four years, but in some cases even longer. The subset of museums we will discuss herein has used one or many of these social media strategies.

MUSEUMS, PROFESSIONALS, SPACES, AND COMMUNITIES: A SYSTEMIC PERSPECTIVE

In this chapter, we adopt a systemic approach to museum and space. One of the most significant and striking theoretical contributions of a systems approach has to do with notions of *open systems* and interaction with environments. The rise of systems theory was first propelled by the heuristic of the biological system applied to social environments.[4] However, decades after these first and very early receptions of systems theory in the social sciences, researchers started to engage with systems theory as a metaphor[5] for social interactions, especially in the case of organization studies, the discipline from which we approach museums in this chapter. Museums interact with their environments and are influenced by their environments as organizations. However, we wish to emphasize the generative aspects of museums. Accordingly, we adopt an autopoietic view of systems and organizations,[6] building on the following assumptions: (1) organizations are open systems that interact with their environment, (2) the level of interaction with this environment may be so important that organizations may define their environment, and (3) an organization is a network of processes in interaction.[7] Museums and their professionals are not only responding to stimuli and reacting to their environments, influencing their environments simply through their responses to the stimuli. They also create their environments, and the communicational dimension of museum work is a complex network of process that shapes the museum, its structures, and its permanence, while also creating expectation among its audience.

Territorializing the Museum Space: Deleuze and Guattari

The work of Gilles Deleuze and Félix Guattari offers an interesting perspective, combining a theory of space and systems thinking. A Deleuzian approach to systems thinking emphasizes the importance of processes. Museums as organizations are networks of processes that create their environment. In other words, the Deleuzian approach to systems thinking is consistent with the principles of autopoiesis as outlined above.[8] The system is not to be seen as a closed unit, but rather as an open-ended and developing assemblage.

In this systemic and productive relationship, social media is a generative instrument that creates museum communities and spaces. From an empirical perspective, social media is a communicational tool; it does not make an organization, but it *organizes* individual and collective selves; it intersects and connects in communicational fluxes. Building on the work of Deleuze and Guattari,[9] we suggest that social media is used as a tool[10] of displacement to cope with museum nomadism. When museums must close their spaces to the public to reorganize or create a new space, social media becomes a tool that helps museums recompose, explore, and occupy new spaces. In other words, social media helps in the exploration and experimentation of new (becoming) spaces. Social media in this context is a tool of conquest,[11] looking to conquer, build, and make familiar the museum's future spaces.

To characterize the museum space in Deleuzian terms, we develop on the idea of de-territorialization.[12] The process of de-territorialization refers to a displacement; it involves a line of flight from a familiar (museum) space to a new one. To quote Deleuze and Guattari, "to de-territorialize is to quit a habit, to quit forms of sedentary life."[13] De-territorialization is an active process of displacement. Moreover, de-territorialization may even refer to an escape, a departure from "forms of alienation and precise forms of subjectivation."[14] When museums close temporarily to transform their facilities, museums de-territorialize, they make a dramatic rupture with the space they knew, they inhabited, and for which the public knew them. Change management in this context is a form of nomadism; it is a quest for a new territory, for a new museum space. For Deleuze and Guattari, de-territorialization is a transitive moment; it is followed by a re-territorialization—a new space, with new habits and new ways for engagement.

The systemic interaction between museums, professionals, spaces, and communities is operated through the processes of territorialization, de-territorialization, and re-territorialization. These interactions create the museum as an assemblage that changes and transforms over time. In transition, social media acts as means to de-territorialize—as a line of flight toward a new museum space. Social media announces the rupture and the departure from the familiar habit and the known. Not only does social media de-territorialize; it also re-territorializes. In its narratives about spaces, in demonstrating how the new space is becoming and emerging from the change, social media re-territorializes. Social media helps anticipate and develop new ways of being and dwelling in the museums' new spaces, in both practical and symbolic terms; it reassembles its community.

Spaces in Transition

In this chapter, we focus on seven cases of temporary closure. The redevelopment of the Canadian Museum of Science and Technology (CMST), started in 2014, driven by important infrastructure problems from its early days in 1967 all the way to the health hazard situation (mainly poor air quality) that emerged in 2014. The redevelopment of the San Francisco Museum of Modern Art (SFMOMA) involved a closure between 2013 and 2016 to add 235,000 more square feet to the exhibit space. The Hong Kong Museum of Art in the Tsim Sha Tsui area closed its doors in 2015 to transform its architecture and incorporate the beautiful Hong Kong skyline in its place. The Musée Carnavalet, which documents city history in Paris, partially closed in 2016 to redevelop the space in order to find new ways to engage with its audience. The Musée royal de l'Afrique centrale in Belgium is an interesting case. It closed its doors in 2013 for renovation, but the project was also defined as an opportunity to redefine the institution's identity because it was understood and labeled as *the last* colonial museum of Europe. The museum's exhibit and design had remained partially unchanged, though not intact, since the 1960s. These cases present interesting and creative strategies to cope with the absence of space or its temporary virtualization. Finally, we wish to present two additional cases where social media is used not to cope with absence, but as part of a strategy to create enthusiasm and excitement for the *new* space to come. To speak about these uses, we will refer to the marketing of the Pierre Lassonde Pavillion, which opened in 2016 at the Musée national des beaux-arts du Québec. In a similar vein of thought, we will discuss the long odyssey of the National Gallery of Singapore, which finally opened its doors in 2015.

The findings discussed in the next section come from a broader research program that started in 2011 and are based on a small sample of the organizations studied. The material discussed builds during site visits, and when possible, interviews with professionals. In addition, we conducted a documentary analysis (e.g., press releases, annual review, transformation plans, and strategic plans) and social media intervention analysis to better understand how social media was mobilized during these pivotal periods for these organizations.

FROM DE-TERRITORIALIZATION TO RE-TERRITORIALIZATION

Maintaining a Presence and Opening the Black Box of Change

One of the most important uses of social media aims at maintaining presence, using the virtual space as a tool to maintain connections with the museum's community. A good example of such a strategy, which was structured in a planned and well-integrated manner, is SFMOMA's change with its transition identity through its *Museum on the Go* program.[15] The initiative kept the museum brand visible throughout the San Francisco Bay area by partnering with other museums in the area and proposing public art activities to pursue its programming despite the closure of its downtown exhibit space. It structured the narrative and provided material to organize the communication campaign through social media.

A closer look at SFMOMA's communicational activities through social media (i.e., Facebook, Twitter, and Instagram) during that period reveals a number of interesting patterns of communication change to de-territorialize and re-territorialize the museum's identity as an identity in flux. The communication patterns during the transition disclosed how professionals, objects, and spaces were *on the go* and still interacting during the museum's closure to the public. Communications were also structured around different museum professionals, engaging with them to understand their work, preferences, or role during the museum's transformation. Social media was also used to maintain the museum in the arts narrative, to celebrate the anniversaries of artists or special days that brought art and community together. Some forms of communication during change expressed more deliberate attempts to engage with the public (e.g., who are the five women artists you admire?). In the last months of the transition, the museum's narrative refocused on a countdown mode, and most communications were inviting the community back into the museum space.

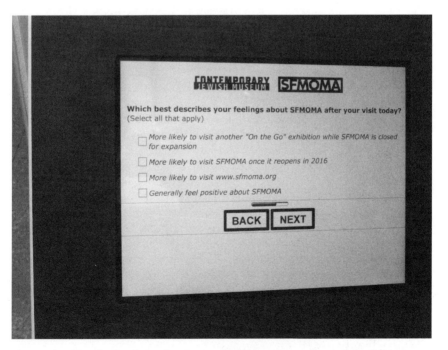

Figure 11.1. On the Go Campaign. Interactive Visitor Survey Form at the Contemporary Jewish Museum in San Francisco. *Source*: Author.

Similar narratives of institutional change can be found in the #MyMuseum2017 communication campaign of the Canada Museum of Science and Technology (CMST), a national museum of Canada. Once again, the communication campaign gives institutional change an identity through social media combined with the science mobile team's off-site activities in the nation's capital region. Using video on its YouTube channel, the CMST is narrating its de-territorialization—that is, the disappearance of its exhibit space—while also alluding to its territorialization, in a utopian fashion, where museum professionals and members of the change team are asked to discuss the future exhibit spaces with image juxtapositions and architect plans to create a sense of value and rationale for the coming museum spaces. On Twitter, the museum maintains its operations; it connects with the broad museum community and communicates about its collections and research to ensure that the CMST pursues its communicational and educational mandate as a public service subsidized by the federal government.

Similarly, for some organizations, the capacity to pursue their educational mission and outreach to a specific community is at stake during museum closure. For the Musée Carnavalet in Paris, the change is an opportunity for organizational learning and for further developing its social media capacity. While the change is narrated, the museum insists on *ephemerides*[16] and on communicating key aspects of their collection, mission, and relation to Paris in the virtual space. In this change that could unfold in 2019, the museum is re-territorializing its operations in a virtual space, and through ephemerides of art and social life in Paris, it keeps a consistent narrative to which a community of learners could easily connect. In other words, they create educational expectations and a consistent offering based on their collection and research work and expertise.

In many cases, these social media strategies are also about opening the hidden, or invisible, dimension of institutional change. The cases of the SFMOMA and the CMST, among others, all use social media to create a window to organizational change. In addition, the Musée royal d'Afrique centrale in Tervuren, Belgium, has put together a blog page to narrate its institutional change. This blog acts as common place where the invisible aspects of institutional changes are being narrated by different professionals, and these can then become material for social media, mainly Twitter and Instagram. These examples speak to a fascination about museum space that are emptied, gutted out of its structures, or even restructured, followed by a re-population with its precious museum objects and artifacts. These create expectations for the spaces to come, but in addition, they provide material and archives for the museum's institutional history. The age of social media has even opened new possibilities for researchers on organizational change; the digital traces that narrate the change can provide useful information that would be otherwise without trace, or left to architect materials and strategic plans.

Narrating Institutional Transformation

In other circumstances, the de-territorialization of the museum spaces during institutional change leads to a more profound operation of institutional identity construction. In these cases, the museum uses social media to narrate another future for the relationship between museum and community. The Hong Kong Museum of Art launched its social media campaign in August 2015 as the *Hong Kong Museum of Art on Wheels* primarily through Facebook and Instagram. In collaboration with the Hong Kong Leisure and Culture Department and with the support of the Jockey Club of Hong Kong, this transformation on social media is presenting a museum that tries to develop roots with the local and global community.

Figure 11.2. Hong Kong Museum of Art's Esplanade. *Source:* **Author.**

The museum is well anchored in the Asian and global art scene as a leading museum of art in Asia, but its social media communications allude to an attempt to get closer with its community. The use of Instagram anchors the museum as still operating during its transformation, communicating with youth and local citizens. More than an architectural change, the museum is also trying to further its outreach and its presence, and the social media strategy conveys a will to get the museum's institutional identity closer to the values of cultural engagement with the arts. Its social media strategy involves people in social situations outside the museum, engaging with museum promotional material and in other outreach activities. Social media in this sense narrates not only architectural change, but it narrates a will to transform and reshape the museum's institutional and organizational identity.

Similarly, the Musée royal d'Afrique centrale in Belgium has also used its architectural change as a springboard to engage publicly with its institutional history, as being a museum associated with Belgian colonial history in central Africa. The institutional change has opened a window where museum professionals no longer have to defend a space or carry the weight of the museum's institutional history, enabling new discursive capacities where the museum can perform and circulate a postcolonial look at the collection more widely. Further, more creative and productive narratives of collaboration can be performed between Belgium and central Africa. From a systemic perspective, in this case, Twitter and Instagram have participated in the ethical re-articulation of the relationship between museum and community as space was suspended before the creation of a new space. In this case, the narration of change through social media is simultaneously symbolic and transformative as it speaks to the rarely acknowledged weight of spaces and architecture in museums.

Creating Communities and Introducing New Spaces

From a systemic perspective, integration and dynamic equilibrium are important properties of a system. In this area, social media has also been used in transformations to speak about new and sometimes contentious spaces. In the case of the Musée national des beaux-arts du Québec (MNBAQ), in Québec City, a social media strategy was used to value the construction of a new pavilion. The new Pierre-Lassonde Pavilion was an ambitious project aimed at bringing additional exhibit spaces, more room for contemporary art from Québec artists, and new spaces to create additional social activities. The Pierre-Lassonde Pavilion is the consecration of a transformation of the institution moving away from the more austere architecture and layout of the conventional gallery. Social media activities presented the new space and introduced it to the museum's public, while also reaching out—in style and communicational efforts—to connect with people who may not have been the usual public of this institution.

In some cases, social media has played a vital role for years. The National Gallery of Singapore is an interesting case in point. In fact, the museum project developed incrementally between 2005 and 2015. The museum existed through small temporary exhibits and its staff, but it also existed widely through social media before it officially opened its permanent location in the former supreme court building in 2015. Over five years of activities on Twitter and other social media, the museum managed to develop a brand in absence of an actual space. The virtual space of social media was material for the museum's territorialization, creating a sense of community and generating an audience for this museum to take roots.

Figure 11.3. National Gallery Singapore. Space Opening Event on November 24, 2015. *Source:* **Author.**

Figure 11.4. National Gallery Singapore, Main Building. *Source*: Author.

CONCLUSION

Museums are always open. In the digital age, professionals who highlight the significance of backstage activities and the wealth of other events programmed to maintain the museum's presence in its city and community vehemently challenged any idea that the museum is inaccessible. While this assertion is partly true, the reality is that museums and their professionals always undergo a paradoxical sense of anxiety and excitement when the main museum space is inaccessible. Social media enables museums to compensate for the absence of spaces. It can also help produce a narrative for an absence, creating enthusiasm for a space to come. While the social media supposes interaction, most of these narratives are developed through platforms and strategies that enable an official story of organizational change to be produced, polished, and told to the audience. From a systemic perspective, social media enables a new form of archive and renders some of the museum's interactions more visible, generating vital traces. From a more critical reception, social media enables interaction and can possibly bring in new publics to engage with museums. However, there is also the potential to reinforce the power of dominant classes and the influence of the museum's pre-established publics. In social media, public relations activities are being performed in new and interesting ways. But from a Bourdieusian perspective,[17] one still wonders if the social interactions performed through social media are giving even more powers to the dominant public, which encourages prudence when performing social media activities.

BIBLIOGRAPHY

Bourdieu, Pierre, and Alain Darbel. *L'amour de l'art: Les musées d'art européens et leur public.* Paris: Les Éditions de Minuit, 1966.

Burrell, Gibson, and Gareth Morgan. *Sociological Paradigms and Organizational Analysis.* London: Heineman, 1979.

Davallon, Jean. "Le musée est-il vraiment un media?" *Publics et musées* 2, no. 1 (1990): 99–103.

Deleuze, Gilles. *Pourparlers 1972–1990.* Paris: Les Éditions de Minuit, 1990.

Deleuze, Gilles, and Félix Guattari. *L'anti-Œdipe: Capitalisme et schizophrénie.* Paris: Les Éditions de Minuit, 1972.

———. *Mille Plateaux: Capitalisme et schizophrénie 2.* Paris: Les Éditions de Minuit, 1980.

Goffman, Erving. *The Presentation of Self in Everyday Life.* New York: Anchor, 1959.

Gombault, Anne. "La nouvelle identité organisationnelles des musées." *Revue Française de gestion* 142, no. 1 (2003): 189–203.

Hillier, Bill, and Kali Tzortzi. "Space Syntax: The Language of Museum Space." In *A Companion to Museum Studies*, edited by Sharon MacDonald, 282–302. London: Blackwell, 2006.

Kawamoto, Hideo. "Autopoïèse et l'individu en train de se faire." *Revue philosophique de la France et de l'étranger* 136, no. 3 (2011): 347–63.

MacLeod, Suzanne. *Reshaping Museum Space: Architecture, Design, Exhibitions.* London: Routledge, 2005.

Mingers, John. "A Comparison of Maturana Autopoietic Social Theory and Giddens Theory of Structuration." *Systems Research* 13, no. 4 (1996): 469–82.

———. "An Introduction to Autopoiesis—Implications and Applications." *Systems Practice* 2, no. 2 (1989): 159–80.

Morgan, Gareth. *Images of Organizations.* Thousand Oaks, CA: Sage, 2006.

San Francisco Museum of Modern Art. "SFMOMA Presents Innovative Off-Site Programming While Building is Closed for Expansion." Press Release, June 19, 2012, last updated May 06, 2014. https://www.sfmoma.org/press/release/sfmoma-presents-innovative-off-site-programming-w/.

Silverstone, Roger. "Les espaces de la performance: Musées, science et rhétorique de l'objet." *Hermès* 22, no. 1 (1998): 175–88.

Yanow, Dvora. "Space Stories: Studying Museum Buildings as Organizational Spaces While Reflecting on Interpretive Methods and their Narration." *Journal of Management Inquiry* 7, no. 3 (1998): 215–39.

NOTES

1. Jean Davallon, "Le musée est-il vraiment un media?" *Publics et musées* 2, no. 1 (1990): 99–103; Anne Gombault, "La nouvelle identité organisationnelles des musées," *Revue*

Française de gestion 142, no. 1 (2003): 189–203; Bill Hillier and Kali Tzortzi, "Space Syntax: The Language of Museum Space," in *A Companion to Museum Studies*, ed. Sharon MacDonald (London: Blackwell, 2006), 282–302.

  2. Erving Goffman, *The Presentation of Self in Everyday Life* (New York: Anchor, 1959).

  3. Dvora Yanow, "Space Stories: Studying Museum Buildings as Organizational Spaces While Reflecting on Interpretive Methods and their Narration," *Journal of Management Inquiry* 7, no. 3 (1998): 215–39; Roger Silverstone, "Les espaces de la performance: Musées, science et rhétorique de l'objet," *Hermès* 22, no. 1 (1998): 175–88; Suzanne MacLeod, *Reshaping Museum Space: Architecture, Design, Exhibitions* (London: Routledge, 2005).

  4. Gibson Burrell and Gareth Morgan, *Sociological Paradigms and Organizational Analysis* (London: Heineman, 1979).

  5. Gareth Morgan, *Images of Organizations* (Thousand Oaks, CA: Sage, 2006).

  6. John Mingers, "An Introduction to Autopoiesis—Implications and Applications," *Systems Practice* 2, no. 2 (1989): 159–80; John Mingers, "A Comparison of Maturana Autopoietic Social Theory and Giddens Theory of Structuration," *Systems Research* 13, no. 4 (2006): 469–82.

  7. Hideo Kawamoto, "Autopoïèse et l'individu en train de se faire," *Revue philosophique de la France et de l'étranger* 136, no. 3 (2011): 347–63.

  8. Ibid.

  9. Gilles Deleuze and Félix Guattari, *L'anti-Œdipe: Capitalisme et schizophrénie* (Paris: Les Éditions de Minuit, 1972); Gilles Deleuze and Félix Guattari, *Mille Plateaux: Capitalisme et schizophrénie 2* (Paris: Les Éditions de Minuit, 1980).

  10. We use the expression tool or instrument to refer to the idea of machine defined with a greater philosophical depth in the work of Deleuze and Guattari, *Mille Plateaux*, 460.

  11. Gilles Deleuze, *Pourparlers 1972–1990* (Paris: Les Éditions de Minuit, 1990), 50.

  12. Deleuze and Guattari, *Mille Plateaux*.

  13. Deleuze and Guattari, *L'anti-Œdipe*, 162.

  14. Ibid.

  15. San Francisco Museum of Modern Art, "SFMOMA Presents Innovative Off-Site Programming While Building is Closed for Expansion," press release, June 19, 2012, last updated May 06, 2014, https://www.sfmoma.org/press/release/sfmoma-presents-innovative -off-site-programming-w/.

  16. Ephemerides are a form of commemoration based on a calendar. They are also a form of historical and literary communication that associates a day of a calendar year with an important event that occurred on the same day in the past.

  17. Pierre Bourdieu and Alain Darbel, *L'amour de l'art: Les musées d'art européens et leur public* (Paris: Les Éditions de Minuit, 1966).

12

The Evaluation of Public Goods

Systems Thinking in the Case of Circuito Liberdade

Ana Flávia Machado, Diomira M. C. P. Faria,
Sibelle C. Diniz, Bárbara F. Paglioto, Rodrigo C. Michel,
and Gabriel Vaz de Melo

The *Circuito Liberdade* (CL) is a complex of cultural entities (museums, libraries, and cultural centers) surrounding the *Praça da Liberdade* (see figure 12.1), a square in the central area of Belo Horizonte, in the state of Minas Gerais, Brazil. It was inaugurated in 2010, after the transference of the state (Minas Gerais) government headquarters to a new area located in the north end of the city in the same year. The former government buildings were completely refurbished to accommodate the cultural amenities. Some of those buildings date from the late nineteenth and early twentieth century, while others were reformed solely to compose the main cultural center of the city.

The following cultural organizations currently occupy the CL: *Arquivo Público Mineiro* (Public Archive of Minas Gerais); *Biblioteca Pública Estadual Luiz de Bessa* (Luiz de Bessa State Public Library); *Palácio da Liberdade* (Palace of Liberty); *Museu Mineiro* (Museum of Minas Gerais); *Centro de Formação Artística* (Center of Artistic Formation); *Centro de Arte Popular CEMIG* (CEMIG Center of Popular Art); *BDMG Cultural* (Cultural BDMG); *Academia Mineira de Letras* (Minas Gerais Academy of Letters); *Horizonte Sebrae-Casa da Economia Criativa* (Sebrae Horizon-House of Creative Economy); *Casa Fiat de Cultura* (Fiat House of Culture); *Centro Cultural Banco do Brasil* (Banco do Brasil Cultural Center); *Espaço do Conhecimento UFMG* (UFMG Knowledge Space); *Memorial Minas Gerais Vale* (Memorial Minas Gerais Vale); *MM Gerdau-Museu de Minas e do Metal* (MM Gerdau-Museum of Mines and Metal).[1]

Figure 12.1. Circuito Liberdade, Cultural Circuit of Belo Horizonte, Minas Gerais, Lucia Sebe, Portal PBH. All rights reserved. Available in: https://www.flickr.com/ photos/portalpbh/sets/72157638355730985/, accessed on May 4, 2015.

The CL seeks to replicate international experiences that used the culture as central in the process of regeneration of urban areas, such as Bilbao (Spain) and Medellín (Colombia). However, one major difference from those cases is that the construction of the CL did not involve civil society actors (residents and local institutions directly affected by the intervention) in the planning process. In addition to the public institutions composing the CL, the government created public-private partnerships that assigned public buildings—owned by the government of the state of Minas Gerais— to private companies for a certain period (five years renewable). These companies are responsible for the maintenance of their buildings, exhibitions, and events, as well as management of specific programs.

The facilities of the CL have a cooperative relationship. Although the managers have autonomy to plan the artistic and cultural activities developed in each institution, five committees with representatives from all institutions of the CL and of the IEPHA (State Institute of Historical and Artistic Heritage of Minas Gerais)[2] discuss issues at monthly meetings.

In their meetings, the five committees discuss issues relevant to the cultural spaces. The education committee deals with programs and actions concerning the museums' schedules, especially visits by public schoolchildren. The communication committee is concerned with issues related to the disclosure of events and ways to increase the communication efficiency of each institution through collective strategies. The heritage committee works with issues concerning heritage maintenance, assignment of spaces, and accessibility. The scheduling committee defines the agenda of the events organized by the whole organization, such as weekly events in museums and Christmas and vacations programs. Lastly, the management committee gathers the directors of each facility to discuss proposals prepared by the other committees and common management issues, such as local traffic, audience, security, and others. The committees comprise representatives from workers of correlated areas of the cultural organizations (educators, journalists, architects, program developers, and directors) that compose the CL and also with representatives of IEPHA. This allows the cultural institutions to work in collaboration and to establish a more comprehensive relationship with the public.

Due to this collaborative administrative arrangement of the CL and its willingness to understand the impact on the public, we use the systems thinking approach in researching how the public values the CL and how their perspectives can be incorporated in the CL's practice. In the words of Walker et al.,

> Systems thinking is an approach to defining [*sic*] problems and formulating and testing potential solutions. It focuses on identifying the underlying causes of problems and . . . evaluating the consequences of management responses and other scenarios. In combination with the "learning organization" concept, the approach can be used to achieve group or team learning about a problem.[3]

By conducting research on how people evaluate and think about the CL as a public good, this study intends to find any underlying issues with the CL in connecting with its audiences. The results can be adopted by the CL in making it a cultural complex where the leadership and management value the perspectives of the audiences that are most affected by the practices of the CL.

Like museums and cultural centers, the CL is considered a public good.[4] According to economic theory, public goods are defined by being meritorious, as they carry social and symbolic values, and they are non-rival and non-excludable; thus people cannot be excluded from their consumption. Unlike private goods, in which their value can be calculated in real markets, public goods require other valuation methods. Researchers have developed different methods to measure the social value of something not subjected to market laws of pricing. In this study, we resort to the contingent valuation (CV) method, where simulated markets are created from the measurement of the willingness to pay (WTP) of current and potential users.

In 2014 we carried out field surveys as a pilot project.[5] We supplied questionnaires to a selected sample of passersby in the surroundings of the CL, including regular visitors and bystanders, or non-visitors.[6] We aimed to use the results to calculate not only the WTP for the services of the CL, but also the evaluation of the institutions, socioeconomic characteristics, and cultural habits of the respondents. Thus, we can analyze the factors associated with the WTP to use the facilities of the CL and estimate a value for them.

Aligned with the systems thinking approach, the valuation perception of the public goods by visitors and non-visitors to the cultural institutions of the CL contributes to support the definition of conjoined strategies that could be adopted by these organizations in order to make the provision of services more adequate to its objectives—in other words, the objective of consolidation of different public profiles. In the rest of the chapter, we present a short literature review about public goods and their evaluation, the methodology of our project, and the results.

CULTURAL INSTITUTIONS, PUBLIC GOODS, AND WILLINGNESS TO PAY: A BRIEF REVIEW OF LITERATURE

Museums and cultural centers are the best examples of community cultural goods, because they preserve the community's memory and expose its artistic creativity. For those reasons, they have value that transposes their economic and social impact. Bille and Schulze argue that there are four dimensions of the valuation of cultural heritage (which includes museums and cultural centers) and its influence in regional development: (1) value option, given by the possibility to enjoy a good or service; (2) existence value, derived from the knowledge of the existence of the good and service; (3) prestige value, extracted from the recognition of local or regional wealth; and (4) heritage value, derived from the possibility of future generations to access the good or to use the service.[7]

The social and historical significance of museums and cultural centers combined with budgetary constraints (these facilities are usually government-owned, so they need funding from taxes) requires that these public goods must be systematically evaluated. It is necessary to have mechanisms or instruments to measure the social value of the public good in order to assess the decisions on construction, expansion, and maintenance of museums and cultural centers. The evaluation method of CV is one of those instruments. It consists of asking the users of a specific good or service directly how much they would be willing to pay for the implementation, improvements, or access to the public good. From the information obtained, the method estimates values for the good or service in question, making it an evaluation marker.

It is an evaluation marker, because, following Klamer, the allocation of value in a monetary metric to something with subjective content (such as a cultural good) boosts idiosyncrasies of respondents, on top of different experiences.[8] The values do not inform our actions as economic agents, since the context in which the processes take place is what matters. In other words, besides the difficulty of people treating values with economic measures, even if methods are available, there is an implicit degree of subjectivity in these evaluation levels that eventually describes group principles (i.e., the sample) who express their preferences.

In the literature of cultural goods evaluation, there are three main approaches: the maximum willingness to make donations to museums,[9] the willingness to purchase tickets,[10] and the effects of a free admission day on the revenues of the institution.[11]

However, the method has biases. We want to emphasize three of them: (1) the warm glow effect, in which respondents may express a positive willingness to pay because they feel good about the act of giving for a social good; (2) the embedding effect, happening when the respondents treat, without taking in consideration a cost-benefit analysis, the investment in one or more institutions as something unique; and (3) the protest, in which they would refuse to pay for a public good.[12]

In order to deal with these biases and produce accurate results, we followed Ardila et al. and adopted better procedures.[13] For the pilot study, we pre-analyzed the sample by organizing focus meetings with user groups, aiming to identify possible values of willingness to pay of a sample of the population studied. We also conducted additional pilot surveys to test the forms and the scenarios built on the good or service to be evaluated and to test which questions should be included in the WTP questionnaire and the response to proposed values, which allowed us to determine which result we should expect. The obtained results were then used to plan the definitive questionnaire and to estimate the sample size.

In summary, despite being a controversial method of allocating values to public goods, contingent valuation is an economic tool that contributes to the formulation of public policies. As Klamer reflected,[14] each CV study can only work for its own object of study. In other words, we cannot apply the same questionnaire to other places or studies because our questionnaire and the results it yields can only be applied to the study for which it was designed, namely the CL area.

The contingent valuation method searches for an objective evaluation starting from the users of the cultural facilities and their possible influences over the management of these spaces. By listening to the respondents and connecting their needs to the practice of the CL, the management of the CL can fully apply systems thinking approach, identifying underlying problems, potentials, and limitations of these spaces and improving the shared management of the CL for its audiences by adopting a culture of learning.

METHODOLOGY

With the results obtained by the pilot studies described in the last section, we prepared a questionnaire to present to a sample of visitors and non-visitors. In order to estimate the respondents' WTP, the survey questionnaire proposed hypothetical situations to the subjects. There are three types of questions: (1) open-ended questions about monetary value (direct question on how much the subject is willing to pay); (2) a list of possible preestablished values to the selection of maximum amount that the respondent is willing to pay; and (3) questions in which the subject votes "yes" or "no" (referendum method). In the questionnaire, we must propose a reference value. We have found that it costs roughly R$10 (US$3.84)[15] by each taxpayer to maintain the CL. Thus, we have adopted R$10 as a reference to our subjects (that is, the respondent will decide if they are willing to pay equal, less, or more than the reference value).

In addition to the questions presented above, we asked two more questions: (1) if they thought that the public investment in cultural activities in the state of Minas Gerais was: (a) very high; (b) sufficient, (c) low; or (d) no answer; and (2) for what reasons the CL should be valued: (a) for its existence; (b) leisure option; (c) transmission of knowledge; (d) creating employment and income; (e) attracting tourists; (f) creating a distinction for Belo Horizonte in the national and international cultural context; (g) none of the reasons above or no answer. In the second question, the respondent could mark more than one answer. We included these questions to qualify the information provided by the WTP quantitative questions. Yet, in the same line of good practices in CV, we also asked questions about cultural habits. The reasoning behind this is that there is a high correlation between visiting cultural facilities (like the CL) and consuming cultural goods (e.g., books, theater, and musicals).

We defined the sample limit considering the monthly average of spontaneous visitors to the CL (see table 12.1). In the defined limit, a total of 154 recurring visitors and 59 non-visitors were surveyed. Thus, in the final study, 213 surveys were conducted over three weeks, on Thursdays, Saturdays, and Sundays.

PROFILE OF RESPONDENTS

This section presents a profile of the respondents. Table 12.2 summarizes their socioeconomic profile. Among visitors, the percentage of women is slightly higher than men. In our sample, the modal age ranges are sixteen to twenty-five and twenty-six to thirty-five years old. For visitors, about 67 percent were between sixteen and thirty-five and for non-visitors 61 percent were between sixteen and thirty-five years old. Given that about 40 percent of visitors and about 30 percent of non-visitors are in the sixteen to twenty-five years range, it can be said that the results corroborate the literature, that is, since young people have more time for leisure, they tend to consume more cultural goods.[16]

As for level of education, the visitors of the CL have, on average, eight more years of education than non-visitors. We observed a similar pattern concerning household income. The higher income ranges include more visitors than non-visitors, that is, visitors are relatively wealthier than non-visitors. The majority of both visitors and non-visitors live in the city of Belo Horizonte (76 percent), while 13 percent come from other municipalities in the metropolitan region, 4 percent from other municipalities of the state of Minas Gerais, 5 percent from other states in Brazil, and 2 percent from other countries (Peru, Spain, and France).

The relation between visits and cultural habits was captured by a set of questions on reading habits and frequency to cultural events, museums, and cultural centers.[17] Since the visiting frequency to other cultural facilities is low, reading and movie going are the most common cultural habits. Our study also tried to identify the presence of behavior that Stigler and Becker associate as the *positive addiction*[18]—in other words, the relationship between the present consumption of culture and previous

Table 12.1. Number of Visitors per Month and in 2013 Circuito Liberdade Spaces*

Sector	Jan	Feb	Mar	Apr	May	Jun	Jul	Aug	Sep	Oct	Nov	Dec	Total
Overall Total	52,650	31,836	48,053	55,538	58,540	46,350	62,162	65,922	104,475	95,398	109,819	69,474	800,218
Total Education	1,754	1,771	8,330	10,788	9,431	7,224	5,695	10,061	22,930	9,047	9,081	2,341	98,453
Total Spontaneous	39,965	25,589	33,105	38,716	40,725	32,270	47,821	43,616	39,480	39,734	38,503	39,678	459,202
Total Events	12,847	5,086	7,130	6,717	9,812	7,492	10,416	14,350	41,924	47,635	60,407	35,128	258,944
Total Visitation	52,812	30,675	40,235	45,433	50,537	39,762	58,237	57,966	81,404	87,369	98,910	74,806	718,146
Total Virtual	87,551	73,708	105,078	107,816	98,632	89,083	84,844	88,344	107,935	168,788	159,919	32,100	1,204,298
Visitors 2010–2013	-	-	-	-	-	-	-	-	-	-	-	-	2,538,651

Source: Sérgio Magnani Cultural Institute.

*Public Archive of Minas Gerais, Luiz de Bessa State Public Library, Palace of Liberty, Museum of Minas Gerais, CEMIG Center of Popular Art, Banco do Brasil Cultural Center, TIM UFMG Knowledge Space, Museum Minas Gerais Vale, Museum of Mines and Metal, Inhotim School, Queen of Scrap.

Table 12.2. Socioeconomic Characteristics of Respondents (Percent)

	Non-visitors	Visitors
By sex		
Male	52.54	47.44
Female	47.46	52.56
By age group		
Up to 15 years	1.69	3.18
16–25 years	30.51	40.76
26–35 years	30.51	26.11
36–45 years	11.86	7.64
46–55 years	11.86	11.46
56–65 years	10.17	4.46
Over 65 years	1.69	5.10
Did not answer	1.69	1.27
By education		
No schooling	0.00	0.64
Incomplete Primary Education	10.17	1.27
Complete Primary Education	13.56	1.27
Incomplete High School	15.25	8.28
Complete High School	32.20	18.47
Incomplete Undergraduate	13.56	29.94
Complete Undergraduate	5.08	22.93
Graduate	10.17	17.20
By monthly household income range (R$)		
Up to 720	0.00	1.27
More than 720 to 1,200	18.64	7.64
More than 1,200 to 2,000	30.51	10.19
More than 2,000 to 4,000	16.95	19.11
More than 4,000 to 6,000	10.17	16.56
More than 6,000 to 8,000	1.69	7.01
More than 8,000 to 10,000	3.39	7.01
Over 10,000	8.47	8.92
Could not answer	10.17	22.29
By place of residence		
Belo Horizonte	67.80	75.80
Other locations	32.20	24.20

Source: Author.

exposure or past consumption levels. Table 12.3 shows the number of respondents who reported reading habits. Visitors tend to read more books, both in print format (82 percent) and e-books (29 percent) and to use the Internet more (69 percent) than non-visitors.

Table 12.3. Number of Respondents Who Reported Habit of Reading, According to the Format

	Newspaper	Magazine	Book	Internet	e-book	Other	Total Respondents
Non-visitors	49.15%	40.68%	49.15%	50.85%	6.78%	6.78%	59
Visitors	45.86%	43.31%	82.17%	69.43%	29.30%	2.55%	157
Total	37.50%	42.59%	73.15%	64.35%	23.15%	3.70%	216

Source: Author.

The CL visitors tend to frequent cinemas, theaters, and dance performances almost twice as often as non-visitors. They also tend to go to the movies and the theater at least five times a year. They also participated in other cultural activities more frequently, but in minor proportions (see table 12.4).

Table 12.4. Number of Respondents Who Reported Attending Cultural Activities More Than Five Times a Year

	Cinema	Theater	Concert	Show	Dance	Total respondents
Non-visitors	35.59%	11.86%	8.47%	22.03%	6.78%	59
Visitors	61.15%	21.66%	10.83%	31.21%	17.20%	157
Total	54.17%	18.98%	10.19%	28.70%	14.35%	216

Source: Author.

We built a cultural habits index (CHI) using the principal component analysis (PCA) procedure. The PCA reduces the volume of the data under analysis and facilitates the interpretation of the correlations between the variables.[19] In our case, we used the number of books read and the attendance to cinemas, theaters, concerts, shows, and dance performances in the last year. Thus, we applied the weights of this first component to calculate the indicator shown in table 12.5 in standardized form.[20] The average and median of the CHI for visitors (0.54 and 0.53 respectively) are higher than those of non-visitors (0.38 and 0.37), a tendency that occurs throughout all the distribution. This suggests that visitors have a higher profile of culture consumers.

Table 12.5. Distribution of Cultural Habits Index (CHI)

	Obs.	Average	Standard deviation	Percentiles		
				25%	50%	75%
Non-visitors	59	0.38	0.20	0.26	0.37	0.46
Visitors	157	0.54	0.19	0.41	0.53	0.67

Source: Author.

Therefore, it is understood that the CL visitors are also regular consumers of other cultural goods, such as literary, visual, and performing arts. Although the admission ticket is free in all institutions, we simulated a contingent market, asking which value the respondents would be willing to pay for the acquisition of a hypothetical weekly pass, using the reference value. This question sought to evaluate the CL from the economic point of view and to compare it with the valuation in cultural terms.

The results also show that non-visitors would pay an average weekly pass of US$13.44, higher than the visitor group (approximately US$8.70). This implies that the non-visitor group assigns a major value to the cultural services compared to the visitor group (see table 12.6). One possible explication for this fact is that non-visitors do not know the real cost of a cultural service, since they do not have the custom of visiting it. In other words, non-visitors tend to overrate the value of cultural goods and services they do not consume and for which they do not have a reference price. On the other side, we must be aware of the possibility that non-visitors may have a *strategic* behavior, seeking for status or acceptation from the surveyor giving the *right answer*, and so respond with a high value for the public good (the *warm glow* effect).

Table 12.6. Number of Respondents According to Willingness to Pay Ranges and Average Value of the Weekly Pass (R$)

	0	>0–10	>10–50	>50–100	>100	NR*	Total	AVP
Non-visitors	7	11	20	4	3	14	59	34.96
Visitors	33	36	54	5	3	26	157	22.62
Total	40	47	74	9	6	40	216	25.77

Source: Author.
*Did not answer or did not know.

Among the visitors, there seems to be no relation between the average CHI and WTP, suggesting that, for this group, the WTP is defined by other reasons not related to cultural habits (see figure 12.2).

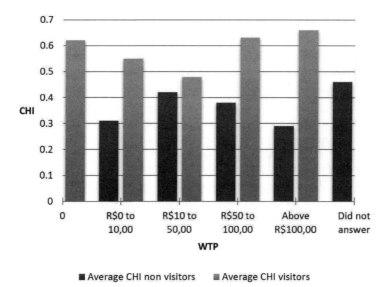

Figure 12.2. Average CHI and Willingness to Pay Ranges (US$1 Equivalent to R$2.6).
Source: **Author's elaboration from survey research in 2014.**

The given economic value (price of the weekly pass) is combined with the satisfaction and valuation reasons of the CL. From table 12.7, we see that, as expected, the WTP is directly related to the satisfaction with the visit. Even those people who chose "minimally satisfied" are willing to pay some amount for a weekly pass, which suggests the presence of the dimensions of use value identified by Bille and Schulze.[21] Use value, in this case, is associated with the possibility of a person enjoying visiting the cultural institution, even if this person has never done it before. The presence of the museum or cultural center by itself constitutes a value.

Table 12.7. Number of Visitors According to Willingness to Pay (R$) Ranges and Evaluation of Circuito Liberdade

	0	0 to 10	10 to 50	50 to 100	Over 100	NR*	Total	Mean
Unsatisfied	1	0	0	0	0	0	1	0.00
Minimally satisfied	3	1	2	0	0	1	7	10.00
Satisfied	9	13	16	1	1	6	46	23.05
Very satisfied	17	19	33	4	1	18	92	22.58
NR*	3	3	3	0	1	1	11	31.00
Total	33	36	54	5	3	26	157	22.62

Source: Author.
*Did not answer or did not know.

FINAL CONSIDERATIONS

The results of the WTP for the CL are similar to those found in the international literature. Moreover, the application of the CV method was appropriate to appreciation of value of non-market goods and services such as the CL. In addition to the question of WTP, other issues of cultural and social values allowed us to identify opportunistic behavior of respondents, such as the warm glow effect. Another result from our analysis is that visitors value the facilities based on their frequency in cultural activities.

Although the CV method has faced criticism,[22] the method is still an important tool to evaluate public policies in the cultural sector, for two main reasons: first, in this topic, where there is a difference between cost and social return, it is necessary to have an evaluation not only for construction, maintenance, and repair of cultural facilities, but also to validate their existence and use by the population that attends it or only contributes through tax payments; second, the respondents, when asked to express their opinion on the subject, are encouraged to reflect on the public heritage of a place. Consequently, this reflection can stimulate a sense of identity and belonging, key aspects for public education in culture.

Last, we presented these results to the managers of the institutions; the results can further influence the practice of the CL in the future. For example, the survey result indicated that there are non-visitors to the CL who value what the CL has to offer. Yet they are not coming. Aligned with the systems thinking approach described at the beginning of the chapter, while the study helped identify some of the underlying issues of the CL—its visitors are not very diverse and share common characteristics and there are people who value the CL who do not use its facilities—the study also suggests that with further visitor and non-visitor studies, the CL can determine what would make non-visitors come to the CL, expanding the offerings to wider audiences and diversifying existing audiences. In addition, it has also been organized to expose contents and execute activities and workshops that reflect the local culture rather than emphasize the artistic production from other states or countries in an effort to appeal to local audiences and attract more community members to the CL. These changes and possibilities show how evaluations of museums and other cultural facilities can interact with the systems thinking approach in identifying potentials and limitations of the cultural facilities and to allow them to be better used by the public. Public consultations must occur with a greater frequency because it affects the management process with actual results and allows the voice of the public to be heard. When this continues, the CL can become a learning organization where its collaborative management teams and leaders continue to study visitors and non-visitors and reflect their changing needs and interests into its practice.

BIBLIOGRAPHY

Ardila, Sergio, Ricardo Quiroga, and William J. Vaughan. *A Review of the Use of Contingent Valuation Methods in Project Analysis at the Inter-American Development Bank.* Washington, DC: Inter-American Development Bank, 1998.

Ateca-Amestoy, Victoria. "Determining Heterogeneous Behavior for Theater Attendance." *Journal of Cultural Economics* 32, no. 2 (2008): 127–51.

Bedate, Ana Maria, Luis César Herrero, and José Ángel Sanz. "Economic Valuation of a Contemporary Art Museum: Correction of Hypothetical Bias Using a Certainty Question." *Journal of Cultural Economics* 33, no. 3 (2009): 185–99.

Bille, Trine, and Günther G. Schulze. "Culture in Urban and Regional Development." In *Handbook of the Economics of Art and Culture,* edited by Victor A. Ginsburgh and David Throsby, 1051–99. Oxford: North-Holland Elsevier, 2006.

Borgonovi, Francesca. "Performing Arts Attendance: An Economic Approach." *Applied Economics* 36, no. 17 (2004): 1871–85.

Diamond, Peter A., and Jerry A. Hausman. "Contingent Valuation: Is Some Number Better Than No Number?" *Journal of Economic Perspectives* 8, no. 4 (1994): 45–64.

Klamer, Arjo. "A Pragmatic View on Values in Economics." *Journal of Economic Methodology* 10, no. 2 (2003): 191–212.

Ringstad, Vidar, and Knut Løyland. "The Demand for Books Estimated by Means of Consumer Survey Data." *Journal of Cultural Economics* 30, no. 2 (2006): 141–55.

Santagata, Walter, and Giovanni Signorello. "Contingent Valuation of a Cultural Public Good and Policy Design: The Case of 'Napoli Musei Aperti.'" *Journal of Cultural Economics* 24, no. 3 (2000): 181–204.

Sanz Lara, José Ángel, and Luis César Herrero Prieto. "Valoración de bienes públicos relativos al patrimonio cultural: aplicación comparada de métodos de estimación y análisis de segmentación de demanda." *Hacienda Pública Española* 178 (2006): 113–33.

Steiner, Faye. "Optimal Pricing of Museum Admission." *Journal of Cultural Economics* 21, no. 4 (1997): 307–33.

Stigler, George J., and Gary S. Becker. "De gustibus non est disputandum." *American Economic Review* 67, no. 2 (1997): 76–90.

Throsby, David. *Economics and Culture.* Cambridge: Cambridge University Press, 2001.

Walker, Paul A., Richard Greiner, David McDonald, and Victoria Lyne. "The Tourism Futures Simulator: A Systems Thinking Approach." *Environmental Modelling & Software* 14, no. 1 (1998): 59–67.

NOTES

1. *Sebrae* is the Brazilian institution that supports small and medium enterprises; Fiat is a multinational automotive producer; *Banco do Brasil* is the largest of the Brazilian public banks; BDMG is the Development Bank of Minas Gerais; CEMIG is the electricity company of Minas Gerais; UFMG is the Federal University of Minas Gerais; *Vale* is a multinational mining company; and Gerdau is a Brazilian steel company.

2. IEPHA is currently responsible for the management of CL. Between 2013 and 2015, this management was under responsibility of the *Instituto Cultural Sérgio Magnani* (Cultural Institute Sérgio Magnani), a civil society organization of public interest.

3. Paul A. Walker, Richard Greiner, David McDonald, and Victoria Lyne, "The Tourism Futures Simulator: A Systems Thinking Approach," *Environmental Modelling and Software* 14, no. 1 (1998): 60.

4. David Throsby, *Economics and Culture* (Cambridge: Cambridge University Press, 2001).

5. This research was funded by *CNPq/Ministério da Cultura* through the call n. 80/2013 *CNPq/SEC/Ministério da Cultura*. The field research was authorized by the COEP-UFMG on October 6, 2014.

6. Please contact Prof. Ana Flávia Machado (afmachad@cedeplar.ufmg.br) for the questionnaires.

7. Trine Bille and Günther G. Schulze, "Culture in Urban and Regional Development," in *Handbook of the Economics of Art and Culture*, ed. Victor A. Ginsburgh and David Throsby (Oxford: North-Holland Elsevier, 2006), 1051–99.

8. Arjo Klamer, "A Pragmatic View on Values in Economics," *Journal of Economic Methodology* 10, no. 2 (2003): 191–212.

9. Walter Santagata and Giovanni Signorello, "Contingent Valuation of a Cultural Public Good and Policy Design: The Case of 'Napoli Musei Aperti,'" *Journal of Cultural Economics* 24, no. 3 (2000): 181–204.

10. José Ángel Sanz Lara and Luis César Herrero Prieto, "Valoración de bienes públicos relativos al patrimonio cultural: aplicación comparada de métodos de estimación y análisis de segmentación de demanda," *Hacienda Pública Española* 178 (2006): 113–33; Ana Maria Bedate, Luis César Herrero, and José Ángel Sanz, "Economic Valuation of a Contemporary Art Museum: Correction of Hypothetical Bias Using a Certainty Question," *Journal of Cultural Economics* 33, no. 3 (2009): 185–99.

11. Faye Steiner, "Optimal Pricing of Museum Admission," *Journal of Cultural Economics* 21, no. 4 (1997): 307–33.

12. Peter A. Diamond and Jerry A. Hausman, "Contingent Valuation: Is Some Number Better Than No Number?" *Journal of Economic Perspectives* 8, no. 4 (1994): 45–64.

13. Sergio Ardila, Ricardo Quiroga, and William J. Vaughan, *A Review of the Use of Contingent Valuation Methods in Project Analysis at the Inter-American Development Bank* (Washington, DC: Inter-American Development Bank, 1998).

14. Klamer, "Pragmatic View."

15. The Real/Dollar exchange rate was approximately R\$2.60/US\$1 during the project.

16. Victoria Ateca-Amestoy, "Determining Heterogeneous Behavior for Theater Attendance," *Journal of Cultural Economics* 32, no. 2 (2008): 127–51; Francesca Borgonovi, "Performing Arts Attendance: An Economic Approach," *Applied Economics* 36, no. 17 (2004): 1871–85; Vidar Ringstad and Knut Løyland, "The Demand for Books Estimated by Means of Consumer Survey Data," *Journal of Cultural Economics* 30, no. 2 (2006): 141–55.

17. To capture cultural habits, we used questions traditionally adopted in the cultural consumption literature. They are related to reading habits, cinema, theater performances, musical concerts, museums, and cultural centers. We recognize that we are disregarding the importance of popular art manifestations in Brazilian cultural context, but we seek to maintain the same approach to international literature, in order to not lose comparability.

18. George J. Stigler and Gary S. Becker, "De gustibus non est disputandum," *American Economic Review* 67, no. 2 (1977): 76–90.

19. The PCA methodology is used when we have a large quantity of variables to analyze one single problem. The method searches for common characteristics in the database and separates them into *components* for groups of variables that have the same characteristics. This method used a covariance matrix to search the similarities and create the component, so we are able to reduce a large number of variables into some components.

20. The indicator values were normalized in order to vary between 0 and 1. The closer to 1, the higher the habit of reading and attendance in cultural areas.

21. Bille and Schulze, "Culture in Urban and Regional Development."

22. Diamond and Hausman, "Contingent Valuation."

Part VI

Take Action

1. In Paquette and Nelson's chapter regarding rebranding museums through social media narratives, the authors propose using the notions of *de-territorializing* (undoing former territorial boundaries with audiences) and *re-territorializing* (establishing a new narrative and building new relationships with the community). How is your museum currently using social media as an inclusive and narrative approach to building new relationships with the community or expanding existing conceptualizations of your museum? Are your social media posts haphazard or do they follow a plan for creating consistent and inclusive messages that build stories?

2. Machado, Faria, Diniz, Paglioto, Michel, and Vaz de Melo examine strategies of a cultural institution complex in Brazil to focus on visitorship and local community. To understand community members' evaluation of the complex and their cultural preferences better, they interviewed visitors and non-visitors. How might your museum gain access to non-visitors (including those who walk right by your front doors and those participating in other venues across the community)? Who might you collaborate with to develop this kind of evaluative work? How would you use the findings to take next steps for connecting with new or formerly excluded audiences? How would you use external communication including marketing, social media, and other approaches to connect with these audiences?

Part VII

SYSTEMS THINKING IN COMMUNITY ENGAGEMENT

Beyond communication, how are museums including community members in the process of developing museum programs and exhibitions? External communication may take various forms; some examples and best practices are discussed in the previous part. However, some museums go much further in including community inputs after finding out about their needs and interests. The chapters in this part address effective ways to include the community in the process of creating museum content and experiences beyond communication.

The Museum (the fictional museum based on a real museum first introduced in the Part I introduction) tries to include community input in its programs and exhibitions but its approach to community engagement is often lip service or its community is very narrowly defined as shown in the Part VI introduction (i.e., the museum only gets input from its existing members and donors). For example, the museum has a community advisory committee yet its members' ideas are not included in major programming and exhibition decisions. They are invited to sit passively in a meeting where the decision is already made by museum staff who present it to them; they then are forced to approve as the projects are often already under way and resources already spent. A group of museum donors acts as community liaisons between the museum and its community. However, this group is composed of people who rarely represent the local predominately blue-collar community. This type of community engagement is not an inclusive one that actively engages diverse groups of community inputs and perspectives in programming and exhibition efforts based on the social, cultural, educational, and political needs of local communities.

The two chapters in this part show how museums include community concerns, issues, and perspectives into the heart of museum exhibitions and programming through inviting community members to be on the exhibition and programming teams. Guido Ferilli, Sendy Ghirardi, and Pier Luigi Sacco in chapter 13 see museums as part of local communities and urge them to be community forums by inviting community members to contribute content and be part of programming development. Two best case studies included in this chapter, the Israel Museum of Jerusalem, Israel, and the Castello di Rivoli in Turin, Italy, address community issues year-round, not just for a one-time special event. The authors further analyze these cases to show commonalities between them, which can be applied to other museums in engaging their communities. In order for museums to be truly community focused, they should involve all levels and positions of museum staff, utilize a multidirectional communication system, give community authorship, and follow the model of partnership.

Swarupa Anila, Amy Hamilton Foley, and Nii Quarcoopome in chapter 14 share the community engagement model that the Detroit Institute of Arts used to include community perspectives in its Asian permanent collection reinstallation project. The model is visitor centered, thinking about the visitor first when reinstalling collections rather than following an art historical or Western view of organizing artworks. The museum actually included a group of paid community consultants deliberately organized to be diverse and having direct or indirect Asian background and interests. The team of diverse positions of museum staff and community members together made decisions for the museum's permanent collection reinstallation, valuing shared authority and multiplicity in perspectives, thereby challenging the traditional object-based and museum-centered installation process.

13

The Museum as a Catalyst of Social Development

Best Practices to Engage the Community

Guido Ferilli, Sendy Ghirardi, and Pier Luigi Sacco

Museums are cultural ecosystems in themselves and part of wider cultural ecosystems embedded in a societal space, whose influence on community life is manifold and profound,[1] even if sometimes not properly appreciated in the full richness of its implications. To appreciate the consequences of this perspective fully, it is necessary to analyze museums from a holistic viewpoint,[2] and not as isolated units or self-contained institutions.

Connecting the museum with the local environment and communities is natural, but neither obvious nor easy. It necessarily enables local actors to understand and empathize with others and to jointly develop a community perspective that organically dialogues with their own. The museum cannot be regarded as a closed realm people occasionally visit when looking for some moments of leisure or spiritual cultivation, but as a lively and essential part of the social and institutional infrastructure of the community. Therefore, the museum can become a relevant actor when dealing with a variety of problems of different natures—connected with education, public health, social cohesion, and so on. In this way, the museum can qualify as a proper *cultural hub* that is recognized as a collective asset by a large local constituency.

To achieve this goal, the museum must be an enabling agent for the local community, by providing appropriate tools to different players in diverse capacities. First, the museum must create the conditions for a high level of cultural participation of the local community, which is not just the result of promotion and marketing or of high-budget blockbuster events, but of a steady, coherent, and effective year-round policy of community engagement. Through a high level of local participation, the museum can harness forms of creation of social value that would be unattainable otherwise.[3]

The participatory dimension of the museum is primarily linked to the creation of *capability building experiences* that constitute the main building block of the enablement process by helping people develop various social and cognitive skills, such as intercultural dialogue, addressing and framing unfamiliar experiences and contexts, and harnessing ingenuity in challenging situations. Consequently, the participatory museum can be regarded as an accelerator for the creation of assets such as human, social, cultural, and symbolic capital.

To credibly qualify as a participatory museum, it is necessary to define a specific approach aimed at effectively facilitating the engagement of community members and visitors with their diverse characteristics. In systems thinking terms, the participatory museum acts as a socio-cognitive regulator of community functioning via cultural participation. To this purpose, the museum must give up a mono-directional line of communication (i.e., being a content provider to the passive audience), learning to dialectically shape its interface through an in-depth conversation with its public.[4] The museum is a temple of knowledge and culture, but also a forum. It preserves and showcases objects that transmit cultural and social knowledge, represent a heritage, and embody values and worldviews, but also stimulate debate and innovative forms of expression and creativity.[5] When fully performing this double function, the museum actually cultivates the collective intelligence of its reference community.

Participation may take different forms. It is not a binary yes or no concept, but a nuanced continuum, from mere transmission and exchange of information to the public designing and even implementing the whole project. Participatory programs give the public a central role in terms of authorship, coauthorship, or partnership. They also require the involvement of the whole staff, from management to front line, and not only of those who directly interact with visitors. The museum can share some responsibility with the public, asking for an active creative contribution, responding to the needs and interests of local stakeholders, and even moving its activities outside its gates into public space. In all these cases, there is ample room to deploy participatory practices, explore possibilities, or run experiments of joint discovery with the public.

In this chapter, we focus upon two emblematic case studies that illustrate some best practices on how to engage the community and become effective facilitators: The Israel Museum of Jerusalem, Israel (IMJ), and the Castello di Rivoli in Turin, Italy (CRT).

CASE STUDIES: IMJ

IMJ has become an incubator of civic responsibility and a reference for the city community. Art education is a core focus and has always been part of IMJ's core mandate. Among the variety of activities offered by the educational department, the Youth Wing, the *community projects* deserve special attention. They involve different local communities including Ethiopian immigrants, Arabic and Hebrew students and kids, youth in distress, and soldiers. IMJ is deeply aware of the social context and is a dynamic machine that engages the visitor as a provider of knowledge, abilities and learning styles, and interpretive strategies.[6] Jerusalem's inhabitants are heterogeneous in social, cultural, and religious terms, and the museum fully caters to such diversity by inviting community members to contribute content, involving them in the museum's activities, or encouraging the museum to reach out to community spaces.

Here are a couple of examples. *Window Dialogue: Community Outreach and Art Education in the Arab Sector*, funded by the Fine Foundation of Pittsburgh and started in 2008, is a project that allows the IMJ staff to teach art in high schools in the Arab community. The goal is to break down social, cultural, and religious barriers due to the cooperation of the participants and to the universal language of art. The museum staff and the teachers work together to create an art education program for the students, who would rarely visit the museum otherwise.

Another project is *Bridging the Gap*, funded by the Association of Friends of the Israel Museum of Germany. It enables young Arabs and Jews to create art together in the museum space to break down reciprocal negative stereotypes and to visit and appreciate together the museum through guided tours. Four Jerusalem schools are involved, two Arab schools from East Jerusalem and two Jewish schools from West Jerusalem. Teachers and Arab-Jewish artists of the museum staff provide instruction. This project contributes to the establishment of a new and intercultural community platform through the transition from individual to collective participation and practice.

These examples show the varied outreach of the IMJ and how the museum manages to actively engage very different types of publics, offering through their projects cutting-edge approaches to some of the key social and political criticalities of the city. Rather than through communication campaigns, the museum attracts visitors through its ability to become part of the fabric of the daily life of Jerusalem's troubled social and cultural scenery.

CASE STUDIES: CRT

Castello di Rivoli (CRT) is a contemporary art museum in Turin, Italy, that also responds to the needs and requests of local constituencies in innovative ways. With the project *Il Cantiere dell'Arte* (*the Art Construction Site*), CRT's educational department has launched a partnership with the nonprofit foundation *Medicina a Misura di Donna*, operating at the Sant'Anna Hospital of Turin, with the purpose of changing the negative perception of the hospital spaces through art forms, thus developing a new art-centric hospital environment that engages staff, patients, and visitors alike. The project followed a bottom-up approach, characterized by the involvement of the hospital community, starting with focus groups collecting opinions regarding hospital spaces, the hospital environment, and its possible improvements. Communities of artists, sports teams (such as the local Turin softball team), and even bank managers were involved in collaborating with the museum and the foundation during their team-building practices, creating the wall-paintings in the hospital. The project has radically changed the physical aspect of the hospital spaces, improving both the quality of the experience of patients and their families and fostering belongingness through creative collective actions that improve daily life in the workplace, with the contribution of the whole hospital population.

CRT's multi-annual initiative *Il Tappeto Volante* (*The Flying Carpet*) is another example that started in 1996, through the collaboration with the Municipal Nursery School Bay of San Salvario, a neighborhood of Turin. The school's teachers asked the museum's department of education to help them to cope with ethnic tensions in the school population and among the neighborhood residents through an innovative approach to contemporary art, jointly experienced by all participants as a moment of deep interpersonal communication facilitated by museum educators. Art provides the basis for a socially shared imagination that helps build a new sense of community. The word *carpet* was used as a metonymic device for guiding intertwining activities that teach acceptance of diversity and how to live it as a resource, starting from actual collective carpet making by teachers, museum staff, students, and parents. Activities, both in the museum and at school, last for the entire school year, and prepare the final events that mark significant moments in the life of the San Salvario community. Over the years, the project network has been extended to all local schools and neighborhood associations, the department of education of the City of Turin, and the foundation for School-Compagnia di San Paolo. The project's collaborative planning is a key social benefit: all educational activities over the years have been designed collaboratively, leading to shared practices and experimentation that unveiled the needs and expectations of the neighborhood's local constituencies.

UNDERSTANDING THE EFFECTS OF PARTICIPATION: THE ACTION WORKFLOW APPROACH

The brief analysis of two case studies above allowed us to exemplify a few different modes of participation and sketch some common traits of a pathway to effective community engagement. Despite the projects' obvious differences, a few basic elements may be recognized.

Both examples illustrate the importance of community awareness for effective involvement, and how local community engagement may become a powerful platform of social cohesion. Also, the participatory process involves the activation of an intense social exchange between the museum and its reference communities, as a part of an intrinsically relational process. We can make sense of these aspects by means of the *Action Workflow* (AW) model of business process reengineering,[7] which interprets processes as a homeostatic interaction that generates relations and intangible assets. The AW model, in turn, is based upon the Speech Act Theory.[8] We can regard it as a structure of commitment that enables a transaction between two constituencies, a *customer* and a *performer*, to accomplish a purpose. Such purpose will often change and be rearticulated as the two parties work together, develop new insights and learning, and get a clearer understanding of what is possible and what is needed.

The AW thus adopts the Language-Action Perspective,[9] first introduced in the field of information systems, to capture the fact that human beings are fundamentally linguistic beings and act through language. It was argued that language is used not only for exchanging information, but also to perform actions. Mazzei and Esposito summarized this approach into a few key practices: exploring, setting, acting, and valuing, and applied them to a corporate communication plan.[10] We can translate their practices into a sequence of phases that characterize the process through which the museum engages its reference communities, adapting the framework accordingly to the specificities of museum environments (see table 13.1 for a summary of the four phases).

Exploring is the first step and is the analysis of the starting situation. It includes three sub-processes: museum mission awareness, context analysis, and community actors' analysis.

Museum mission awareness is fundamental to understanding the direction the museum wants to take and to defining the objectives to achieve. The participation of local communities must be considered a core point of this agenda. According to Mark O'Neill,[11] museums must go beyond the elite model (focusing on collections) and the welfare model (focusing on improving visitor services for a select public), to the social justice model that strategically integrates public engagement into the structures and makes it a responsibility of all staff. Context analysis helps identify the environmental factors and the institutional dynamics in which the museum is embedded. Making the social, economic, and cultural conditions explicit allows for the designing of specific projects that target key environmental issues effectively. The analysis of community actors allows the understanding of the needs, interests, and expectations of the local constituencies, in order to engage them appropriately.[12]

In each of the projects reported above, the museum staff is aware of the educational mission of the museum and identifies participation as a core goal. Both IMJ and CRT strive to meet the interests and the needs of their communities, providing tailored programs for the different constituencies that inhabit the city (IMJ), and addressing the needs and requests of some specific local stakeholders (CRT). The exploring phase is thus ideal for the museum staff to put into focus the strategic objectives of the institution, the key features and constraints of the external context, and the basic demands and expectations of the museum's key constituencies. In the exploring phase, two intangible assets are generated: the *awareness* of the reality in which the museum operates and interacts and the *legitimacy* to act within the community.

Setting is the process of negotiating the project. It consists of three sub-processes: building local networks, defining goals, and designing the project. Building local networks is an important step to defining the strategy of the project and to financing it. Defining goals is the key step where the museum and the other stakeholders arrive at a shared view of the objectives that the project design needs to accomplish. Designing the project, in turn, means identifying which activities to provide, how, and to what purpose. Again, the exemplified museum projects reflect this part of the methodology; they are all realized through a collaboration with other territorial actors (e.g., schools, hospital, foundations, and associations), which together with the museums work to build the programs step by step. During this phase, the intangible values of *sharing* and *socialization* are generated through close cooperation between the museum and the local stakeholders.

The *acting* phase implements the planned initiatives. It includes two sub-processes: developing the project activities, and engaging the community and developing relations. Again, it entails a close collaboration between the museum staff and the museum constituencies. This is where the museum has a chance to reach both the already engaged constituencies and previously unengaged ones. In our examples, both IMJ and CRT moved beyond their own physical walls and worked within the city spaces to build new relations—even with marginal groups not directly involved in the project. This phase helps to generate assets of *active participation* and *partnership* within and outside the museum and its physical space.

Finally, in the *valuing* phase, the knowledge generated during the participation process must be capitalized, leveraged, and deposited. It includes the evaluation of the programs' initiatives and of the system-wide effects generated by the projects. The former kind of evaluation consists of measuring the outputs of participation activities, analyzing the characteristics of the engaged public, and assessing the effects of the activities on the participants in terms of changes in attitudes and behavior and of whether such changes persist over time. The latter kind of evaluation, which targets the projects' spillover effects, helps to elucidate the impact of active cultural participation on the territory as well as beyond the project itself. The intangible resources generated at the *valuing* stage are *learning* to further improve engagement and participation, and *problem-solving expertise* as a basis for a new cycle of goal setting and projects.

Table 13.1. The Four Phases of the Action Workflow Approach, Their Sub-Processes, and the Resultant Intangible Assets

Phases	Sub-processes	Intangible assets
Exploring	• Mission awareness • Context analysis • Community actors' analysis	• Legitimacy • Awareness
Setting	• Building local networks • Defining shared goals • Designing projects	• Sharing • Socialization
Acting	• Developing project activities • Engaging the community	• Active participation • Partnership
Valuing	• Evaluations of program and initiatives • Evaluation of spillover effects	• Learning • Problem-solving expertise

Source: Author.

Through the AW approach, it is possible to pursue a concrete strategy of embedding of the museum cultural ecosystem into the wider socioeconomic environment of the city, and to promote a new vision of the museum as a platform for the creation of social value beyond the traditional mission of the museum, as a starting point for new forms of culture-based experimentation and social innovation.

BIBLIOGRAPHY

Austin, John L. *How to Do Things with Words*. 2nd ed. New York: Oxford University Press, 1976.

Bateson, Gregory. *Steps to an Ecology of Mind*. Chicago: University of Chicago Press, 2000.

Cameron, Duncan F. "The Museum: A Temple or the Forum." *Journal of World History* 14, no. 1 (1972): 189–204.

Falk, John H. *Identity and the Museum Visitor Experience*. London: Routledge, 2016.

Hooper-Greenhill, Eilean. *The Educational Role of the Museum*. London: Routledge, 1999.

Jung, Yuha. "The Art Museum Ecosystem: A New Alternative Model." *Museum Management and Curatorship* 26, no.4 (2011): 321–38.

Mazzei, Alessandra, and Annamaria Esposito. "Il piano di comunicazione da strumento a processo organizzativo e relazionale. Il caso Henkel Italia." *Mercati e Competitività* 9, no. 1 (2012): 95–113.

Medina-Mora, Raul, Terry Winograd, Rodrigo Flores, and Fernando Flores. "The Action Workflow Approach to Workflow Management Technology." In *Proceedings of the Conference on Computer-Supported Cooperative Work*, 281–88. New York: ACM, 1992.

O'Neill, Mark. "Museums—Culture Welfare or Social Justice." In *Creativity, Regional Development and Heritage*, edited by Christina Wistman, Sofia Kling, Peter Kearns, and Jamtli Förlag, 14–27. Ostersund: PASCAL International Observatory, 2011.

Sacco, Pier Luigi, Guido Ferilli, and Giorgio Tavano Blessi. "Culture 3.0. Cultural Participation and the Future of Cultural Policies: A European Perspective." Working paper, IULM University, 2016.

Searle, John R. *Speech Acts: An Essay in the Philosophy of Language*. Cambridge: Cambridge University Press, 1969.

Simon, Nina. *The Participatory Museum*. Santa Cruz, CA: Museum 2.0, 2010.

Winograd, Terry. "A Language/Action Perspective on the Design of Cooperative Work." In *Computer Supported Cooperative Work: A Book of Readings*, edited by Irene Greif, 623–53. San Mateo, CA: Morgan Kaufman, 1986.

Winograd, Terry, and Fernando Flores. *Understanding Computers and Cognition: A New Foundation for Design*. Boston: Addison Wesley, 1987.

NOTES

1. Yuha Jung, "The Art Museum Ecosystem: A New Alternative Model," *Museum Management and Curatorship* 26, no. 4 (2011): 321–38.

2. Gregory Bateson, *Steps to an Ecology of Mind* (Chicago: University of Chicago Press, 2000).

3. Pier Luigi Sacco, Guido Ferilli, and Giorgio Tavano Blessi, "Culture 3.0. Cultural Participation and the Future of Cultural Policies: A European Perspective," working paper, IULM University, 2016.

4. Nina Simon, *The Participatory Museum* (Santa Cruz, CA: Museum 2.0, 2010).

5. Duncan F. Cameron, "The Museum: A Temple or the Forum," *Journal of World History* 14, no. 1 (1972): 189–204.

6. Eilean Hooper-Greenhill, *The Educational Role of the Museum* (London: Routledge, 1999).

7. Terry Winograd and Fernando Flores, *Understanding Computers and Cognition: A New Foundation for Design* (Boston: Addison Wesley, 1987); Raul Medina-Mora, Terry Winograd, Rodrigo Flores, and Fernando Flores, "The Action Workflow Approach to Workflow Management Technology," in *Proceedings of the Conference on Computer-Supported Cooperative Work* (New York: ACM, 1992), 281–88; Alessandra Mazzei and Annamaria Esposito, "Il piano di comunicazione da strumento a processo organizzativo e relazionale. Il caso Henkel Italia," *Mercati e Competitività* 9, no. 1 (2012): 95–113.

8. John R. Searle, *Speech Acts: An Essay in the Philosophy of Language* (Cambridge: Cambridge University Press, 1969); John L. Austin, *How to Do Things with Words*, 2nd ed. (New York: Oxford University Press, 1976).

9. Terry Winograd, "A Language/Action Perspective on the Design of Cooperative Work," in *Computer Supported Cooperative Work: A Book of Readings*, ed. Irene Greif (San Mateo, CA: Morgan Kaufman, 1986), 623–53.

10. Mazzei and Esposito, "Il caso Henkel Italia."

11. Mark O'Neill, "Museums—Culture Welfare or Social Justice," in *Creativity, Regional Development and Heritage*, ed. Christina Wistman, Sofia Kling, Peter Kearns, and Jamtli Förlag (Ostersund: PASCAL International Observatory, 2011), 14–27.

12. John H. Falk, *Identity and the Museum Visitor Experience* (London: Routledge, 2016).

14

Systems Thinking for Visitor-Centered, Community-Engaged Interpretive Planning

Swarupa Anila, Amy Hamilton Foley, and Nii Quarcoopome

The Detroit Institute of Arts (DIA) has a well-established history of experimentation and innovation in visitor-centered interpretive processes, planning, and development. The museum invests significant energy and resources to hone visitor-centered design of art experiences during exhibition planning and development. Consistent work with visitors before art is installed and galleries are opened to the public often brings to light nuanced observations, sensitivities, and issues that influence the decisions exhibition teams make in creating overall exhibition experiences.

As the DIA prepares to reinstall its Asian permanent collections, the museum enters the realm of co-creation on the premise that there is powerful potential in connecting art, individuals, communities, and the museum during the interpretive planning process. To discuss this project, this chapter examines internal systems for developing exhibitions and permanent collection installations. It also explores relationships between the museum and communities, the adaptations of DIA systems and processes, and philosophical and practical goals for new permanent collections galleries that are both visitor centered and community engaged in their presentations of art.

SYSTEMS THINKING—THEORETICAL LEANINGS

This chapter situates its analysis of the DIA's case study in the understanding of systems thinking as "a discipline for seeing wholes . . . a framework for seeing interrelationships rather than things, for seeing patterns of change rather than static snapshots. . . . Systems thinking is a discipline for seeing the 'structures' that underlie complex situations."[1]

Glenn Sutter argues that "many conventional museums are limited in their capacity to contribute to this work because of their focus on reductionism."[2] However, two aspects of systems thinking become particularly useful in considering interpretive planning at the DIA. The first is to consider the practice of identifying the systems, structures, and full interactions required to create art installations to be a worldview. This worldview calls for a cyclical approach between analysis and synthesis, in other words, to examine individual issues but remaining mindful of the need to balance those particular issues in the context of the broader museum ecosystem. As a worldview, systems thinking assumes that no phenomenon or person in the exhibition development process may be considered in isolation from its relationships to other phenomena and individuals.

The second aspect of systems thinking that is critical to visitor-centered interpretive planning and that is challenging to traditional modes of museum work is multiplicity—the recognition that "each system or subsystem, because it is complex and entails a multitude of various individual, empirical, social, and political relationships, needs to be analyzed from multiple perspectives."[3] These systems-thinking approaches that emphasize interconnectedness, non-separability, nonlinearity, and polyvocality—from within the museum and without—allows new modes of interpretive planning to flourish in creating dynamic, inventive, and fresh installations of art. These approaches pressure traditional models of museum work.

REINSTALLATION 1.0: SYSTEMS THINKING FOR A VISITOR-CENTERED APPROACH

The DIA's mission, written in 2007, is to help each visitor find personal meaning in art and with each other.[4] While visitor-centeredness may seem to have been established as a philosophical foundation of the DIA's identity for over a decade now, developing processes to support, sustain, and expand that foundation in disciplines across the museum have had to aggregate over the course of many years. From 2003 to 2007, the DIA planned and reinstalled the majority of its permanent collection to serve a broad public by shifting presentations of art from strictly disciplinary art historical installations to interdisciplinary, human-centered themes that could appeal to non-expert audiences. For example, decorative arts that were once shown in galleries organized as *Eighteenth-Century French Art* were reinstalled in a suite of galleries called *Splendor by the Hour* that explore the proliferation of fine objects used by European aristocracy to support their lavish daily rituals of leisure (see figure 14.1).

The DIA recently reinstalled its Ancient Near Eastern collection in a gallery renamed *Ancient Middle East*. Other art museums typically organize these collections by ancient culture, for example, Sumerian, Babylonian, and Assyrian. The DIA's new gallery examines the interplay of art and technology in the development of the world's earliest civilizations and empires (see figure 14.2).

Figure 14.1. Visitors Engage with an Immersive Video of an Eighteenth-Century Banquet Surrounded by Decorative Arts for Dining in the Evening Gallery of the *Splendor by the Hour* suite. *Source*: Detroit Institute of Arts.

Figure 14.2. Dynamic Projected Text Asks Visitors "When is art . . . Technology?" Prompting Them to Enter the Ancient Middle East Gallery. *Source*: Detroit Institute of Arts.

This visitor-centered approach hinges on understandings and crucial insights about who is likely to visit the gallery, what stories might interest them, and what they might feel and do when they visit. This also entails striving for installations of art, interpretation, and design that are welcoming, accessible, insightful, thought-provoking, interactive, and also engaging on multiple levels, including offering opportunities for visitors to form and express their own opinions.

A team-based approach to exhibition planning was established that broke with the traditional practice of the curator as single source for concepts and installation ideas. The new systems brought together people of different expertise at various stages of the process, including large cross-divisional teams at the early concept phase. The teams included representatives from diverse departments including curatorial, interpretation (then called education), development, conservation, and marketing.

Visitor-centered installations necessitated establishment, expansion, and growth in two areas of professional expertise: first, interpretation grounded in education theory and user-based design; and second, evaluation grounded in visitor studies and research. Both became critical to integrating the direct needs and interests of visitors in planning as well as the development of diverse, dynamic means for engaging them as central users of exhibitions.[5] In addition, visitors and non-visitors would require space in the system. Their voices and perspectives were included through evaluation methods such as visitor panels and as advisors. If a system will not function well or must adapt when a new component is added, then the ancillary is true as well and perhaps with greater challenge. When multiple components (e.g., interpretation, evaluation, and visitor voice) are added, the existing system (centering mainly on curatorial, exhibition, and design) not only becomes strained by their inclusion but splinters or breaks and new systems are born.

The early team-based approach sought to diminish siloed work within the museum and to integrate skill sets and multiple internal perspectives at the earliest phases of ideation. In the years since the 2007 reinstallation project, a struggle ensued to consider which aspects of the reinstallation, including team-based work, would continue for special temporary exhibition development—"to determine what goals or purposes the system has, or what goals it should have, and how these are prioritized, since the goals a system has will affect its structure and interrelationships."[6] At the core, and in order to continue visitor-centered work, a key set of relationships between curatorial, interpretive, and evaluation expertise rose to prominence and required adaptive systems change.

Yet oftentimes, the lack of the requisite understanding of interrelationships makes for a very delicate ecosystem. The use of the word *delicate* here is noteworthy; it acknowledges the tenuous nature of the visitor-centered interpretive practices because of its relative infancy in art museums. As such and especially in recent years, the DIA has not engaged a perfectly harmonized system as roles expand, shift, or realign.[7] Perceptions of power lost or diluted—and even those of too-rapid growth of responsibilities and work demands—can be painful, upsetting, and destabilizing. Correspondingly, J. C. Minger warns of disruptions when "systems analysis fails to recognise [*sic*] the distinctive character of its subjects—purposeful, self-defining, reflexive human beings and the context within which the creation and agreement of objectives and values take place."[8] Flaws reside in the assumption that everyone will think and act toward the same goals. Unevenness of staff commitment and expertise aside, there are behavioral and attitudinal expectations. These include but are not limited to humility, generosity of spirit, collaboration, and inclusion. Such intangibles cannot be easily measured and quantified.

Adaptive and successful systems foster internal culture to create investment in the mission and align staff to goals and a clear picture of the interdependencies of work. In the intervening years since the 2007 reinstallation, the team-based approach remained. However, cultural understanding and internal support for the shift from object- and scholarship-centered interpretive development to one inclusive of visitor-centered work has not always been stable. Over a decade's work of culture change to adapt to visitor-centeredness meant, and still means, attending to the mindset and motivations of staff. The pronoun *we*, as opposed to *I*, is encouraged as the operative word in all aspects of the process. Shared authority underscores the broad consensus around the criticality of interdependence, mutual respect, and complementarity as foundational to the team process and goals of deepening visitor experiences with art. But beyond regular communications training for teamwork and periodic workshops or lectures to align work to visitor-centeredness, there are some museum professionals who might require thorough reeducation. Every staff person on the team, regardless of station and specialty, works in tandem with others. As such, museum professionals directly involved in the core business of art installations and exhibitions need to reexamine their practices and be willing to contribute to how the museum engages a diverse array of audiences.

IDENTIFYING THE PROCESSES THAT SUPPORT THE SYSTEM

In order to understand internal DIA processes for developing visitor-centered installations with more clarity and precision, to alleviate mounting frustrations over missed deadlines, and to identify efficiencies and opportunities for improvement, a team of DIA directors and managers recently engaged in a year-long review of the overall exhibition process. Staff from exhibitions, interpretive planning, curatorial, collections management, and other areas of the museum analyzed and assessed the process of exhibition development from conception to installation and de-installation to identify dependencies, bottlenecks, and inefficiencies. The exercise aimed to map the DIA's process in a framework that would be defined through attention to multiple perspectives across museum disciplines.

What emerged was a detailed understanding of the complex interplay of departmental work, but also frustration. The DIA's many departments work within a highly interdependent, multidimensional system that is difficult to define in a two-dimensional model on paper. Indeed, the exercise revealed that "few systems are merely linear and few are closed systems that are not constantly in dynamic processes of changing and reinventing themselves."[9]

However, the exercise also generated an understanding of the system's flexibility to account for the unique challenges of any given project. Size, scope, and timing of installations, as well as shared understanding of purpose and goals, would require adaptations by different departments at different moments. This foundational understanding showed that the DIA's development process could adapt and be adaptive to new initiatives that were soon to be implemented. Strategizing efficiencies and flexing all parts of the system is expected. Doing so for a single project all at once heightens frustrations.

REINSTALLATION 2.0—SYSTEMS THINKING FOR CO-CREATED INSTALLATIONS

In 2015, the DIA began long-term planning for its next run of permanent collection gallery reinstallations, starting with the Asian collections. Leadership from curatorial, learning and interpretation, exhibitions, and collections discussed resetting logistics and infrastructure to accommodate a series of long-term, large-scale projects. The plan included again implementing cross-divisional concept teams that had been so innovative in leading to the success of the DIA's 2007 reinstallations.

The new starting point also provided the opportunity for broader critical reflection, using a methodology that intersects systems thinking with moral imagination. Patricia Werhane invokes the notion of the moral imagination, defined by Edmund Burke to be an ethical responsibility to consider the human experience beyond the self, and poses a new challenge for systems thinkers. Werhane asks "managers and companies to think more imaginatively . . . [to] step back from established practices and traditions, to develop a new mental model of what *should* be."[10]

That step back for the DIA reinstallation process required an examination of current and future needs. Perhaps most importantly, it required considering the DIA's relationship and commitments to the communities in which it lives and serves. In 2012, voters in three counties approved a homeowner's tax to support up to 70 percent of the museum's operating funds for ten years while the museum raises endowment. The tax agreement with the counties includes funding for school visitation, which has significantly increased the number of students served, and free general admission for tri-county residents, which has increased attendance and the diversity of our visitors. In 2015, the city of Detroit survived a bankruptcy through a *grand bargain* in which the DIA contributed $100 million to support city pension funds. Each of these events created new obligations and relationships to residents of the region.

Perhaps more importantly, the combined systems thinking and moral imagination approaches challenge institutions to reinvent themselves to solve "what often appear to be intractable problems created by systemic constraints for which no [one] individual appears to be responsible."[11] The problem that could be addressed through a reconsidered process for the DIA's Asian reinstallation involves social justice issues of racial representation and cultural definition within traditional American art museums. Presentations of diverse, global creative expressions in art museums, including the DIA, are often fraught with narrow and exclusionary interpretations. Asian collection displays in art museums are typically organized by taxonomies of culture, period, medium, and religion. Even when well-intentioned practices produce more fulsome cultural, religious, and political contexts, the tools of examination and interpretation of those very contexts are shaped for and from Westernist and Euro-centric art historical worldviews. Systems thinking, which relies fundamentally on the inclusion of multiple perspectives, can begin to fracture those static and limited worldviews.[12]

With these larger contexts and potential opportunities in mind, the DIA leadership team made the decision to engage in co-creation, a process that operates on interconnected social and meaning-making systems with a core strength and reliance on multiple perspectives: "it is probably never possible to take account of all the networks of relationships involved, and surely never so given that these systems interact over time, a multiple perspectives approach forces us to think more broadly, and to look at particular systems or problems from different points of view."[13] Therefore, rather than creating a cross-disciplinary team of only museum staff, the Asian project concept team was designed to reserve positions for community members. Residents of the region applying for positions on the team were selected based on their self-identification as Asian in heritage or of having relationships with Asian communities. Candidates were also considered for their ability to work collaboratively, flexibility of thought, and community involvement. Age, gender, and other factors were considered to build a balanced team. The community team members self-identified as Korean, Indian, Taiwanese, Filipino, Japanese, Thai, and of mixed Asian heritage. They ranged in occupations as a retired physician, a journalist, a recent college graduate, homemakers, an engineer, and business owners. As paid consultants, the community consultants joined the curator and interpretive planner as full-throated team members charged with learning the objects and discussing and exchanging perspectives to generate a list of potential big ideas that would move into the next phases of development by the staff team.

To accommodate this co-creative approach, a new architecture for meetings, agendas, communications, and support systems had to be developed to facilitate the inclusion of non-museum voices as team members and to ensure that museum goals would be met. An existing oversight group reformed as the *gallery strategies team*[14] shaped its purpose to oversee development, create milestones, and define parameters for the reinstallation practices, and to guide what would be loosely referred to as the *community consultant concept team* (see figure 14.3).

Figure 14.3. The Asian Early Concept Team, Inclusive of Staff and Community Members, Brainstorms Big Ideas in a Gallery Converted to a Meeting Room Visible to Museum Visitors in the Asian Wing. *Source*: Detroit Institute of Arts.

Despite the incomplete definition of the DIA's logistical processes, the system has proven relatively adaptable as new structures for co-creation merge with existing methods that provide checks and balances, such as focus group testing, inclusion of interdisciplinary content advisors, and in-community consultations.[15] The Asian collections were divided to test the new methodologies. The process was piloted for the Japanese collection in January 2016 to work through challenges and unforeseen complications and to anticipate needs for the overall Asian project. Some key observations from the Japan pilot reveal that because the pilot for Japan overlapped with the onset of the Asian project, little time was left for course corrections or for deep reflections to serve the rest of the project. As the pilot unfolded, it became necessary to reiterate frequently goals and rationale, as well as descriptions of the impact and outcomes envisioned to inspire a sense of purpose and permeate the minds of those involved. For those on staff who were quietly uncomfortable about the co-creation process, such reminders of purpose changed mindsets when they also witnessed the momentum of enthusiasm and critical giving by people traditionally outside but now inside of the museum. This could be attributed to the growing realization of the power, influence, voice, and connectivity beyond museum walls. Simultaneously, those on staff disinclined or actively resistant toward co-creation had dramatically negative impact on team culture, morale, and productivity. This situation required added care from the oversight group and firm communication if only because the inclusion of community members affects internal relationships. Perhaps because people outside of the museum acted as witness to DIA culture and process, issues of roles and power that arise in staff-only teams were not as close to the surface and perhaps were subsumed entirely. At the same time, over-politeness between all team members—staff and community consultants alike—at key moments were suspected of risking the positive tension that pushes innovative thinking.

As the early community consultant concept team phase ended, the process transitioned to established internal practices. Testing through other aspects of well-established DIA interpretive practice (focus group evaluations and in-community consultations) furthered the work that was presented back to the community consultants for their critical review and to ensure that they saw their work and ideas reflected in the concept that would organize the installation.

CONCLUSION

The DIA's Asian reinstallation project seeks to recognize and cultivate interdependencies between individuals inside and outside the DIA to increase its social capital[16]—in other words, the aggregated potential resources through relationships of mutual acquaintance and recognition. Investing in the involvement of community members acts on the assumption that at any given moment, each individual is connected to dozens if not thousands of others in multivalent, shifting, and often overlapping communities.

Because the mission of this art museum is fundamentally directed to the work of facilitating meaning-making, it is theorized that inclusivity, shared authority, and community engagement all deepen and expand potential meaning-making opportunities through systems thinking approaches for co-creative permanent collections galleries development. Care for the human interactions at stake and a broad sense of interconnectedness require ongoing reflection on the museum's internal processes and external relationships but most importantly, on the systems that hold all together as interdependent.

BIBLIOGRAPHY

Anila, Swarupa. "Visitors Enter Here: Interpretive Planning at the Detroit Institute of Arts." In *Interpreting the Art Museum: A Collection of Essays and Case Studies*, edited by Graeme Farnell, 16–41. Boston: MuseumsEtc, 2015.

Blackwell, Ian. "Community Engagement: Why Are Community Voices Still Unheard?" *Journal of Education in Museums* 30 (2009): 29–36.

Bourdieu, Pierre. "The Forms of Capital." In *Handbook of Theory and Research for the Sociology of Education*, edited by John Richardson, 241–58. New York: Greenwood, 1986.

Czajkowski, Jennifer W. "Changing the Rules: Making Space for Interactive Learning in the Galleries at the Detroit Institute of Arts." *Journal of Museum Education* 36, no. 2 (2011): 171–78.

Czajkowski, Jennifer W., and Shiralee Hudson-Hill. "Transformation and Interpretation: What Is the Museum Educator's Role?" *Journal of Museum Education* 33, no. 3 (2008): 255–63.

Czajkowski, Jennifer W., and Salvador Salort-Pons. "Building a Workplace that Supports Educator-Curator Collaboration." In *Visitor-Centered Exhibitions and Edu-Curation in Art Museums*, edited by Pat Villeneuve and Ann Rowson Love. Lanham, MD: Rowman & Littlefield, 2017.

Edson, Robert. *Systems Thinking: Applied.* Falls Church, VA: ASystT Institute, 2008. Available online http://www.anser.org/docs/systems_thinking_applied.pdf.

Korn, Randi. "The Case for Holistic Intentionality." *Curator* 50, no. 2 (2007): 255–65.

Minger, John C. "Towards an Appropriate Social Theory for Applied Systems Thinking: Critical Theory and Soft Systems Methodology." *Journal of Applied Systems Analysis* 7 (1980): 41–48.

O'Neill, Mark, and Lois H. Silverman. Foreword to *Museums, Equality and Social Justice,* edited by Richard Sandell & Eithne Nightingale, xx–xxi. London: Routledge, 2012.

Penney, David. "Reinventing the Detroit Institute of Arts: The Reinstallation Project 2002–2007." *Curator* 52, no. 1 (2009): 35–44.

Senge, Peter. *The Fifth Discipline: The Art and Practice of the Learning Organization.* New York: Doubleday, 2006.

Sutter, Glenn. "Thinking Like a System: Are Museums Up to the Challenge?" *Museums & Social Issues* 1, no. 2 (2006): 203–18.

Werhane, Patricia H. "Moral Imagination and Systems Thinking." *Journal of Business Ethics* 38, no. 1/2 (2002): 33–42.

NOTES

1. Peter Senge, *The Fifth Discipline: The Art and Practice of the Learning Organization* (New York: Doubleday, 2006).

2. Glenn Sutter, "Thinking Like a System: Are Museums Up to the Challenge?" *Museums & Social Issues* 1, no. 2 (2006): 203.

3. Patricia H. Werhane, "Moral Imagination and Systems Thinking," *Journal of Business Ethics* 38, no. 1/2 (2002): 35.

4. The mission, written in 2007, read, "The DIA creates experiences that help each visitor find personal meaning in art." In 2016, "and with each other" was added to acknowledge the social nature of meaning-making in museums.

5. Jennifer W. Czajkowski and Shiralee Hudson-Hill, "Transformation and Interpretation: What Is the Museum Educator's Role?" *Journal of Museum Education* 33, no. 3 (2008): 255–63.

6. Werhane, "Moral Imagination," 36.

7. Jennifer Czajkowski and Salvador Salort-Pons write at length about new balances of roles and responsibilities; Jennifer W. Czajkowski and Salvador Salort-Pons, "Building a Workplace that Supports Educator-Curator Collaboration," in *Visitor-Centered Exhibitions and Edu-Curation in Art Museums*, ed. Pat Villeneuve and Ann Rowson Love (Lanham, MD: Rowman & Littlefield, 2017).

8. John C. Minger, "Towards an Appropriate Social Theory for Applied Systems Thinking: Critical Theory and Soft Systems Methodology," *Journal of Applied Systems Analysis* 7 (1980): 47.

9. Werhane, "Moral Imagination," 35.

10. Ibid., 33–36.

11. Ibid., 33.

12. See DIA case studies: Swarupa Anila, "Visitors Enter Here: Interpretive Planning at the Detroit Institute of Arts," in *Interpreting the Art Museum: A Collection of Essays and Case Studies*, ed. Graeme Farnell (Boston: MuseumsEtc, 2015).

13. Werhane, "Moral Imagination," 36.

14. The three authors serve on the gallery strategies team.

15. Anila, "Visitors Enter Here," 18.

16. Pierre Bourdieu, "The Forms of Capital," in *Handbook of Theory and Research for the Sociology of Education*, ed. John Richardson (New York: Greenwood, 1986).

Part VII

Take Action

1. Both chapters in this section share approaches for community involvement and engagement. How could you invite community perspectives in your exhibitions and programs involving meaningful participation?
2. In Ferilli, Ghirardi, and Sacco's chapter, the authors analyzed two museums' approaches at the Israel Museum of Jerusalem, Israel, and the Castello di Rivoli in Turin, Italy, before proposing that museums apply an *action workflow* model for building community engagement and participation. How might you incorporate the phases—exploring, setting, acting, and valuing—in your museum using table 13.1? What representatives from across museum departments should be involved in the planning? How could community partners participate?
3. Anila, Foley, and Quarcoopome share the team-based process established at the Detroit Institute of Arts for developing reinstallations of permanent collections that include community involvement. In upcoming reinstallation projects, what community voices would be important to include in your museum? How would you structure the teamwork including staff and community participation?

Part VIII

SYSTEMS THINKING IN FUNDRAISING AND FINANCIAL SUSTAINABILITY

This part discusses the systems way of thinking about museum fundraising and financial sustainability. While museums tend to be nonprofits in the United States and pubic organizations in some Asian and European countries, just like for-profit businesses, museums cannot survive without sustainable income and support from their communities. What is unique about nonprofit organizations is that they can fundraise. In fact, most of museum revenue in the United States is composed of private contributions and grants (38 percent comes from individual, foundation, and corporation giving) and public grants (24 percent from government agencies) which are considered unearned income, mainly raised from fundraising activities.[1] Practices related to fundraising and financial sustainability are interlinked to museums' main services and community engagement. For example, *The Museum* (the fictional museum based on a real museum first introduced in the Part I introduction) does not have adequate connections with its diverse community groups and organizations and its revenue sources therefore are not diverse enough. In other words, the museum relies on a small group of donors, who are already appealed to by other arts and cultural organizations in town, to support its operation. This model is risky and unsustainable; losing one of the few important donors would affect the museum in a negative manner financially. *The Museum* also does not properly utilize more market-oriented strategies in generating funds for the museum, such as opening the museum's café for lunch and dinner (the museum's café has been closed for more than five years) and partnering with local hotels and tourism related industries to attract more visitors.

Susan Mann in chapter 15 analyzes a closed museum fundraising and financial sustainability model that was utilized by a failing museum, the Mary Brogan Museum of Art and Science, which was located in Tallahassee, Florida. Using a hard systems methodology of game theory and the concept of network, she talks about two predecessor museums, one an art museum and the other a science museum, that together became the Mary Brogan Museum. The art museum operated like a closed system, utilizing connections only in the narrow, closed art world within Tallahassee, while the science museum explored a broad network of resources and partnerships. When these two organizations combined to form a bigger museum, its closed system model for seeking financial resources and community support was more heavily adopted, eventually leading to a permanent closure of the museum. This chapter demonstrates that unhealthy and isolated museums *die* just like unhealthy species in natural ecosystems.

On the contrary, chapter 16 describes a successful fundraising and financial sustainability model, the global museum network of the Guggenheim Foundation. By examining the Bilbao Guggenheim branch closely, Natalia Grincheva describes museums as part of the global market and economy and discusses how the Guggenheim created a network of its museum branches all over the world. The Guggenheim is an open system that interacts with the extended environment, especially the economy, adjusting to reach the state of *dynamic equilibrium*[2] by tapping into neoliberal systems and global franchising. Resources and information flow through the networked organizations (branches) and these organizations also affect the local economy in a positive manner by bringing in tourists and culture to accommodate the changes. By putting its brand name in the global market, the Guggenheim attracts more funding from foreign governments and corporations, which helped raise the unearned revenue (e.g., contributions) of the foundation.

NOTES

1. Ford W. Bell, *How Are Museums Supported Financially in the U.S.?* (Washington, DC: US Department of State, Bureau of International Information Programs, 2012), http://iip digital.usembassy.gov/st/english/pamphlet/2012/05/201205155699.html

2. Ludwig von Bertalanffy, "The Theory of Open Systems in Physics and Biology," *Science* 111, no. 2872 (1950): 23–29.

15

The Application of Systems Thinking to Museum Sustainability

Susan Mann

The Great Recession of 2007–2011 rippled through the arts world as granting organizations temporarily reduced the dispersal of funds[1] while the US government worked to avoid economic collapse. Arts organizations struggled to balance the financial deficits and devalued endowments by reducing staff and salaries, raising prices for admissions and programs, canceling or postponing programs, and implementing furloughs in order to lower costs.[2] Once the economy stabilized, arts organizations continued to experience reduced support from all levels of government with a general decline in contributions from foundations, corporations, and individual donors.[3] In 2011, the slow economic recovery of the arts witnessed all types of nonprofit arts organizations falter and fail as the number of registered 501(c)(3) arts organizations decreased from 113,000 to 95,000.[4]

ASSESSING THE ECONOMIC ENVIRONMENT

The traditional approach to financial sustainability in the arts, utilizing endowments invested in funds and financial management, proved inadequate to deal with the economic chain reactions that resulted in the Great Recession. The Mary Brogan Museum of Art and Science, a mid-size museum that closed just after the end of the Great Recession,[5] offers the conditions to explore financial resource management within the context of systems methodology, game theory, and networks; the complexity of factors involved makes an exploration of an existing museum difficult without a complicated computer simulation or a retroactive application to an event or situation. Systems methodology offers a variety of approaches and techniques for small to mid-size museums to assess the nature of their organizations within a larger commercial ecosystem to proactively build sustainable financial resources. The application of game theory through networks allows museums to examine the financial components within the organization's economic environment. Game theory, a type of hard systems methodology and the foundational basis of networks,[6] is the mathematical modeling of conflict and cooperation, invented as a tool for studying economic and strategic decision making linked to goals.[7]

THE CASE OF THE MARY BROGAN
MUSEUM OF ART AND SCIENCE

On February 12, 2013, WTXL Channel 27 in Tallahassee, Florida, reported the official closing of the Mary Brogan Museum of Art and Science (MOAS).[8] One year earlier, the board of directors had voted to close the doors to the museum on January 13, 2012, to meet outstanding financial obligations.[9] The MOAS board made the decision to temporarily continue with the children's educational camp program as the means to pay down the organization's debt. After a year of educational camps and selling off the collection and other assets, the museum was unable to reorganize its finances and eliminate its debt, leaving an outstanding deficit of $30,000 before the final dissolution.[10]

The narrative of the Mary Brogan Museum contains the thread of financial struggle from the inception of the museum's first nonprofit predecessor throughout its twenty-two-year existence. Kalin Wilson, a former employee of MOAS,[11] recorded the evolution of the museum in her master's thesis for Florida State University's Department of Anthropology, providing insights into the museum's early struggles. Her thesis, "The Mary Brogan Museum of Art and Science: The Genesis of a Museum in Tallahassee, Florida,"[12] traces the inception of the social, political, and financial events that chronicle the origins of the Museum of Art/Tallahassee (MA/T) and the Odyssey Science Center and their eventual merger that resulted in the Mary Brogan Museum. The research narrative employs an ethnographic methodology with interviews and personal experiences during Wilson's tenure. The early chapters trace the community interest in creating a cultural institution in Tallahassee that resulted in the creation of the Museum of Art/Tallahassee and the parallel interest in the establishment of the Odyssey Science Center. The chapters show the different evolutionary paths that MA/T and Odyssey used to create their individual organizations.

GAME THEORY AS A GAME CHANGER

The choice of game theory as a tool for museum fiscal management is a practical one; the cultural policy of the United States emphasizes the importance of strategic decision making in the arts because of the need for accountability in spending public funds. Game theory is a type of hard systems methodology. Unlike soft systems methodology, which has an emphasis on discovery, learning, and taking purposeful action to manage real situations,[13] hard systems methodology is about the identification and formulation of real-world problems and the search for an efficient means of resolution to achieve the defined purpose of the system.[14]

Application of Game Theory

Game theory and networks are the keys to building a strong financial community for small and mid-sized museums. In order to analyze the life and eventual demise of the Mary Brogan Museum of Art and Science systemically, it becomes necessary to identify whether the system is closed or open as well as the constituent components. A closed system is one considered isolated from the environment, in which no material enters or leaves.[15] An open system is one in which there is a continual import and export of material in relation to the environment outside the system.[16] Every organism is essentially an open system that is neither static nor always containing identical components.[17]

The history of MOAS recorded by Wilson supplied the information necessary to track the IRS Form 990s for MA/T, the Odyssey Science Center, MOAS, and the Capital Cultural Center, a third nonprofit organization created to disperse the grant funds for building the MOAS facility. Other documents produced by the City of Tallahassee, such as the earlier cultural development plan for the museum facility and the minutes from city council meetings from the closing of MOAS, were collected to gain a wider perspective of the financial environment of the Brogan Museum. The analysis of these and other documents[18] helps identify the complex factors that led to the demise of MOAS and illustrate the application of systems thinking to navigate other museums toward a proactive financial strategy.

Museum of Art/Tallahassee: A Closed System

The early origins recorded by Wilson's research analyzed with the financial documents provide the necessary information to conclude that the Museum of Art/Tallahassee predecessor organization was representative of a closed system. The art museum feasibility study was only conducted within the art community of Tallahassee.[19] The narrow focus of the art community environment continued with the MA/T fundraising efforts that concentrated on fundraising dinner parties within the same art community, as well as the limited pursuit of grant funds from the State of Florida and the tax revenue from a utilities rate increase referendum proposed by the City of Tallahassee.[20] The self-limiting and insular actions of the smaller art community produced results that failed to engage the support of the general community and greater financial input for the art museum, thus provoking a negative reaction in the Tallahassee community for MA/T that contributed to the failure of the referendum. The arts community found it necessary to expand its closed system and undertake actions to generate broader community support to ensure the passage of a second referendum.[21]

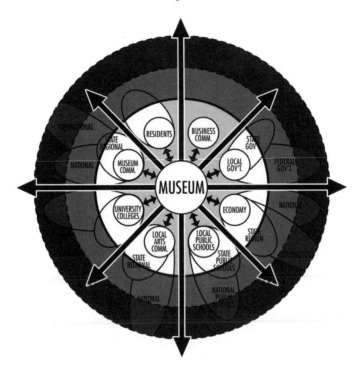

Figure 15.1. Closed System: In a Closed System, the Museum Does Not Recognize the Artificial Constructs Limiting Their Understanding of the Diverse Network within Their Unique Community Ecosystem. *Source*: James I. Zipperer.

The Odyssey Science Center: An Open System

The Odyssey Science Center displayed the characteristics of an open system. Nancy Armstrong,[22] a community organizer and the driving force behind Odyssey, contacted a variety of national science museums and built a community network with city government, Leon County schools, Tallahassee Community College, Florida State University, Florida A&M University, local science teachers, and parents. Odyssey's fundraising efforts included securing foundation and government grants outside the Tallahassee area, and a membership to a science consortium that resulted in the award of exhibits built by the Pacific Science Center in Seattle, Washington. Local partnerships with the Leon County school board and Tallahassee Community College resulted in the Exploration Station, a place for school groups and Tallahassee residents to explore science through a hands-on approach.[23] The rent-free Odyssey retail museum store in a Tallahassee mall not only generated funds, but also built community support and goodwill for the science center.[24] The proactive approach by Armstrong to develop an open system that functioned within a wider environment generated a diverse range of inputs for Odyssey, allowing it to take the actions that built a solid foundation of community support and generated needed financial resources. The positive outcomes fostered a proactive approach that further stimulated Odyssey's financial momentum.

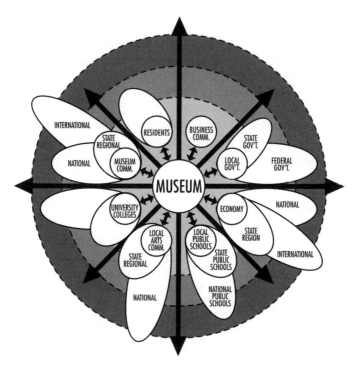

Figure 15.2. Open System: In an Open System, the Museum Recognizes the Diverse Network Interactions within Their Community Ecosystem. The Museum Actively Expands the Diversity of Their Network Relationships to Build Organizational Sustainability. *Source*: James I. Zipperer.

Game Theory and Networks

The article "Prosperity Is Associated with Instability in Dynamical Networks"[25] discussed the prosperity associated with the growth and decline of social and economic networks using a game theoretical model to form dynamic networks.[26] Within the article, a network consists of nodes designated as either cooperator or defectors nodes. A node can represent an individual agent or contact point.[27] From a museum or arts organizational perspective, a node could be another museum, a city council, a bank, or a community leader. Nodes link to form a network. A cooperator node is one that pays a cost for another node to receive a benefit.[28] In a network, one cooperator node can contribute to other nodes through their shared connections. A defector node does not pay for the benefits of other nodes, yet it reaps the same rewards as the cooperator nodes.[29] A defector node does not produce a revenue stream or have an over-reliance on outside funding, such as an arts organization that receives most of its income from grant funds. The authors found that cooperation leads to prosperity, which was associated with increased connectivity, but exposed the network to invasion by defectors with the potential for network collapse.[30]

When new nodes connect with established nodes, they imitate the behaviors and social networks of those network nodes perceived to be models of success. The imitated behaviors are known as strategies, while the imitated social networks are known as connections.[31] Unless examined as part of a computer simulation where the inputs and outputs are trackable, the only way to recognize the difference between a cooperator node and a defector node in a network is usually in hindsight. When a newcomer to the network arrives and begins to model its imitated behaviors, the new node has no way to discern if it is modeling its strategies on a cooperator or defector node, nor is the network able to discern if the new node is a defector attaching to a prosperous environment.

The earlier review of the histories of MA/T and Odyssey chronicled their behaviors within their particular systems. When these systems are placed within the social network of Tallahassee, the action strategies of MA/T and Odyssey reveal their respective node designations. The MA/T existed within the narrow environment of the art community. Its fundraising efforts raised the charge of elitism when the City of Tallahassee attempted to fulfill its obligation to construct an art museum facility with a small tax increase. To achieve its goal, MA/T appeared to adopt some of the connective community strategies displayed by Odyssey through educational engagement activities. On the surface, MA/T had the appearance of a successful organization.

Odyssey's proactive strategies and collaborative alliances established a fundraising campaign that subsidized the exhibition and educational programming of the young science organization, as well as paying for most of the construction of a three-story facility. When the City of Tallahassee compelled the partnership between the two organizations, Odyssey brought the greater contribution of financial and operational resources. Therefore, MA/T can be designated as the defector node and Odyssey as the cooperator node before the two organizations merged to become the Mary Brogan Museum of Art and Science. After the merger, the financial and management strategies adopted by MOAS was the MA/T defector approach within a closed system, as revealed in the later review of the compiled MOAS documents. The defector designation is reinforced by the final year of the museum's existence when the defector core that was the original MA/T organization was cut out of the Brogan, leaving the cooperator core of the original Odyssey organization to function and generate enough money to pay down the debt to $30,000 at the official dissolution.

CONCLUSION AND FINAL THOUGHTS

The Great Recession of 2007–2011 set off a chain of events in the arts that resulted in reduced foundation and governmental funding. The consequences of the slow recovery witnessed the loss of 18,000 nonprofit arts organizations with governmental and philanthropic giving returning to pre-Recession levels in 2014. The Mary Brogan Museum of Art and Science always struggled with the problem of financial sustainability, a familiar experience for many museums. The Great Recession fostered the economic conditions that undermined the accustomed channels of reliable contributed income habitually used to support the Brogan Museum.

Systems thinking offers a new approach to financial stability, and game theory contributes the tool of networks to increase future sustainability. An analysis of the funding sources for a museum can easily determine if the organization is a closed system that habitually relies on the same small funding pool, or an open system with several divergent funding sources. The identification of system assists the museum in dealing with the complexities involved in the purpose and functions of a museum. An open system is one that continues to seek out and build support within the community, such as the example of the Odyssey Science Center. The application of game theory and networks has the potential to help museums utilize rational decision making to build a strong financial network. The identification of collaborator and defector models will assist museums in the development of fundraising strategies and financial network building with several nodes of equal funding strength instead of relying on a network of a few, powerful nodes vulnerable to funding cutbacks in the event of future economic downturns.

In order to prevent similar results from another inevitable recession, museums need the tools to examine their approach to financial stability to adapt and survive in a changing environment. The systems approach of game theory, applied through network systems theory, provides museums with the ability to leverage their collaborative strengths within a systems framework to pursue their mission.

BIBLIOGRAPHY

Burge, Stuart. "An Overview of Hard Systems Methodology." *Systems Thinking: Approaches and Methodologies* (2015). Accessed October 1, 2016. http://www.burgehugheswalsh.co.uk/Uploaded/1/Documents/Hard-Systems-Methodology.pdf.

Cavaliere, Matteo, Sean Sedwards, Corina E. Tarnita, Martin A. Nowak, and Attilla Csikász-Nagy. "Prosperity Is Associated with Instability in Dynamical Networks." *Journal of Theoretical Biology* 299 (2012): 126–38. doi:10.1016/jtbi.2011.09.005.

Checkland, Peter. *Systems Thinking, Systems Practice*. West Sussex, UK: Wiley, 2004.

Checkland, Peter, and Jim Scholes. *Soft Systems Methodology in Action*. West Sussex, UK: Wiley, 1990.

Davis, Morton O. *Game Theory: A Nontechnical Introduction*. Mineola, NY: Dover, 1983.

Haines, Stephen G. *The Systems Thinking Approach to Strategic Planning and Management*. Boca Raton, FL: St. Lucie Press, 2000.

Kage, Krystof, and City of Tallahassee. "Summary of Commission Meeting: January 11, 2012." *Talgov.com*, February 1, 2013. Accessed October 1, 2016. https://www.talgov.com/uploads/public/documents/commission/pdf/meetings/ja12.pdf.

Kushner, Roland J., and Randy Cohen. *2013 National Arts Index*. Washington, DC: Americans for the Arts, 2013. http://www.artsindexusa.org/national-arts-index.

Miringoff, Marque-Luisa, and Sandra Opdycke. "The Arts in a Time of Recession." *International Journal of the Arts in Society: Annual Review* 4, no. 5 (2010): 141–68. doi:10.18848/1833-1866/CGP/v04i05/35726.

Morreale, Joseph C. "The Impact of the 'Great Recession' on the Financial Resources of Nonprofit Organizations." Wilson Center for Social Entrepreneurship, Paper 5, 2011. Accessed October 1, 2016. http://digitalcommons.pace.edu/cgi/viewcontent.cgi?article=1004&context=wilson.

Nowak, Martin A. "Five Rules for the Evolution of Cooperation." *Science* 314, no. 5805 (2006): 1560–63. http://www.jstor.org/stable/20032978.

Nowak, Martin A., Corina E. Tarnita, and Tibor Antal. "Evolutionary Dynamics in Structured Populations." *Philosophical Transactions of the Royal Society B* 365, no. 1537 (2010): 19–30. doi:10.1098/rstb.2009.0215.

Schweitzer, Frank, Giorgio Fagiolo, Didier Sornette, Fernando Vega-Redondo, Alessandro Vespignani, and Douglas R. White. "Economic Networks: The New Challenges." *Science* 325, no. 5939 (2009): 422–25. http://www.jstor.org/satble/20536695.

von Bertalanffy, Ludwig. *General System Theory: Foundations, Development, Applications*. New York: George Braziller, 2015.

Wilson, Kalin. "The Mary Brogan Museum of Art and Science: The Genesis of a Museum in Tallahassee, Florida" (master's thesis). Tallahassee: Florida State University, 2003.

Wilson, Ty. "The Mary Brogan Museum is Shut Down by Board of Directors." WTXL-TV online. Tallahassee, FL. February 12, 2013. Accessed October 1, 2016. http://www.wtxl.com/news/local/the-mary-brogan-museum-is-shut-down-by-board-of/article_1ef79bf8-756a-11e2-bbdb-0019bb30f31a.html.

NOTES

1. Joseph C. Morreale, "The Impact of the 'Great Recession' on the Financial Resources of Nonprofit Organizations," Wilson Center for Social Entrepreneurship, Paper 5 (2011), http://digitalcommons.pace.edu/cgi/viewcontent.cgi?article=1004&context=wilson.

2. Marque-Luisa Miringoff and Sandra Opdycke, "The Arts in a Time of Recession," *International Journal of the Arts in Society: Annual Review* 4, no. 5 (2010), doi:10.18848/1833-1866/CGP/v04i05/35726.

3. Ibid.

4. Morreale, "The Impact of the 'Great Recession'"; Roland J. Kushner and Randy Cohen, *2013 National Arts Index* (Washington, DC: Americans for the Arts, 2013), http://www.artsindexusa.org/national-arts-index.

5. The author was employed at the Mary Brogan Museum from late 2009 until the organization closed its doors to the public on January 12, 2012.

6. Matteo Cavaliere, Sean Sedwards, Corina E. Tarnita, Martin A. Nowak, and Attilla Csikász-Nagy, "Prosperity Is Associated with Instability in Dynamical Networks," *Journal of Theoretical Biology* 299 (2012): 126–38, doi:10.1016/jtbi.2011.09.005.

7. Ludwig von Bertalanffy, *General System Theory: Foundations, Development, Applications* (New York: George Braziller, 2015); Morton D. Davis, *Game Theory: A Nontechnical Introduction* (Mineola, NY: Dover, 1983); Martin A. Nowak, Corina E. Tarnita, and Tibor Antal, "Evolutionary Dynamics in Structured Populations," *Philosophical Transactions of the Royal Society B* 365, no. 1537 (2010): 19–30, doi:10.1098/rstb.2009.0215.

8. Ty Wilson, "The Mary Brogan Museum is Shut Down by Board of Directors," WTXL-TV online, Tallahassee, FL, February 12, 2013, accessed October 1, 2016, http://www.wtxl.com/news/local/the-mary-brogan-museum-is-shut-down-by-board-of/article_1ef79bf8-756a-11e2-bbdb-0019bb30f31a.html.

9. Krystof Kage, and City of Tallahassee, "Summary of Commission Meeting: January 11, 2012," *Talgov.com*, February 12, 2013, accessed October 1, 2016, https://www.talgov.com/uploads/public/documents/commission/pdf/meetings/ja12.pdf.

10. Wilson, "Brogan Museum is Shut Down."

11. Kalin Wilson was a graduate student when she was employed by the Mary Brogan Museum of Art and Science. She resigned her position to finish her master's thesis.

12. Kalin Wilson, "The Mary Brogan Museum of Art and Science: The Genesis of a Museum in Tallahassee, Florida" (master's thesis, Florida State University, 2003).

13. Peter Checkland and Jim Scholes, *Soft Systems Methodology in Action* (West Sussex, UK: Wiley, 1990).

14. Stuart Burge, "An Overview of Hard Systems Methodology," in *Systems Thinking: Approaches and Methodologies*, 2015, accessed October 1, 2016. http://www.burgehugheswalsh.co.uk/Uploaded/1/Documents/Hard-Systems-Methodology.pdf; Peter Checkland, *Systems Thinking, Systems Practice* (West Sussex, UK: Wiley, 2004); Stephen G.Haines, *The Systems Thinking Approach to Strategic Planning and Management* (Boca Raton, FL: St. Lucie Press, 2000).

15. von Bertalanffy, *General System Theory*; Haines, *Systems Thinking Approach*.

16. von Bertalanffy, *General System Theory*.

17. Lord Cultural Resources conducted feasibility studies for an art museum, a science museum, and a performing arts center for the City of Tallahassee. The feasibility study for the art museum was only conducted within the Tallahassee arts community, while the study for the science museum was broadly conducted within the population of Tallahassee; Wilson, "Mary Brogan Museum."

18. Along with the stated documents, the author consulted her personal notes taken during her employment at the Mary Brogan Museum.

19. von Bertalanffy, *General System Theory*.

20. Wilson, "Mary Brogan Museum."

21. Ibid.

22. Nancy Armstrong thought Tallahassee needed a hands-on science center, was the driving force behind the creation of the Odyssey Science Center, and led the nonprofit development; ibid.

23. The Exploration Center was a converted warehouse located on the campus of Tallahassee Community College that served as temporary housing for the hands-on exhibitions and science education programming for Odyssey; ibid.

24. Ibid.

25. Cavaliere et al., "Prosperity Is Associated with Instability."

26. Ibid.

27. Frank Schweitzer, Giorgio Fagiolo, Didier Sornette, Fernando Vega-Redondo, Alessandro Vespignani, and Douglas R. White, "Economic Networks: The New Challenges," *Science* 325, no. 5939 (2009): 422–25, http://www.jstor.org/satble/20536695.

28. Martin A. Nowak, "Five Rules for the Evolution of Cooperation," *Science* 314, no. 5805 (2006): 1560–63, http://www.jstor.org/stable/20032978.

29. Ibid.

30. Cavaliere et al., "Prosperity Is Associated with Instability."

31. Ibid.

16

Sustainable Fundraising in the Twenty-First Century

Behind the Scenes of the Global Guggenheim Success

Natalia Grincheva

APPLYING SYSTEMS THINKING TO THE "GUGGENHEIM BILBAO" PHENOMENON

According to systems thinking theory, a system can be defined as "a group of inter-related components that form a complex whole, a configuration of parts that are connected through a web of direct and indirect relationships."[1] Within museum literature, a systems thinking approach usually helps to explore a museum as a complex structure, a set of relationships between various internal organizational departments and a larger context in which they exist and operate. The larger context constitutes an "external system, which is composed of local and global environments that in turn affect the museum's internal system."[2] This approach emphasizes strong interdependencies that occur in and outside museums, as autonomous organizations with their own institutional cultures and codes of conduct, and external environments that can exert significant influence upon them or can be affected by them on various levels, including economic, political, social, or cultural.

One of the most important dimensions of external systems that can considerably affect museums, and conversely then influence back, is the economy. As Latham and Simmons argue, museums "depend on their local economy in both direct and indirect ways"; at the same time they "may have a profound effect on their local economy."[3] A classic example is the Guggenheim *Bilbao effect*, the first successful museum franchise experience in the world that dramatically influenced the economic landscape of the small provincial city in Spain, transforming it into a premier tourist destination.[4] The Guggenheim Bilbao was the first satellite museum in the worldwide network

181

of museums and cultural partnerships of the Solomon R. Guggenheim Foundation. With the main museum in New York, the foundation has branches also in Venice and Bilbao as well as building new franchises in Abu Dhabi and Helsinki. Starting from the first year (in 1997) of its operation, the Bilbao museum attendance figures nearly tripled the originally projected numbers. In 1998, 1.3 million visited the Guggenheim Bilbao; in 1999, the attendance number was 1.1 million.[5] These visits had a positive effect on the city's economy, improving the general level of tourism, which increased nearly 120 percent.[6] In the first years of its operation the museum employed over 4,415 local residents in various capacities.[7] A 1998 economic report revealed that museum visitors "had spent over €50 million on accommodations, €14 million on transportation, €80 million on entertainment, €62 million on shopping, and €30 million at the museum itself on ticket sales, shopping, and at the museum restaurant."[8]

Framing this case within systems thinking theory helps to look at the Bilbao effect as a result of a complex relationship between cities and museums that can generate economic activity in their local communities and significantly contribute to economic development. Indeed, the Guggenheim Bilbao has been discussed in museum scholarship as a ground-breaking phenomenon that turned museums into important actors in a post-industrial economy of contemporary cities.[9] With this successful experience, museums started to be understood as powerful agents in their local communities accelerating cultural, social, and economic changes.[10]

While much has been written already about the Bilbao effect in terms of economic impacts,[11] there is no dedicated research yet that would explain why the Guggenheim Bilbao phenomenon came into existence and what external forces and consequences directly contributed to its development. Moreover, it is even more fascinating to find out how this successful economic experiment influenced the Guggenheim's further development. Did the Bilbao effect have an essential impact on the Guggenheim's global growth? If so, how exactly did this phenomenon aid the museum to pursue its mission on the global scale?

Applying a systems thinking approach, this chapter looks at the Guggenheim Foundation as an *open* system that continuously interacts with the external environment and constantly "adjusts to a new equilibrium if a change occurs in the way the parts are arranged" within a larger context.[12] Understanding global economic reality as *external environment* in which museums operate, the chapter looks at the Guggenheim as a complex system within a larger economic reality, going far beyond the US context. It explores how stepping outside the local borders by developing a franchising network across different countries expanded the Guggenheim's opportunities and brought fundraising practices to a new global level. The chapter analyses the Guggenheim example to demonstrate that staying attuned to global economic changes, or in other words, adequately adjusting the museum's *system* to changes in a larger environment, has a profound impact upon institutional development. The Guggenheim case illustrates how a strategic reconfiguration of fundraising approaches in the twenty-first century can help large and internationally known museums to tap into resources available for them in the global context.

Furthermore, this chapter employs a systems thinking framework to demonstrate that franchising practices have emerged in the conditions of economic globalization as an extension of the museum's fundraising activities in pursuit of new international opportunities for growth and development. The chapter reveals that economic conditions of the global neoliberal regime shape favorable conditions pushing large and internationally recognized museums, such as the Guggenheim, to *go global*. It exposes that the emergence of the Guggenheim Bilbao was a logical step in the development of the museum's fundraising efforts in the era of economic globalization.

FRANCHISING AS GLOBAL FUNDRAISING: THE GUGGENHEIM APPROACH

Fundraising is an important part of nonprofit management; it is a process of soliciting contributions of money or in-kind support from external sources that can include central or local government agencies, commercial companies, international or national foundations and charitable trusts, or individual patrons.[13] The majority of museums, as nonprofit organizations, strongly rely on fundraising activities to maintain their financial sustainability. Museums raise funds to support their programming, organize exhibitions and special events, or take care of their collections through conservation and research programs.[14] Fundraising is a complex process that includes not only identifying, approaching, applying, and gathering funds, but also establishing and maintaining an appealing, trustworthy, and reliable image of an art organization. As Varbanova stresses, "the general rule is that people always give to people; therefore, fundraising is about building up friendships, not just financial relations."[15] In a museum context, Walhimer confirmed that fundraising is a "complex sale. It is a part personal relationship, part trust, and part hope."[16] The focus on fundraising activities that have recently emerged in the era of economic and cultural globalization meets external pressures to construct an institutional identity not only within a local community, but in a larger international environment. This type of fundraising relies on the development of a global organizational brand.

Brand, as a marketing concept, has been adopted by contemporary museums to construct and promote their distinctive identities as cultural institutions on the cultural market.[17] "The essence of a successful brand is its high level of name awareness and the positive associations which attach to the name and are called to mind by the name."[18] Within a museum context, the aim of branding is to "add symbolic value" to a museum reputation, making it appealing and recognizable among potential audiences.[19] The main strategies for reinforcing the museum's brand on the global scene have traditionally included international exchange activities bringing museums' collections to new audiences in new geographic locations, for example traveling exhibitions or blockbusters. The Guggenheim pioneered a new approach for global brand management, such as museum franchising.

In the business world, franchising is known as a contract-based practice of granting the right to use the company brand name and utilize a well-developed business model in different places to distribute goods or sell services in new markets.[20] Museum franchising is "the culmination of global changes in the management of museums," leading to a more entrepreneurial style of operations within the professional museum community.[21] Vivant suggests that museum franchising practices help to build a strong international reputation, which as cultural capital can be translated into economic capital.[22] By opening a new branch in a different geographic location, the Guggenheim was able not only to significantly enlarge its exhibitory spaces and strengthen its infrastructures, but, more importantly, to reinforce its global brand, which multiplied international fundraising opportunities. The successful franchising experiment in Bilbao turned out for the Guggenheim as a robust fundraising platform enabling the museum to establish new partnerships and attract direct contributions from international patrons and governments.

For example, in the case of the Guggenheim Bilbao, Basque officials agreed to finance the entire operation, which included both the construction of the building (estimated at $100 million) and operating costs of the finished museum.[23] They also provided a $50 million new acquisitions budget and, most importantly, the Basque government donated $20 million to the Solomon R. Guggenheim Foundation before the museum was even constructed—a donation referred to in Spain as a *rental fee*.[24] This rental fee, charged by the Guggenheim as a tax-deductible donation, "set the precedent for incorporating a Guggenheim franchise fee in future deals."[25] Without direct investment costs for the Guggenheim Foundation itself, the satellite museum significantly improved the budget of the foundation and enlarged the Guggenheim's exhibitory spaces in Europe. Even more importantly, it proved that the "'global' museum can work," making "the Guggenheim the most attractive museum for global capital."[26]

The Guggenheim Bilbao symbolized the power of the museum brand's attractiveness in promoting the city as a tourist destination.[27] The museum in Bilbao gave rise to a so-called Bilbao effect with its almost immediate economic returns, described earlier in this chapter. Following the success of the Bilbao franchise, many cities began to evaluate their investment capacities to invite a new branch of the Guggenheim to their locations.[28] In 2000 the former director of the Guggenheim, Thomas Krens, shared that since the opening of the satellite in Bilbao, the museum "received more than 60 requests to participate in urban development and cultural infrastructure projects from . . . governments all over the world."[29]

With such a demand for Guggenheim museums in different countries, the foundation acquired a strong brand identity that reinforced the marketability of the franchise idea. Guggenheim developed a standard franchise agreement that was proposed to all those who wanted to assess their capacities to build a new branch in their locations. The conditions of this agreement obliged future franchise owners to cover all the costs of a new museum building and to make a charitable contribution to the foundation ranging between $20 million and $30 million. In return for this donation, the Guggenheim agreed to lend satellite museums its name, its administrative expertise, and art collections.[30] Peter Lawson-Johnston, who oversaw the development of the Guggenheim Foundation as its board president and chair for more than forty years, once shared, "these international arrangements have in most cases provided substantial net revenue to the Guggenheim, helping to close the gap in our own operating budget. Without global growth, the Guggenheim New York would be a substantially poorer institution—financially and artistically."[31]

Within the systems thinking framework, the Guggenheim franchising network can be understood as a system of interrelated nodes manifested in satellite museum spaces in various geographic locations. Each of them plays a crucial role in a larger network, in which resources and information flow among different parts of the system.[32] In terms of direct museum impacts, this flow of resources among the interconnected parts in the system translates into a robust infrastructure facilitating a more efficient development of the museum in the global context. Thus, the Bilbao franchise significantly reinforced the Guggenheim global brand to be known not only as a museum of contemporary art, but as a powerful actor of urban regeneration and economic development.

Most recently, the director of the Guggenheim, Richard Armstrong, shared: "it's a rare week when [he] doesn't receive at least one request to build a museum somewhere in the world."[33] One of the largest of such ongoing projects is Abu Dhabi Guggenheim, "a $27 billion luxury property development on a once-uninhabited sandbar just off the Abu Dhabi coastline," a deal with the United Arab Emirates' Tourism Development & Investment Company.[34] Furthermore, plans are under way for a brand-new franchise museum in Helsinki in cooperation with the Finnish government to help the city "prosper in an increasingly interconnected and competitive world."[35]

However, global brand development expanding the Guggenheim network further is not the only contribution to the museum fundraising efforts. The chair of the Guggenheim's board of trustees explained, "as Guggenheim 'brand recognition' grows, we have also been successful in gaining financial support from image-conscious foreign corporations now operating in the United States."[36] For example, since the late 1990s Hugo Boss, a global luxury fashion and style company of German origin, has been "one of the most important and long standing corporate patrons. . . . In addition to funding several exhibitions, it also completely funds the biennial Hugo Boss Prize— a major, juried contemporary art invitational whose winner receives $50,000 and a show at the Guggenheim."[37] Among the most recent examples is the 2014 Guggenheim UBS MAP Global Art Initiative, engaging curators and artists from the Middle East, Asia, Africa, and Latin America. This long-term project is organized in cooperation with UBS Wealth Management, a global financial services firm headquartered in Zurich and Basel, which donated $40 million to this initiative.[38] The patronage of all these Guggenheim projects by transnational companies can be explained by the donors' financial stakes in dynamic regions where the corporations have significant interests. Furthermore, these international patrons enjoy continual recognition in all

Guggenheim museum sites in different locations.[39] In this way, the global presence of the museum creates a stronger appeal to its potential donors, tapping into their need to reach new geographic markets. In terms of systems thinking, the franchising practices establish additional connections and relations between the museum and a larger external environment. These new connections build strong foundations for the Guggenheim to expand its international fundraising opportunities, inviting new corporate sponsorships and donations from transnational actors seeking to capitalize on the Guggenheim's name.

THE "OTHER" SIDE OF THE GLOBAL FUNDRAISING

Even though this approach might seem too commercial for a nonprofit museum, it works well for the Guggenheim to attract global capital, allowing it to pursue its mission to celebrate contemporary art and "explore ideas across cultures through dynamic curatorial and educational initiatives and collaborations" on the global scale.[40] Indeed, the Guggenheim is a museum, where inherited American commercialism, populism, and financial adventurism go far beyond accepted or practiced norms within the professional world of American museums. The Guggenheim's corporate approach has always generated a lot of criticism, detractors accusing the museum of transforming into a neoliberal institution, "increasingly dependent on corporate gifts rather than public funding; that privileges traveling exhibitions over permanent collections, aspirational leisure over education, risk and innovation over cultural preservation."[41]

However, as the famous American art critic and journalist Deborah Solomon once pointed out, the Guggenheim is "a model of frankness and American pragmatism. . . . It does not pretend that art is religion or that the museum is church."[42] The chair of the foundation himself revealed that the real secret of the Guggenheim's success in the world of art is a strong business acumen and talents.[43] The museum does employ nontraditional, maybe even too commercial strategies for a successful global fundraising which, however, do ensure a sustainable institutional development in the neoliberal economic reality.

The expansion of global tourism, the rise of creative and cultural industries as the main drivers of national economies, and the emergence of transnational actors on the economic and cultural markets have become the key twenty-first-century developments that influenced the Guggenheim strategies to *go global* and to pursue a truly international course of organizational growth. Trying to explain the main drives behind the development of the franchise museum model, Krens repeatedly emphasized that the institution was relying more on the exogenous factors in a larger international context. "Globalization is not an environment that we are shaping," Krens pointed out; "It is being shaped around us. To try to resist these forces, or to somehow pretend they don't exist, I think, is suicidal from an institutional standpoint."[44] This commitment to globalism has been instrumental in developing a successful museum brand that could attract various types of powerful international patrons, whether governments or transnational corporations. The Guggenheim brand has become one of the important tools of the foundation in its efforts of global fundraising.

In terms of systems thinking, the Guggenheim franchising practices were brought to life by key changes in the external environment, provoked by increasing forces of economic and cultural globalization. In turn, the successful franchise experiments accelerated institutional development, making it more responsive and adaptable to external pressures, thus creating a more favorable ecosystem in which the museum enjoys a more economically secured position in the international arena.

BIBLIOGRAPHY

Ambrose, Timothy, and Crispin Paine. *Museum Basics*. New York: Routledge, 2006.

Bradley, Kim. "The Deal of the Century: Planning Process for Guggenheim Museum Bilbao, Spain." *Art in America* 85 (1997): 48–55.

Caldwell, Niall. "The Emergence of Museum Brands." *International Journal of Arts Management* 2, no. 3 (2000): 28–34.

Colbert, Francois. "Changes in Marketing Environment and Their Impact on Cultural Policy." *Journal of Arts Management Law and Society* 27, no. 3 (1997): 177–86.

Conn, Steven. *Do Museums Still Need Objects?* Philadelphia: University of Pennsylvania Press, 2010.

Corbett, Rachel. "Guggenheim Goes Global." Accessed January 18, 2017. http://artnt.cm/1LJ81DJ.

Decker, Darla. *Urban Development, Cultural Clusters: The Guggenheim Museum and Its Global Distribution Strategies*. New York: New York University, 2008.

Dicke, Thomas S. *Franchising in America: The Development of a Business Method, 1840–1980*. Chapel Hill: University of North Carolina Press, 1992.

Ellis, Adrian. "A Franchise Model for the Few—Very Few." *The Art Newspaper* 184 (2007).

Guasch, Ana María and Joseba Zulaika, eds. *Learning from the Bilbao Guggenheim*. Reno, NV: Center for Basque Studies, 2005.

Guggenheim. "About." Accessed October 26, 2016. https://www.guggenheim.org/about-us.

Guggenheim. "Helsinki Explores Possible Guggenheim Museum in Finland 2011." Accessed March 10, 2015. http://bit.ly/192HNdo.

Guggenheim. Press release, September 27, 2000. "Guggenheim Alliance with Gehry and Koolhaas." Accessed March 10, 2015. http://bit.ly/1NkMZZ7.

Krens, Thomas. Lecture at the Art Show, Manhattan's Seventh Regiment Armory, New York, February 20, 1999.

Latham, Kiersten F., and John E. Simmons. *Foundations of Museum Studies: Evolving Systems of Knowledge*. Santa Barbara, CA: ABC-CLIO, 2014.

Lawson-Johnston, Peter. *Growing Up Guggenheim: A Personal History of a Family Enterprise*. New York: Open Road Media, 2014.

Lord, Gail, and Ngaire Blankenberg. *Cities, Museums and Soft Power*. Washington, DC: AAM Press, 2015.

Chapter 16

Martinez, Jill. *Financing a Global Guggenheim Museum.* Columbia: University of South Carolina, 2001.

Marwick, Peat. *Impact of the Activities of the Fundacion del Museo Guggenheim Bilbao on the Basque Country.* KPMG, 1998.

Mediguren, Ibon. "Boomtown Basque." *The Art Newspaper* 12, no. 111 (2001).

Rauen, Marjorie. "Reflections on the Space of Flows: The Guggenheim Museum Bilbao." *Journal of Arts Management, Law, and Society* 30, no. 4 (2001): 283–300.

Sylvester, Christine. *Art/Museums: International Relations Where We Least Expect It.* London: Paradigm, 2009.

Thompson, Don. *The $12 Million Stuffed Shark: The Curious Economics of Contemporary Art.* New York: Palgrave Macmillan, 2008.

Trilupaityte, Skaidra. "Guggenheim's Global Travel and the Appropriation of a National Avant-Garde for Cultural Planning in Vilnius." *International Journal of Cultural Policy* 15, no. 1 (2009): 123–38.

Varbanova, Lidia. *Strategic Management in the Arts.* New York: Routledge, 2013.

Vivant, Elsa. "Who Brands Whom? The Role of Local Authorities in the Branching of Art Museums." *Town Planning Review* 82, no. 1 (2011): 99–115.

Walhimer, Mark. *Museums 101.* Lanham, MD: Rowman & Littlefield, 2015.

Werner, Paul. *Museum Inc.: Inside the Global Art World.* Chicago: Prickly Paradigm, 2005.

Wise, Michael. "An Open Design Competition for a New Museum in the Finnish Capital Reflects a Change in the Foundation's Global Strategy." *Art News*, August 25, 2014. http://www.artnews.com/2014/08/25/rethinking-the-guggenheim-helsinki/

Wyma, Chloe. "1% Museum: The Guggenheim Goes Global." *Dissent* 61, no. 3 (2014): 5–10.

Zulaika, Joseba. *Guggenheim Bilbao Museoa: Museums, Architecture, and City Renewal.* Reno: University of Nevada Press, 2003.

Zulaika, Joseba. "Krens's Taj Mahal: The Guggenheim's Global Love Museum." *Discourse* 23, no.1 (2001): 100–18.

NOTES

1. Kiersten F. Latham and John E. Simmons, *Foundations of Museum Studies: Evolving Systems of Knowledge* (Santa Barbara, CA: ABC-CLIO, 2014), 39.

2. Ibid., 40.

3. Ibid., 45.

4. Kim Bradley, "The Deal of the Century: Planning Process for Guggenheim Museum Bilbao, Spain," *Art in America* 85 (1997): 48–55; Darla Decker, *Urban Development, Cultural Clusters: The Guggenheim Museum and Its Global Distribution Strategies* (New York: New York University Press, 2008).

5. Ibon Mediguren, "Boomtown Basque." *The Art Newspaper* 12, no. 111 (2001).

6. Adrian Ellis, "A Franchise Model for the Few—Very Few." *The Art Newspaper* 184 (2007).

7. Mediguren, "Boomtown Basque."

8. Peat Marwick, *Impact of the Activities of the Fundacion del Museo Guggenheim Bilbao on the Basque Country* (KPMG, 1998).

9. Steven Conn, *Do Museums Still Need Objects?* (Philadelphia: University of Pennsylvania Press, 2010).

10. Gail Lord and Ngaire Blankenberg, *Cities, Museums and Soft Power* (Washington, DC: AAM Press, 2015).

11. Joseba Zulaika, *Guggenheim Bilbao Museoa: Museums, Architecture, and City Renewal* (Reno: University of Nevada Press, 2003); Ana María Guasch and Joseba Zulaika, eds., *Learning from the Bilbao Guggenheim* (Reno, NV: Center for Basque Studies, 2005).

12. Latham and Simmons, *Foundations of Museum Studies*, 39.

13. Lidia Varbanova, *Strategic Management in the Arts* (New York: Routledge, 2013).

14. Timothy Ambrose and Crispin Paine, *Museum Basics* (New York: Routledge, 2006).

15. Varbanova, *Strategic Management in the Arts*.

16. Mark Walhimer, *Museums 101* (Lanham, MD: Rowman & Littlefield, 2015).

17. Francois Colbert, "Changes in Marketing Environment and Their Impact on Cultural Policy," *Journal of Arts Management, Law, and Society* 27, no. 3 (1997): 177–86.

18. Niall Caldwell, "The Emergence of Museum Brands," *International Journal of Arts Management* 2, no. 3 (2000): 28–34.

19. Elsa Vivant, "Who Brands Whom? The Role of Local Authorities in the Branching of Art Museums," *Town Planning Review* 82, no. 1 (2011): 111.

20. Thomas S. Dicke, *Franchising in America: The Development of a Business Method, 1840–1980* (Chapel Hill: University of North Carolina Press, 1992), 2.

21. Paul Werner, *Museum Inc.: Inside the Global Art World* (Chicago: Prickly Paradigm, 2005).

22. Vivant, "Who Brands Whom?"

23. Marjorie Rauen, "Reflections on the Space of Flows: The Guggenheim Museum Bilbao," *Journal of Arts Management, Law, and Society* 30, no. 4 (2001): 288.

24. Ibid., 288.

25. Jill Martinez, *Financing a Global Guggenheim Museum* (Columbia: University of South Carolina, 2001), 32.

26. Joseba Zulaika, "Krens's Taj Mahal: The Guggenheim's Global Love Museum," *Discourse* 23, no. 1 (2001): 112.

27. Bradley, "Deal of the Century"; Decker, *Urban Development*.

28. Skaidra Trilupaityte, "Guggenheim's Global Travel and the Appropriation of a National Avant-Garde for Cultural Planning in Vilnius," *International Journal of Cultural Policy* 15, no. 1 (2009): 125.

29. Guggenheim, Press release, September 27, 2000, "Guggenheim Alliance with Gehry and Koolhaas," accessed March 10, 2015, http://bit.ly/1NkMZZ7.

30. Don Thompson, *The $12 Million Stuffed Shark: The Curious Economics of Contemporary Art* (New York: Palgrave Macmillan, 2008), 125.

31. Peter Lawson-Johnston, *Growing Up Guggenheim: A Personal History of a Family Enterprise* (New York: Open Road Media, 2014), 136.

32. Latham and Simmons, *Foundations of Museum Studies*, 39.

33. Michael Wise, "An Open Design Competition for a New Museum in the Finnish Capital Reflects a Change in the Foundation's Global Strategy," *Art News*, August 25, 2014, http://www.artnews.com/2014/08/25/rethinking-the-guggenheim-helsinki.

34. Chloe Wyma, "1% Museum: The Guggenheim Goes Global," *Dissent* 61, no. 3 (2014): 5–10.

35. Guggenheim, "Helsinki Explores Possible Guggenheim Museum in Finland 2011," accessed March 10, 2015, http://bit.ly/192HNdo.

36. Lawson-Johnston, *Growing Up Guggenheim*, 136.

37. Ibid.

38. Rachel Corbett, "Guggenheim Goes Global," accessed January 18, 2017, http://artnt .cm/1LJ81DJ.

39. Lawson-Johnston, *Growing Up Guggenheim*.

40. Guggenheim, "About," accessed October 20, 2016, https://www.guggenheim.org/.

41. Wyma, "1% Museum."

42. Christine Sylvester, *Art/Museums: International Relations Where We Least Expect It* (London: Paradigm, 2009), 119.

43. Lawson-Johnston, *Growing Up Guggenheim*, 10.

44. Thomas Krens, lecture at the Art Show, Manhattan's Seventh Regiment Armory, New York, February 20, 1999.

Part VIII

Take Action

1. Mann's chapter explores the most undesirable museum outcome—financial instability leading to closure. Looking back analytically, she uses the lens of game theory to make sense of lost financial opportunities. Consider closed and open network possibilities at your museum. Are your funding sources dependent upon specific donors, corporations, and nonprofit sources or have you established a flexible network of alternative sources at the local, state, national, and even international levels? What are new directions and opportunities for exploring funding sources? How are your board, staff (all staff), and community represented in development and financial management planning?

2. Rare is the museum that can work on the global level to the same degree as the Guggenheim as described in Grincheva's chapter. What are takeaway lessons your museum can adapt appropriate for the size and scope of your museum? What are the possibilities for developing a regional, national, international presence or building new partnerships through social media, exhibitions, collections, merchandising, tourism, and other relevant areas?

Part IX

SYSTEMS THINKING IN PHYSICAL SPACES

This part addresses a rethinking of the physical spaces of museums as more inclusive and interactive for all visitors and their needs and interests. Systems thinking approaches reorient museum spaces from aesthetic or architectural works of art to interactive, comfortable, and yet exciting places for all. Traditionally, museum buildings are often built without visitors in mind. In addition, some museum buildings and spaces built many decades ago had different purposes that no longer suit the roles of today's museums. *The Museum*'s building (the fictional museum based on a real museum first introduced in the Part I introduction) is considered by many a work of art. While a world-renowned architect imagined and designed it, he had little understanding of this specific community. It is often criticized as not fitting the aesthetics of the community and not being a comfortable place for community members to visit; it is described by many as foreign, cold, and uninviting. The building ended up being too big for the size of the community; many first-time visitors to the building describe the museum as an empty fancy space. The museum is now stuck with this massive building, without many options to make the museum building more inviting. The initial designing process rarely included visitors' perspectives and community input, hence the undesirable space.

While some newer museum buildings are designed with community and visitors as well as universal design in mind, most museum buildings are built already and are difficult to retrofit for the new functions and community engagement roles of many museums. The chapters in this part describe how museum spaces can be re-envisioned through conceptualizing spaces as both reflective and interactive places and through a visitor-centered and inclusive remodeling process. Ann Rowson Love (coeditor of the book) and Morgan Szymanski, authors of chapter 17, explore the changing concepts of spaces in museums. While museums are places for quiet contemplation as represented in the notion of *the third eye*, more museums are becoming *the third place* where active community participation, conversations, and social actions happen. The authors combine the traits of third places with the feminist systems thinking in order to reconceptualize museum places and spaces as inclusive of the marginalized—ultimately changing organizational culture and taking social actions that matter to the community. They use new space initiatives in the Tate Exchange at the Tate Modern and the Target Studio for Creative Collaboration at the Weisman Art Museum in Minnesota as examples to demonstrate how this reconceptualization of museum spaces as the inclusive third places is implemented in real life settings.

Chapter 18 describes the remodeling and redesign process of Vischering Castle, a heritage site in Muensterland, Germany. Tom Duncan, the architect of the remodel and author of this chapter, approached the castle remodeling process by thinking the visitor experience as a complex system that requires deep understanding from visitor perspectives in order to improve visitor satisfaction, thus imagining and forecasting visitor expectations and requirements. In order to incorporate visitor perspectives, he performed a series of innovative workshops with the project team and group of volunteer tour guides. The two types of workshops included participants doing emotional mapping of visitors over time—thinking through duration of time from arriving to getting tea at the café using a map of the castle—and role playing—imagining the visitor perspectives by putting themselves in the shoes of visitors using the cutout characters and describing their movements and requirements in the first-person perspective. He not only theorizes visitor experience as a system but also shares some practical ways to improve multiple connections and layers that affect visitor experience in a positive manner.

17

A Third Eye or a Third Space?

Systems Thinking and Rethinking Physical Museum Spaces

Ann Rowson Love and Morgan Szymanski

I (Ann) recall during the weeks following 9/11, there was a concerted effort by the museums in New York City and across the country, including my art museum in New Orleans, to encourage Americans to find solace, to remember and memorialize, and to gain comfort in our galleries where we could refocus on the power of human creativity rather than the power of terror. Citizens of the country as a whole could find refuge, peace, and a place to remember those lost in the terrorist attacks. In New Orleans, we had no notion that our city would also succumb to a different kind of attack—the natural disaster of Hurricane Katrina—just four years later.[1]

My art museum, the Ogden Museum of Southern Art, was the first museum to reopen in the city several weeks after the storm, when citizens were finally allowed back home. Although the museum offered opportunity to seek solace in the galleries, the more useful approach, if by happenstance, became the new role of our Thursday night music and educational event called *Ogden After Hours*, as a facilitator in gathering friends, neighbors, city officials (who were also just neighbors during that time), and national responders. Since many music venues had yet to reopen, musicians were invited back to the city to play on Thursday nights at the Ogden. While they played, staff and visitors alike took a break from mucking out flooded homes, and shared evacuation stories, welcomed each other home, welcomed newcomers to their overwhelming work in repairing the city, shared drinks, learned about resources, and celebrated the music, art, and culture of our community. We cried and laughed and at the end of the night said, "See you next week!" Although this weekly event is still a popular ongoing program, the first few months after the storm generated a very different sense of place, and literally, a different use of space. The museum became a home away from home. It became a third place.[2] We followed Thursday nights with new Sunday programming that focused on architectural structural tutorials and resources regarding personal and visual culture restoration to help empower our visitors, friends, and community-wide neighbors rebuild their homes and personal collections. We curated new exhibitions (many of them over a short time) that related to topics on the minds of our community. These programs were open to all. Those who attended, whether for the first time or as a regular, were embraced; they became family. We helped each other restore our community and further embedded our museum there.

A third place, as Ray Oldenburg articulated, is a place to rejuvenate and reflect, but more importantly it is about conversation and social action.[3] A third place is the place you go after home and work. It is inclusive, welcoming both *regulars* and *newcomers*.[4] Museums, it seems, want to embrace both approaches—third eye and third space. I refer to the *third eye* as offering spaces for contemplation, even sacred or spiritual reflection. The concept of the *third eye*, as commonly understood, is a raised consciousness, a mindful contemplation. At the same time, as systems thinking moves us toward more community embeddedness and social engagement, many museums seek to become more relevant as third places.[5]

Third places, or spaces, seem aligned with systems thinking theory. They are ecosystems in and of themselves, where shared authority, inclusion, and social action are at the heart of both relaxing and doing good work in the neighborhood or community. Likewise, systems thinking focuses on the interconnectedness of our organizations within communities. I am particularly drawn to Anne Stephens's feminist systems thinking (FST), which emphasizes inclusion of the marginalized, changing organizational culture, and taking social action.[6] I invited my coauthor and graduate student, Morgan, to help me explore the changing ideas about museum spaces, particularly the approaches museums are using to rethink use of spaces, such as those aligned with third spaces. Together, we will look at practices that are emerging in art museums to make them more relevant, connected, participatory, and change oriented.

We aim to do three things in this chapter. First, we introduce an overview of related literature to examine changing notions regarding museum space—function and purpose. These changing ideas indicate movement toward systems thinking, including ideas about museums as third spaces. Second, we introduce feminist systems thinking (FST)[7] applied to Oldenburg's characteristics of third places.[8] Following, we apply the combined elements of FST and third place theories as we consider new space initiatives in museums using examples of the Tate Exchange at the Tate Modern and the Target Studio for Creative Collaboration at the Weisman Art Museum, University of Minnesota. We conclude by offering this approach for museum space planning using an FST model and the new skills we need as museum professionals to be prepared to lead new space initiatives.[9]

RETHINKING MUSEUM SPACES: FUNCTION AND PURPOSE

The question of whether museums should focus on the third eye or third space is not a new one. More commonly, this comparison of functions has been called temple versus forum, as presented in the well-known Duncan F. Cameron essay written in 1971.[10] Although Cameron, a museum director and museologist, clearly leaned toward the temple notion, where objects of high importance are displayed for visitors to admire and reflect upon, he recognized that the social turbulence of the time called for opportunities to generate conversation. He states, "While our bonafide museums seek to become more relevant, maintaining their role as temples, there must be concurrent creation of forums for confrontation, experimentation, and debate, where the forums are related but discrete institutions."[11] He equates the forum to a *process* and the temple to a *product*.[12] The call for creating relevance and making room for dialogue continues in more current literature and advances more pluralistic practices about space making; yet, there are relatively few empirical studies specifically regarding space.[13]

Suzanne McLeod coedited and edited, respectively, two books on rethinking museum space making. Common threads among chapters call for more inclusive and pluralistic collections and exhibition display strategies as well as visitor-centered practices.[14] In one introduction, she and her coauthors indicated that museum space-making is multidisciplinary and not limited to the field of architecture, but also includes theater, design, and multimedia approaches, among other disciplines—all in an effort to focus on visitors' experience "as a site where space and placemaking connect with human perception, imagination, and memory."[15] Earlier, McLeod also emphasized, "These shifts are variously characterized as creating spaces for lifelong learning, spaces of mutuality and inclusive spaces, where physical, intellectual and cultural barriers to access may be overcome."[16] Elaine Heumann Gurian calls the perceived barriers to access "threshold fear," where museum visitors may feel prohibited from engaging in experiences developed by museum staff.[17] She hypothesizes that urban planning theories could assist museums in developing more inclusive spaces beyond the architectural novelty to promote practices that include museum staff and community members taking part in architectural planning of new spaces. Changing the architectural planning process to address integral community use requires museum leadership to shift organizational culture.

Similarly, Richard Sandell addresses accessibility as a communication problem involving hierarchies of space in museums, or the privileging of certain objects and cultures over others.[18] He argues for museums to work toward achieving social action and equalizing spaces. He asserts, "In many cultural and sociological analyses of the museum's role there is an inherent problematic in the notion of museums as agents of positive (democratizing, empowering, egalitarian) social change. Rather, the museum has historically been linked to processes of exclusion, division, and oppression."[19] He analyzes ways that museums tried to combat these spatial privileging and communication inequalities. He defines three conceptual approaches museums have used—*compensatory, celebratory,* and *pluralist*—each more or less successful in addressing equality on a continuum of practices. The compensatory approach includes short-term, or "temporary interventions."[20] The celebratory approach provides more prominence, both in space allocation and breadth of display content—usually in special exhibitions. Yet this approach is still short-term. The pluralist approach involves more long-term commitment such as the reinstallation of displays, for instance, and a shift that redefines the organization's culture.

Museums as Third Spaces

In 2009 the Institute of Museum and Library Services (IMLS) gathered professionals, from both inside and outside of museums and libraries, to consider future trends and themes.[21] One of the emergent themes specifically addressed museums as third places.[22] "As opportunities for social engagement outside of private or working life and removed from the profit interests of commercial spaces, museums and libraries have the ability to identify and respond to community needs in ways that other spaces cannot."[23] The American Alliance of Museums' (AAM's) Center for the Future of Museums also predicted a continued trend of museums as third places.[24] "Looking toward the future, third places are being re-shaped by a growing community of designers who merge principles of architecture, social ergonomics and technology-based experiences to reshape our relationships."[25]

Although there have been trend predictions, discussions, and descriptions of example programs that focus on developing museums as third spaces, there has been a relative lack of research-based analysis of these spaces in museums. One notable study, however, provided empirical evidence regarding two arts organizations in London—the Tate Modern and the Southbank Centre—where the researchers conducted interviews with visitors to gain their perceptions,[26] using Oldenburg's traits of third places among other parameters,[27] including Falk and Dierking's museum experience model.[28] In addition to the questions, the researchers asked participants to classify their experiences at the sites as one of the following: "place to see art," "place to meet and hang out," "place to drop into," and "third place." Although visitor responses fit into all categories, the one criterion missing from visitor responses about their space use at the organizations was conversation, an important parameter for third places.[29] More visitors tended to see the Southbank Centre, a visual and performing arts venue, as a third place than the modern art museum. The authors advocated for further research. The lack of research studies opens opportunities for researchers and graduate students to further explore museums as third places, or third spaces. We propose a theoretical and analytical approach that combines feminist systems thinking with third place theories.

THIRD SPACES AND SYSTEMS THINKING

Feminist systems thinking (FST), developed by Anne Stephens, combines the two approaches of critical systems thinking and ecofeminist theories.[30] Both theoretical perspectives focus on *emancipatory* practices, where research participants are empowered to make social change in order to dissuade, illuminate, even eliminate, oppression—cultural, gendered, and environmental. In her resulting theory, FST principles include the following characteristics:

- Be inclusive and pluralistic
- Include voices of the disenfranchised
- Enhance organizational culture
- Advance appropriate methodologies
- Bring about social and systemic change

We propose that this adaptation of FST to museum work,[31] combined with considerations regarding Oldenburg's third places, offers new possibilities for analyzing emerging museum spaces and places that focus on inclusion and social change.

CONSIDERATIONS FOR USE: APPLYING FST/THIRD PLACE TO NEW SPACE INITIATIVES

In the following examples, we briefly analyze two initiatives that are committed to museum innovation focused on collaboration and social change—the Tate Modern and the Weisman Art Museum. Methods for this exploration include applying the parameters presented in table 17.1 to artifacts including museum website information, planning documents, media coverage, and informal personal communication. Both initiatives are new at the time of this writing, so there is little existing evaluation or research about the success of the spaces. We propose that the parameters of our FST and third place approach may offer an analysis to better understand space use.

Tate Exchange, Tate Modern

The Tate Exchange at the Tate Modern in London is a new space in the museum's Switch House, which opened in 2016. The Switch House features new galleries focused on inclusion of more women artists in an overall attempt to equalize gallery spaces.[32] The Tate Exchange has its own floor, but topics and art explorations are museum-wide. The space is designed as a drop-in center that features a multifunctional set of spaces that can be part classroom, artist studio, conversation, and work area.[33] Artists conduct residency projects that open up the exploration of art on a range of topics. In addition to artist residencies, Tate Associates—schools, nonprofit organizations, and universities, to name a few—will participate in longer-term partnerships. Daily visitors are invited to drop in to explore topics and initiatives.

There is an understanding that visitors bring their own perspectives and cultural backgrounds to the museum. In turn, the museum wants to offer safe and nurturing ways to share those perspectives. One example includes the residency conducted by the Guerilla Girls, who created a *Complaints Department*, whereby visitors had the opportunity to "post complaints about art, culture, and politics."[34] All programs and

Table 17.1. Adapted FST for Museums and Considerations for Third Places

Adapted Feminist Systems Thinking for Museums	Considerations for Third Places in Museums
Be inclusive and pluralistic.	• Ensure accessibility for all—a range of operational hours, functions of space, services available, etc. • Prioritize inclusion at all steps—welcoming to all, both regulars and newcomers; conversations include relevant neighborhood or community issues related to inclusion.
Include the voices of the disenfranchised.	• Include underrepresented voices in space planning and use (exhibitions, programming, convening spaces). • Invite voices to assist in advancing equality in museum displays (in an effort to eliminate hierarchies) through collections and exhibitions.
Enhance organizational culture.	• Reorient organizational structures to be more collaborative and inclusive. • Allow resulting conversations to create an organizational culture that embraces learning and change.
Advance appropriate methodologies.	• Advance qualitative research approaches and visitor studies to gain more in-depth understandings about perceptions and experience. • Conduct research that is participatory and empowering.
Bring about social and systemic change.	• Seek social justice through museum practices—take part in the promotion of democratic processes and doing good work for the community.

Source: Author.

initiatives are free and offer many ways for visitors, artists, and community partners to take part in institutional and cultural critique.

During the building and planning process for the Tate Exchange, staff members traveled to US museums, among others, to explore museum spaces and programs that foster unique, in-depth community partnerships that promote and engage in social action.[35] Applying FST and third place considerations, the Tate Exchange focuses on inclusion and accessibility, including cross-generational and sociocultural backgrounds. They are inviting visitors, partners, and artists to take on institutional critique through conversation and arts making. The long duration of the planning process for the new building spaces indicates the commitment among museum leaders to shift organizational practices. Since the space is new, at the time of this writing, research and study regarding the success and challenges of the space are needed and are presumably under way.

The Target Studio for Creative Collaboration, Weisman Art Museum

The Weisman Art Museum (WAM) at the University of Minnesota expanded its institution in 2011 and generated plans to add new spaces including the Target Studio for Creative Collaboration. The studio is one of the five galleries and is intended for creative collaborations across disciplines, which fluidly reiterates the WAM's mission as a place for discovery.[36] The museum brought back the original architect, Frank Gehry, to spearhead the expansion that would later become an architectural presence along the Mississippi River and to students walking across campus.[37] According to the museum, the goal of the space is to make art relevant to all people and disciplines and to encourage them to think about art in ways not normally thought about in an art museum.[38]

Looking at the Target Studio for Creative Collaboration through a critical lens, there is much to consider about the studio aligning with FST and third place considerations. The space has no admission fee and the museum encourages all community members to experience the space.[39] The museum desires to invite and work with all university and community groups to engage in a collaborative process that ultimately results in a unique and timely product (e.g., exhibitions) completely dependent on that group's discussion. In fall 2016, the museum released a position announcement for new curatorial position for the Studio.[40] The curator will act more as a team leader in search of potential collaborators that include but are not limited to fellow museum staff, students, faculty, and staff from the university as well as the surrounding community.[41] What is notable about this new position is that it specifically calls for a new kind of curator, one that can facilitate conversation, collaboration, and new ways to explore collections and exhibitions on an ongoing basis. While there is not much information on what is happening in the studio right now in regard to visitor research and intentionally seeking social action through these collaborations, creating this new position is telling of what is to come for the WAM and the museum field as a whole.

Initiatives like the Tate Exchange and the Target Studio for Creative Collaboration provide examples of new collaborative, socially engaged museums that adhere to the tenets of systems thinking. Feminist systems thinking, when paired with considerations for third places, offers guidelines for planning museum spaces and an approach for researchers, staff members, and community partners to analyze success and challenges. This combination of FST and third place considerations is a new analysis tool that offers possibilities for further articulation through qualitative analyses that explore different approaches to shaping museum space planning and implementation. There is potential to offer a different sense of place through a different use of space—inclusive, empowered, and change oriented—for the museum and the community.

BIBLIOGRAPHY

Adams, Geraldine Kendall. "Tate Exchange to Launch Next Week." *Museums Association News.* Accessed February 24, 2017. http://www.museumsassociation.org/museums-journal/news/21092016-tate-exchange-set-to-launch-next-week.

Cameron, Duncan F. "The Museum, a Temple or the Forum." In *Reinventing the Museum: The Evolving Conversation on the Paradigm Shift*, edited by Gail Anderson, 48–60. Lanham, MD: AltaMira, 2012. First published 1971 in *Curator: The Museum Journal*.

Falk, John H., and Lynn D. Dierking. *The Museum Experience*. New York: Routledge, 2016.

Golden, Garry. "Experience Design and the Future of Third Place." *Center for the Future of Museums Blog*. Last modified April 3, 2012. http://futureofmuseums.blogspot.com/2012/04/experience-design-future-of-third-place.html.

Gurian, Elaine Heumann. "Threshold Fear." In *Reshaping Museum Space: Architecture, Design, Exhibitions*, edited by Suzanne McLeod, 203–14. London: Routledge, 2005.

Hanks, Laura Hourston, Jonathan Hale, and Suzanne McLeod. "Introduction: Museum Making, the Place of Narrative." In *Museum Making: Narratives, Architectures, Exhibitions*, edited by Suzanne McLeod, Laura Hourston Hanks, and Jonathan Hale, xviii–xxiii. London: Routledge, 2012.

Kerr, Euan. "Weisman Art Museum to Open Doors, Show Off New Galleries." *MPR News*, September 30, 2011. Accessed February 20, 2017. https://www.mprnews.org/story/2011/09/30/newweisman.

Kingsman, Fiona (head, Tate Exchange). In discussion with Ann Rowson Love, July 2015.

Love, Ann Rowson, and Pat Villeneuve. "Edu-Curation and the Edu-Curator." In *Visitor-Centered Exhibitions and Edu-Curation in Art Museums*, edited by Pat Villeneuve and Ann Rowson Love, 11–22. Lanham, MD: Rowman & Littlefield, 2017.

———. "Edu-Curator: The New Leader in Art Museums." Paper presented at the National Art Education Association National Convention, Chicago, March 2016.

McLeod, Suzanne. Introduction to *Reshaping Museum Space: Architecture, Design, Exhibitions*, edited by Suzanne McLeod, 1–25. London: Routledge, 2005.

———, ed. *Reshaping Museum Space: Architecture, Design, Exhibitions*. London: Routledge, 2005.

McLeod, Suzanne, Laura Hourston Hanks, and Jonathan Hale, eds. *Museum Making: Narratives, Architectures, Exhibitions*. London: Routledge, 2012.

Oldenburg, Ray. *The Good Great Place: Cafes, Coffee Shops, Bookstores, Bars, Hair Salons, and other Hangouts at the Heart of a Community*. Cambridge, MA: Da Capo, 1999.

Pastore, Erica. *The Future of Museums and Libraries: A Discussion Guide*. Washington, DC: Institute of Museums and Library Services, 2009.

Sandell, Richard. "Constructing and Communicating Equality: The Social Agency of Museum Space." In *Reshaping Museum Space: Architecture, Design, Exhibitions*, edited by Suzanne McLeod, 185–200. London: Routledge, 2005.

Slater, Alix, and Hee Jung Koo. "A New Type of Third Place?" *Journal of Place Management and Development* 3, no. 2 (2010): 99–112.

Stephens, Anne. *Ecofeminism and Systems Thinking*. New York: Routledge, 2013.

"Tate Exchange Launches with Tim Etchells's 'The Give and Take.'" *Art Daily*. Accessed February 24, 2017. http://artdaily.com/news/90540/Tate-Exchange-launches-with-Tim-Etchells-s--The-Give-and-Take-#.WLLxTbQk_ww.

University of Minnesota–Twin Cities. "Curator of the Target Studio for Creative Collaboration." University of Minnesota's Human Resources. Accessed February 20, 2017. https://chroniclevitae.com/jobs/0000331983-01.

The Weisman Art Museum at the University of Minnesota. "The Target Studio for Creative Collaboration at WAM." Accessed February 20, 2017. http://www.research.umn.edu/documents/TARGETplanning.pdf.

NOTES

1. Ann Rowson Love was the founding curator of education at the Ogden Museum of Southern Art in New Orleans from 2000 to 2006.

2. Ray Oldenburg, *The Good Great Place: Cafes, Coffee Shops, Bookstores, Bars, Hair Salons, and other Hangouts at the Heart of a Community* (Cambridge, MA: Da Capo, 1999).

3. Ibid.

4. Ibid., 34.

5. Alix Slater and Hee Jung Koo, "A New Type of Third Place?" *Journal of Place Management and Development* 3, no. 2 (2010): 99–112.

6. Anne Stephens, *Ecofeminism and Systems Thinking* (New York: Routledge, 2013). Our museum education and visitor-centered exhibitions MA/PhD program uses FST as our foundational operating theory.

7. Ibid.

8. Oldenburg, *The Good Great Place*.

9. Ann Rowson Love and Pat Villeneuve, "Edu-Curation and the Edu-Curator," in *Visitor-Centered Exhibitions and Edu-Curation in Art Museums*, ed. Pat Villeneuve and Ann Rowson Love, 11–22 (Lanham, MD: Rowman & Littlefield, 2017).

10. Duncan F. Cameron, "The Museum, a Temple or the Forum," in *Reinventing the Museum: The Evolving Conversation on the Paradigm Shift*, ed. Gail Anderson (Lanham, MD: AltaMira, 2012), 48–60. First published 1971 in *Curator: The Museum Journal*.

11. Ibid., 55.

12. Ibid., 57.

13. Richard Sandell, "Constructing and Communicating Equality: The Social Agency of Museum Space," in *Reshaping Museum Space: Architecture, Design, Exhibitions*, ed. Suzanne McLeod (London: Routledge, 2005): 185–200.

14. Suzanne McLeod, Laura Hourston Hanks, and Jonathan Hale, eds., *Museum Making: Narratives, Architectures, Exhibitions* (London: Routledge, 2012); Suzanne McLeod, ed., *Reshaping Museum Space: Architecture, Design, Exhibitions* (London: Routledge, 2005).

15. Laura Hourston Hanks, Jonathan Hale, and Suzanne McLeod, "Introduction: Museum Making, the Place of Narrative," in *Museum Making: Narratives, Architectures, Exhibitions*, ed. Suzanne McLeod, Laura Hourston Hanks, and Jonathan Hale (London: Routledge, 2012): xviii–xxiii.

16. Suzanne McLeod, introduction to *Reshaping Museum Space: Architecture, Design, Exhibitions*, ed. Suzanne McLeod (London: Routledge, 2005): 1–25.

17. Elaine Heumann Gurian, "Threshold Fear," in *Reshaping Museum Space: Architecture, Design, Exhibitions*, ed. Suzanne McLeod (London: Routledge, 2005): 203–14.

18. Sandell, "Construction and Communicating Equality."

19. Ibid., 187.

20. Ibid., 190.

21. Erica Pastore, *The Future of Museums and Libraries: A Discussion Guide* (Washington, DC: Institute of Museums and Library Services, 2009).

22. Ibid., 9.

23. Ibid., 9–10.

24. Garry Golden, "Experience Design and the Future of Third Place," *Center for the Future of Museums Blog*, last modified April 3, 2012, http://futureofmuseums.blogspot.com/2012/04/experience-design-future-of-third-place.html.

25. Ibid.

26. Slater and Koo, "A New Type of Third Place?"

27. Oldenburg's criteria for third places include accessibility, inclusiveness, open hours, conversation, entertainment, welcoming atmosphere to newcomers, and sense of playfulness, among others.

28. John H. Falk and Lynn D. Dierking, *The Museum Experience* (New York: Routledge, 2016). This work, first published in 1992, presents three contexts of museum experience—personal, social, and physical.

29. Slater and Koo, "A New Type of Third Place?"

30. Stephens, *Ecofeminism and Systems Thinking*.

31. In 2016, Ann Rowson Love and Pat Villeneuve introduced *edu-curation*, a hybrid role of museum educator and curator using an adapted version of Stephens's theory (see table 17.1). The adaptation of Stephens's principles focused on museum exhibition development practices.

32. Geraldine Kendall Adams, "Tate Exchange to Launch Next Week," *Museums Association News*, accessed February 24, 2017, http://www.museumsassociation.org/museums -journal/news/21092016-tate-exchange-set-to-launch-next-week.

33. Fiona Kingsman (head, Tate Exchange), in discussion with the author, July 2015.

34. "Tate Exchange Launches with Tim Etchells's 'The Give and Take,'" *Art Daily*, accessed February 24, 2017, http://artdaily.com/news/90540/Tate-Exchange-launches-with -Tim-Etchells-s--The-Give-and-Take-#.WLI.xTbQk_ww.

35. Kingsman, in discussion with the author, July 2015.

36. "The Target Studio for Creative Collaboration at WAM," Weisman Art Museum at the University of Minnesota, accessed February 20, 2017, http://www.research.umn.edu/ documents/TARGETplanning.pdf.

37. Ibid.

38. Ibid.

39. Euan Kerr, "Weisman Art Museum to Open Doors, Show off New Galleries," *MPR News*, September 30, 2011, accessed February 20, 2017, https://www.mprnews.org/story/2011/ 09/30/newweisman.

40. The position announcement for the new collaborative curatorial position, which is the first endowed curatorial position at the Weisman Art Museum, was listed in fall 2016.

41. "Curator of the Target Studio for Creative Collaboration," University of Minnesota's Human Resources, accessed February 20, 2017, https://chroniclevitae.com/jobs/0000331983 -01.

18

Participative Design Processes for Museums

Tom Duncan

This chapter outlines the input of collaborative workshops on the design process for the redevelopment of the visitor experience at Vischering Castle, a heritage site in Muensterland, Germany. The development of the heritage project includes architectural works[1] to improve access, including an elevator and a new staircase, new infrastructure, and the making of spaces for visitor services and community use. At the center of this research is the design and content development undertaken by the studio Duncan McCauley,[2] responsible for planning the visitor experience and the design of all interpretive elements. This research draws on my practice as an architect in planning the museum experience and investigations into research-led design, and how role playing and thinking in time can be beneficial to the overall design of the museum or heritage site.[3] The three workshops I will report on took place in the castle: the first two during the interpretive programming and feasibility study for the project in November 2014 and January 2015; and the final one at the end of the design phase in July 2016.

The idyllic castle with a moat owned by the same family since 1271 has been a visitor attraction since it opened as a museum in 1973 (see figure 18.1). The castle sits on the outskirts of the market town of Luedinghausen. Along with the castle site, meadowland between the castle and the town is also being developed as a park with a *nature parkour*, where outdoor interpretive elements present stories from the castle in the public realm. It is hoped that the redevelopment of the castle as a landmark project and a center of excellence in the area, together with the parkland, will connect the experience of the castle with the town, thereby increasing visitor numbers to the town and ultimately encouraging urban and economic regeneration. The castle presently has approximately 40,000 visitors a year; the goal of the redevelopment is to create an environment that could accommodate up to 100,000 visitors a year.

The town of Luedinghausen has about 25,000 inhabitants and is in a rural area, but the site is reachable within an hour by car or public transport from a catchment area including cities such as Muenster, Dusseldorf, and Bielefeld. The project is partly funded by *Regionale 2016*,[4] a funding body aimed at increasing the quality of cultural and heritage sites in Muensterland.

Duncan McCauley carried out the three workshops described in this chapter together with the client during the design process. All three workshops were constructive in the way they created a platform for discussion and a means to investigate visitor requirements for the heritage site. They were very much part of an ongoing process rather than defining specific conclusions. The focus of the workshops was on the recognition, design, and development of the visitor experience. Key to recognizing the visitor experience is to think about the possibilities of the interaction of the visitor and the heritage site over time. The goal was to identify, communicate, and prioritize the visitor experience in the planning process over the practicalities of adjacencies of physical space or the complexities of the historical content.

Falk and Dierking describe the museum as having made a transformation from a place for objects to an environment for experiencing something.[5] The physical museum experience emerges in the act of experience making. The interaction of the performative qualities of the visit with the objectivity of the museum creates a

Figure 18.1. A View of Vischering Castle from the Entrance Bridge. *Source:* **Duncan McCauley.**

system that we as designers can recognize and structure appropriately for the visitor and the institution. Roppola talks of the dialogue between museum and visitor in the museum experience and redefines the museum exhibit not as an experience but as a platform for experience.[6] With this statement she recognizes the performative quality of the visit and that a quantifiable visitor experience is only possible with the interaction of visitor and museum. Bagnall described in her empirical study of visitor experiences that the visitors physically, emotionally, and imaginatively map their consumption of the heritage site.[7] She goes on to say how the experience of the visitor of a site is both cognitive but also physical, and that the physical experience often has primacy. In the workshops we tried to imagine through role playing the emotional mapping of a visitor across the site over time to get closer to the visitor's physical experience of the site.

The design of the workshops at Vischering Castle drew on previous experience gained from a collaborative project developed with the Research Centre for Museums and Galleries (RCMG) at the University of Leicester for the Imperial War Museum North (IWMN)[8] in Manchester. The sensibilities of the design process together with academic research and existing visitor analysis from the museum ensured a holistic approach to create a design-led solution. The experimental quality of both the research and the solution-finding process drew on design thinking and research-led design to create solutions for strategic and planning challenges within the museum. There are many intersections of a systems thinking approach and a design thinking process; for example, both involve seeing the challenges through different perspectives in order to unfold new possibilities toward a more human-orientated design solution. With the different expertise of the participants, the aim of one of the workshops was to make the first moves toward designing a structure to facilitate visitor engagement. One of the activities we participated in as a team was the process of mapping an idealized visitor route.[9] As Bagnall points out, the visitor experiences and relates to a site through physical and emotional mapping.[10] I argue that if we as designers can imagine how the visitor's physical and emotional mapping might be structured over a visit to a site, we can better understand the visitor experience. Role playing activities enable the participants of a workshop to alter their perspective and to experience the museum through the eyes of a visitor. By *being* a visitor we can think more closely about the immediate environment and the activities and actions that the visitor is carrying out. This closeness to a visitor allows a more in-depth investigation to inform the design of the visitor experience than only talking about visitors.

SYSTEMS THINKING AND THE VISITOR EXPERIENCE

The contemporary curator is both a curator of objects and a curator of experiences.[11] Similarly the designer is occupied with designing a series of spaces embedded with meaning to be experienced over time. Understanding more about how we do this has become central to museum design research. The visitor experience is about the inter-action between the visitor and the environment of the museum or heritage site. The design of the visitor experience enables this interaction to take place, as Roppola said to create a platform for experience.[12] Considering this, it could be useful to imagine the visitor experience as a system that could potentially allow us to quantify its success.

In a simple mechanical flow diagram (see figure 18.2) of the visitor experience, on the left flowing in are the visitor's expectations and requirements and flowing out on the other side is the visitor satisfaction. In order to improve the quality of the visitor satisfaction flowing out we need to change the design of the visitor experience. The causal loop diagram (see figure 18.3) illustrates a proposed structural model where visitor expectations and visitor satisfaction are key to the system. The movement of the visitor, their interactions with the spaces and the content, their ability to make meaning of it and to communicate about their experience form the inner loop of the diagram. The outer loop is a *feedback loop*. This is initiated by research and evaluation that informs the design process to improve the relevance of the experience for the visitor, creating more meaning-making opportunities, thereby increasing the quality of the visitor experience and ultimately raising visitor satisfaction. The feedback loop shows the importance of research to potentially influence the design process. The research can help to establish the successes and failures in the design of the visitor experience and potentially feed back into the design process to amend and improve it.

According to Meadows, a system is made up of elements, interconnections, and a function or purpose.[13] If we apply this structure directly to the museum visit, the elements could be moments of the visitor's experience, interconnected by their movement through the site. The purpose of the system is to provide a rich and rewarding visitor experience. The visitor satisfaction will always be dependent on factors outside the control of the design team, but the recognition of the need to design the visitor experience and the research around it will provide a basis for a successful museum visit.

Figure 18.2. A Simple Mechanical Flow Diagram of the Visitor Experience. *Source:* Tom Duncan.

Figure 18.3. Systems Diagram Showing the Potential Input of the Visitor in the Design of the Visitor Experience. *Source*: Tom Duncan.

Although this is an oversimplification for the complexities of the relationship between a visitor and a site, it does nonetheless identify the visitor experience as something to be understood and planned in the process of developing a museum or heritage site. Referring to the flow diagram of the system, it follows that in order to design the visitor experience, we need to imagine and forecast our visitors' expectations and requirements. This information forms the brief to design a structure, made of patterns or sequences of events. Furthermore, after the opening of the exhibition or museum, visitor research can produce a feedback loop in the system. This information, gathered from the visitor after their experience in the museum, can influence a change in the structure of the visitor experience to improve visitor satisfaction.

The process and the skill set required to structure and plan the visitor experience lie in a realm between the disciplines of architecture and design and those of a time-based medium such as film. Studying the patterns of the narrative structure used in the medium of film to produce movies may help the design team understand the narrative requirements and the performative qualities of the visitor experience of a museum and give some clues as to how the patterns of events could be structured.[14] It is possible that design processes for museums and exhibitions (including architectural design, 3D exhibit design, 2D graphic design, and audiovisual design) do not prioritize the visitor's expectations and requirements in the same way that the museum as an institution does. If we put the visitor first in the museum, then we also need to put the visitor first in the design process for the museum. The activities in the workshops are an investigation into readdressing this balance, recognizing and planning sequences and dwell times in the visitor experience.

DESIGNING THE VISITOR EXPERIENCE

Using the case study of the redesign of the visitor experience at Vischering Castle, I will describe three activities from three workshops. The first two workshops were carried out with the project team and the third workshop included volunteer tour guides. The workshops attempted to concentrate the focus of the participants on the experience of the visitor rather than on the interpretation of spatial representations of design drawings. The activities that I will discuss all rely on the participants' seeing and feeling from the point of view of the visitor.

The objectives of the first workshop at the feasibility study phase were to form a project team with common goals and to establish the priorities of the content. The participants included the design team, the client body, museum professionals, and representatives from Luedinghausen. The main activity was to map out over a time line an ideal visitor experience.[15] This activity involves thinking through the whole experience from stepping out of the car through to having a cup of tea in the café. It requires the participants to think about the expected dwell times of the visitor and what their requirements, thoughts, or emotional responses might be. As a group, sitting around a table with a long piece of paper stretched out in front of us, we mapped out the thresholds, moments of decision, the frustrations and delights, as well as the basic requirements of orientation, seating, and cloakrooms. Together we decided to base the experience on a two-and-a-half-hour visit and used this as the initial length of the time line. We established a diagram of the varied feelings and practical requirements of the visitor over time. In this activity the imagined visitor was not specified so the participants would switch back and forth between talking about their emotions and requirements and those of other visitor groups such as the elderly or children.

The descriptions in the time line diagram (see figure 18.4) vary from visitor requirements for orientation to their emotional reactions. The convolute of information makes sense regarding the time line, filtering the happenings, requirements, and emotions into an overall experience. Through thinking in time, workshop participants came closer to the actual experience of the visitor as opposed to only considering the spatial adjacencies of the content and activities. It focused the group on what we want the visitors to feel as they move through the site and the exhibitions, so we began to understand what the emotional and physical map of visitors might look like. The conversations around the table brought up issues such as ticketing in the entrance area. Where is the barrier? Can local people enter for free? We also gained an understanding of how long the overall experience would last. For example, by thinking through the dwell times of the visitors it became apparent that two floors of interpretive exhibition space were sufficient when seen in the context of the timing of the overall visit. The third floor is now dedicated to event space and education.

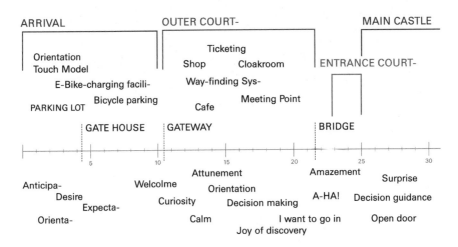

Figure 18.4. Excerpt from a Time Line of a Visitor Mapping Activity at Vischering Castle (translated from German). *Source*: **Duncan McCauley.**

Two months later, in January 2015, we carried out a second workshop with the same participants. They were asked to choose a figure or a group of figures from a selection of hand-drawn characters and to take a few minutes to fill out a visitor identity card including character data such as name, age, how they arrived at the site, where they came from, and what their interests are in visiting the site (see figure 18.5). Before the visit started, the participants shared the details of their characters with the group. This process strengthened the relationship between the participants and their chosen character and gave the whole group a chance to practice talking in first person through the character. For example, "my name is John and I am twelve years old," instead of "my character is called John."

On a large-scale site map, the participants placed their characters and moved them around the site. They took turns telling us about their experiences and engagement with the museum. Talking through the character of a very specific visitor who is of a different age, gender, or social group to the participant brought the participant closer to the actual experience than only talking generally about what the visitor's requirements might be. The workshop gave us an insight into the requirements and expectations of the visitors to the site. It highlighted planning issues that would not

Figure 18.5. Workshop Participants Experience Vischering Castle through Their Visitors at the Feasibility Phase of the Project. *Source*: Duncan McCauley.

have otherwise been discovered. For example, with the arrival of an elderly couple from the next village, it became apparent that despite a new parking lot there was not a designated place for a taxi to pull up. By following the imagined visitors over the site, we can identify important thresholds and moments of decision where the signage and orientation will play a large role in the choices the visitor makes.

After a presentation to the public, a workshop was organized to ensure that the volunteer tour guides were brought on board as part of the design process. The work of the tour guides generates a valuable connection to the visitors and is part of the interpretive concept for the museum. Based on the second workshop, the participants were asked to choose a figure and to develop their character as a visitor to the castle. They then presented their characters to the group. While for the earlier workshops with the project team we worked with the entire site, for this workshop we concentrated on one of the main exhibition floors in the castle, in the hope that through the process of discovering the planned interpretive elements through the visitor's eyes, the volunteer tour guides would become more aware of the requirements of the visitor.

Role playing visitor characters enabled the discussion to be kept focused clearly on what the visitors were going to experience. The reality was that the tour guides mostly discussed from their viewpoint at first, but by moving the characters around the site between the exhibits and identifying key objects, they had a comprehensive understanding of the design and content by the end of the morning. The experience we gained through the participatory process has meant that we have gone on to reappraise the way we present some of the content. Looking at the design through the eyes of the visitor enabled the tour guides to better express the visitor's requirements but also to understand our design principles more thoroughly. Thinking in time allows the museum development team to better comprehend unrealized experiences and to understand curatorial and pedagogical intentions. Participants who are involved with the castle either professionally or on a volunteer basis have attended the workshops. A further development to involve the local community in the design process would be to create a workshop for potential visitors and to have them role playing other visitors.

CONCLUSION

The experiential qualities of the museum visit, the interconnectivity of content, object, and space, require a design process tailored to the museum experience. The tools and methodologies for designing the museum experience can benefit from looking beyond the museum and incorporating design methodologies and structures from a time-based media such as film. Akin to methods in systems thinking, this approach to planning expands the view and considers the interactions of the visitors as part of the design process. It is possible to acknowledge the interaction between the visitor's experience and a museum as a system and thereby understand more about how to plan the structure. Thinking in systems helps define the museum visitor experience as something that needs to be thought about and designed alongside the individual exhibits and spaces of the museum. The systems approach also draws in the importance of research as key to influence change in the system as part of an active ongoing design process.

As architects and designers, we are trained to think spatially, associatively, and metaphorically. The training to experience space in time and through the perspective of a visitor in a museum is not part of our curriculum and must be learned when working with the museum. Adopting the personalities and the back-stories of imagined visitors is a process that has some similarities to how a film director develops the characters in a plot. Role playing activities, as part of the creative process, acknowledge the museum experience as being beyond the functional and aesthetic requirements of the spatial compositions. They encompass the bodily experience of moving through the site and the imagined expectations of the visitor. The process allows the designers to test proposals to a greater depth and for the project team to become more involved, through the imagined visitors, in the planning of the experience.

BIBLIOGRAPHY

Bagnall, Gaynor. "Performance and Performativity at Heritage Sites." *Museum and Society* 1, no. 2 (2003): 87–103.

Falk, John H., and Lynn D. Dierking. *Learning from Museums: Visitor Experiences and the Making of Meaning.* Walnut Creek, CA: AltaMira, 2000.

MacLeod, Suzanne, Jocelyn Dodd, and Tom Duncan. "New Museum Design Cultures: Harnessing the Potential of Design and 'Design Thinking' in Museums." *Museum Management and Curatorship* 30, no. 4 (2015): 314–41.

Meadows, Donella H. *Thinking in Systems: A Primer.* Edited by Diana Wright. White River Junction, VT: Chelsea Green, 2008.

Roppola, Tiina. *Designing for the Museum Visitor Experience.* New York: Routledge, 2012.

NOTES

1. The architects Pfeiffer, Ellermann, Preckel in Munster carried out the planning of the renovation works and changes to the infrastructure of the buildings.

2. Duncan McCauley is a studio for museum planning and exhibition design. The author Tom Duncan, together with Noel McCauley, is a founding member of the studio. On this project Duncan McCauley is working in collaboration with the graphic design studio Polyform.

3. This chapter is part of my research for a practice-centered PhD at the School of Museum Studies, University of Leicester. The PhD is supervised by Dr. Jonathan Hale, Department of Architecture and Built Environment, University of Nottingham and Dr. Suzanne MacLeod, School of Museum Studies, University of Leicester and is funded by the Midlands3Cities Doctoral Training Partnership.

4. *Regionale 2016* is a project to support cultural and economic development in Munsterland, Germany. More information can be found at http://www.regionale2016.de/de/regionale-2016.html.

5. John H. Falk and Lynn D. Dierking, *Learning from Museums: Visitor Experiences and the Making of Meaning* (Walnut Creek, CA: AltaMira, 2000).

6. Tiina Roppola, *Designing for the Museum Visitor Experience* (New York: Routledge, 2012).

7. Gaynor Bagnall, "Performance and Perfomativity at Heritage Sites," *Museum and Society* 1, no. 2 (2003): 87–103.

8. Suzanne MacLeod, Jocelyn Dodd, and Tom Duncan, "New Museum Design Cultures: Harnessing the Potential of Design and 'Design Thinking' in Museums," *Museum Management and Curatorship* 30, no. 4 (2015): 314–41.

9. Ibid.

10. Bagnall, "Performance and Perfomativity."

11. MacLeod, Dodd, and Duncan, "New Museum Design Cultures."

12. Roppola, *Designing for the Museum Visitor Experience.*

13. Donella H. Meadows, *Thinking in Systems : A Primer*, ed. Diane Wright (White River Junction, VT: Chelsea Green, 2008).

14. A comparative study of narrative structures in exhibitions and in the medium of film is an area of research I am currently undertaking.

15. The activity was developed from a workshop carried out at IWMN as described in MacLeod, Dodd, and Duncan, "New Museum Design Cultures."

Part IX

Take Action

1. Love and Szymanski propose using feminist systems thinking and third place considerations for planning, researching, and evaluating outcomes of new museum spaces. Using table 17.1, how might your museum spaces invite conversations among community members about social actions using inclusive and pluralistic approaches? How would you gain input from visitors using more qualitative methodologies that are participatory and empowering?
2. Likewise, Duncan proposes inviting visitor perspectives into the architectural planning process during workshop sessions to imagine their experience and resulting preferences regarding the use of new space. Using emotional mapping and role playing activities, as described in the chapter, how might you invite visitors and non-visitors (potential new audiences) into the architectural planning process of a new museum, new addition, or remodeling of an existing space?

Part X

BECOMING A LEARNING MUSEUM THROUGH SYSTEMS THINKING

Part X is the final part of the book and reinforces the importance of systems thinking in real museum settings. The part also suggests future directions for educating current and future museum professionals and scholars and further developing the systems thinking paradigm in museums through research.

Each part introduction included case vignettes of *The Museum* (first introduced in the Part I introduction), the fictionalized *non-example* of the real-life museum. While the stories of this museum may be a despair to many readers, there is more than what is presented in these stories. In fact, these stories are based on the past practices of an existing museum and the more recent story of this museum is one of hope. With new leadership that understands the systems way of doing museum work, the museum has started developing exhibitions and programs based on teamwork and pursuing cultural relevance to its community by actively reaching out to various community groups and working with community partner organizations. Through these and other systems-based changes in how it operates internally and interacts externally, it is becoming a learning organization. It is also reflective of its past practices by reminding new museum staff of what it was like in the past and using the past mistakes as learning opportunities. Due to these efforts, the perception of the museum by community members has changed dramatically and it is getting more visitors, and more diverse visitors, than ever before. While this museum is learning to be better and more relevant, it shows that systems thinking, when adopted institution-wide, can help even the most dysfunctional and entrenched museum become a learning organization.

The two chapters included in this part will conclude the book. Chapter 19, written by Kiersten Latham and John Simmons, is specifically placed as one of the last chapters of the book because it projects a vision for future museum direction through incorporating systems thinking in education. Latham and Simmons describe how they used systems thinking in both content and pedagogical approaches in educating graduate students by introducing a systems teaching model to a museum studies concentration in the School of Library and Information Science at Kent State University in Ohio. The students in the program go through a comprehensive set of museum courses deliberately designed to provide a holistic understanding of museums as systems and their context in society. Educating future museum professionals and scholars to be systems thinkers is one of the most effective ways to ensure that future museums will stay flexible and healthy and will be responsible and responsive members of larger social ecosystems. Finally, chapter 20, written by Yuha Jung, concludes the book by summarizing and reinforcing the concepts and ideas of systems thinking. She presents characteristics of systems-thinking–based museum practices that are found collectively in many chapters of the book and explores possibilities for future museum practice, training, and research.

19

Using Systems Thinking in Teaching Museum Studies

K. F. Latham and John E. Simmons

In this chapter we explain our approach to teaching museum studies using systems thinking and why it provides an innovative framework for future museum professionals. We explain both *how* we teach in the program (the pedagogical), as well as *what* (the content and concepts). The chapter is organized into three broad areas: (1) an overview of the influences that helped us build and drive our teaching in the program; (2) the model used throughout the suite of courses along with some concepts and examples we use in courses; and (3) how this approach might be useful to the future of museums.

BACKGROUND

In 2011, the Kent State University (KSU) School of Library and Information Science (SLIS) inaugurated a specialization in museum studies within an existing master of library and information science (MLIS) degree program.[1] Students in this specialization acquire the same core information science foundation as library and archive students, but select electives in museum studies. A full museum studies specialization consists of five main courses and one special topics course: *foundations of museum studies, the museum system, museum communication, museum users, museum collections, and museum origins*. These interconnected courses are structured on a perspective of museums as systems so that students gain a holistic understanding of museums and their context in society.

THE INFLUENCES

Our approach to museum studies is informed by several interrelated areas of study (see table 19.1), including phenomenology, systems thinking, design thinking, and complexity science (in curriculum studies). These are connected through holism (the holistic study of a topic), a growing movement across many disciplines, from biological sciences to educational theory.[2] Specifically, in our view the museum is a nested, complex set of ecologies. First, the individual visitor is part of a complicated set of systems; second, the museum system (discussed in more detail below) is a set of systems in which the individual operates; third, the museum system is part of a larger system, which we can call *society* (which also includes a temporal aspect). Of note is that our systems approach emphasizes the importance of the individual in this scenario, be it a visitor, worker, or donor. Within Library and Information Science (LIS), where we have developed this specialization, *system-centered* now has a negative connotation; unfortunately it was used for many years to focus solely on the system rather than the interrelationships between the parts. The new *user-centered* model that replaced it is equally problematic; it often concentrates on just one part of the system rather than the whole and the interactions within. For these reasons, we always work at multiple levels.

Four areas of influence support another aspect of our approach: we teach that binary or dichotomous contrasts in complex systems are not supportable. Binaries appear frequently in museum practice (e.g., object versus ideas, collections versus people, access versus meaning). One of the most detrimental binaries, for example, is the *us and them* attitude we see between collections workers and educators both in programming and at professional conferences.

THE MODEL: THE HOLISTIC MUSEUM ECOSYSTEM

Origins of the Model

Our model is influenced by a long line of museum studies thinkers but especially Humphrey,[3] who conceptualized the museum as a nested system comprised of an inner and an outer museum. Humphrey initially defined the *inner* museum as the collections and the people who study and care for them, and the *outer* museum as "all those translational devices such as exhibits and public programs that make the knowledge of the inner museum available to the lay public."[4] In his view, the inner museum was a hidden system and the outer museum the public face. This model was static because it situated specific activities and staff functions in one of two distinct places. Even so, Humphrey's model is useful to critique the structure and function of different museums; therefore we adapted it to teach students to evaluate structures, functions, and relationships and analyze the museum from different angles. The model is also useful in understanding how museum systems work and have changed over time.

Table 19.1. Four Areas of Influence on the Kent State University School of Library and Information Science Museum Studies Program

	Phenomenology	Systems Thinking	Design Thinking	Complexity Thinking
Definition	The study of phenomena, the way things appear in experience or consciousness[1]	• A worldview[2] • A school of thought that focuses on recognizing the interconnections between the parts of the system and their synthesis into a unified view of the whole[3]	• A human-centered approach emphasizing observation, collaboration, rapid learning, visualization of ideas, rapid concept prototyping, and concurrent business analysis[4] • A methodology for innovation and enablement[5]	• The study of complex systems • Complexity refers to integrated, rich, and varied environments that cannot be understood in simple, mechanistic, or linear ways[6] • A way of thinking and acting[7]
Principles/ Characteristics	No agreed-upon set of principles; intentionality of consciousness and the refusal of subject-object dichotomy are foundational[8]	• "Big picture" thinking • Balancing short-term and long-term perspectives • Recognizing the dynamic, complex, and inter-dependent nature of systems • Accounting for both qualitative and quantitative factors • Everyone is part of the systems in which we function (influence)[9]	• User-centric • Collaborative • Iterative • Holistic • Optimistic • Experimental • Experience design	• Self-organization • Emergence • Interdependence • Feedback • Space of possibilities • Co-evolving • Creation of new order[10]

Source: Author.

Notes

1. David Stewart and Algis Mickunas, *Exploring Phenomenology: A Guide to the Field and Its Literature* (Chicago: American Library Association, 1990).

2. Stephen G. Haines, "Understanding Systems Thinking and Learning," in *The Manager's Pocket Guide to Systems Thinking and Learning* (Amherst, MA: HRD Press, 1998).

3. Virginia Anderson and Lauren Johnson, *Systems Thinking Basics: From Concepts to Causal Loops* (Cambridge, MA: Pegasus, 1997).

4. Thomas Lockwood, *Design Thinking: Integrating Innovation, Customer Experiences and Brand Value* (New York: Allworth, 2010).

5. Ibid.

6. Michael R. Lissack, "Mind Your Metaphors: Lessons from Complexity Science," *Long Range Planning* 30, no. 2 (1997): 294–98.

7. Brent Davis and Dennis Sumara, *Complexity and Education* (Mahwah, NJ: Lawrence Erlbaum, 2006).

8. Stewart & Mickunas, *Exploring Phenomenology*.

9. Anderson and Johnson, *Systems Thinking Basics*.

10. Eve Mitleton-Kelly, *Complex Systems and Evolutionary Perspectives on Organisations: The Application of Complexity Theory to Organisations* (Amsterdam: Pergamon, 2003).

To render it more adaptive and flexible, we were inspired by Keene's museum system model.[5] External influences needed to be included in the model because museums are affected by outside forces including economics, politics, and cultural trends. In our model (see figure 19.1), each museum has an *internal system* (Humphrey's inner and outer museum) but the museum resides within an *external system*, which includes the local and global environments that affect the internal system. The holistic museum model we use in the program consists of these two nested, interacting, dynamic elements.

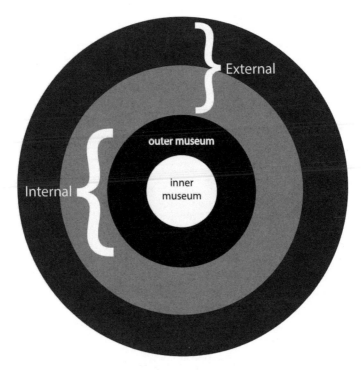

Figure 19.1. The Holistic Museum System Model. *Source*: **Latham and Simmons, 2014.**

The Internal Museum System: Inner and Outer Museum

While no single model is appropriate to describe all museums, a typical museum organization includes a suite of interacting departments (e.g., administration, collections, exhibits, education, public relations, and development). Historically, there has been a distinct line between the inner and outer museums, both figuratively and more literally (figure 19.2, left). For example, not too long ago visitors would rarely encounter or interact with a curator in a gallery. Recent societal changes (e.g., in technology, economics, emphasis on ways of learning, and community involvement) have altered the museum system, making the border between the inner and outer museum more permeable (figure 19.2, right). Today, it is not so unusual to see *curator talks* within the galleries themselves.

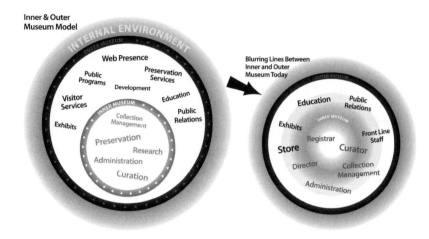

Figure 19.2. The Inner and Outer Museum Model, Shown More Traditionally (A, left) as Well as with Modern Blurring of Borders (B, right). *Source*: **Latham and Simmons, 2014.**

In fact, conventional departmental structures are changing in many museums, making it more difficult to identify museum functions as purely inner museum or outer museum, and the traditional lines are beginning to blur. For example, many museums now use a team approach to developing exhibitions and programs; some even include museum users in the process. As the borderline between the outer museum and the external world has become increasingly porous, a greater flow of information between the museum and the public has taken place. These changes are significant aspects of the growing emphasis in museums on greater transparency, recognizing a new relationship with the public, and more sensitivity to feedback. One result is that it is no longer uncommon to see *inner* museum workers interacting with visitors in the museum galleries, *outer* museum.

In our current model, we continue to use the terms inner and outer museum with our students as devices to discuss shifting practices.[6] We also incorporate the individual experience (whether a worker or visitor) within the museum system, highlighting the personal level within the larger system. Using a systems approach provides a useful way to understand human experience, and in this case the individual experience of museums and museal things, without ignoring equally pertinent social and cultural contexts.

External Systems: The Environment

Museums are not islands, but are situated within a complex of organizational, cultural, and temporal histories and actions; thus they affect and are affected by these external environments (other systems). As a system nested within a set of larger systems, a museum is a relational entity.[7] The changes induced by the museum's relationships may be dramatic or subtle; even seemingly small changes can have far-reaching effects throughout the museum system. Just as the organisms within an ecosystem must constantly adapt to environmental changes, museums also must remain flexible. The external system within which the museum is nested is constantly evolving, with the result that museums must change and adapt, or die. Stresses that cause change to a museum can come from local, regional, national, or global sources.

Everything done in the museum can be connected to external relationships, whether explicitly or implicitly. These relationships include the local community, which involves citizens, politicians, businesses, schools, groups and clubs, and other cultural institutions. Management, vision, and leadership involve understanding and working with these *collisions*, as Haines refers to them.[8] And it is not just museum administrators who must understand the relationships with external systems; even the often-hidden *inner museum* staff has external connections.[9] For instance, although traditionally collections management was considered to take place behind the scenes because it was out of public view, in reality collection managers and registrars must know their communities well. Seeking and managing donations, gathering information about objects, designing exhibitions, writing grants, and raising money usually requires interacting with people and outside agencies.

Concepts

Based on this model and the influences that contributed to it, we use a set of concepts throughout the suite of museum studies courses, both as content and as pedagogical approaches. By applying these concepts across different courses, students are able to understand the interactions within the entire system and make connections from course to course, and thereby from content area to content area.

All of these concepts are built around the notion of the museum as an open complex system. An open system is defined as one with continuous inflow and outflow[10] that maintains creative dynamism in a state of unstable steadiness.[11] It is important to note that not all open systems are complex and adaptive but we consider museums to be complex adaptive systems (CAS), which generally refers to the large number of elements interacting in diverse ways in a system.[12] For a system to be considered complex, there are several necessary qualities: it must be self-organized, emergent from the bottom up; consist of short-range relationships, embedded in a nested structure, ambiguously bounded, organizationally closed (i.e., inherently stable); structure-determined; and far from equilibrium (see Davis and Sumara for detailed definitions of these terms).[13] Complex systems continually transform themselves due to dynamic activity and dissipative structures.[14] In other words, these systems are structured yet slightly imbalanced, and this allows for creativity.[15] Some of the key systems concepts we use in the program to talk about museums include relationships, adaptive and dynamic nature, the coupling of analysis and synthesis, and emergence/co-emergence.

The notion of whole-parts-whole comes not only from systems thinking but also phenomenology. The idea is that an entity exists in a nested relationship in which each whole is composed of interacting parts or elements (the internal system in the model), and is itself a part of a more inclusive whole (what we call external systems in the model).[16] All courses are designed with a whole-parts-whole structure. For example, in the introductory course, students investigate the meaning of museums in society over time (whole) but also discriminate between departmental structures, workers, and tasks in the museum (parts).

Relationships are critical in the museum system. In general, relationships consist of connections between all parts of a system and are essential to maintain an open flow for communication,[17] and ultimately a healthy organization that is relevant to its community. For example, how a museum is positioned in society—as a private or public institution, community organization, within local and global economies, as a memory institution or cultural heritage site, as a representation of national identity, or in a culture of commodity—affects its relationships and functions. Also, the relationships between people and objects are at the heart of the museum concept.[18] In our program, the person-object transaction is taught as one of the most important relationships between the museum and its visitors. A person-object transaction describes the multilayered encounters that museum visitors can have with objects.[19] Whether considering museum workers, visitors, or non-visitors, the museum experience is grounded in the relationships surrounding human beings and museum objects.

The museum system should be adaptive and embrace its dynamic nature. We see the museum as a living system and in this context, adaptive refers to the fact that living systems constantly adapt to changing environments.[20] In such an environment, continuous learning in an organization is important to survival. Dynamic means that although complex adaptive systems are stable in the midst of fluctuation, they are sufficiently sensitive to the environment that transformation can occur as they adjust to internal and external fluctuations.[21] This is a good thing—it means that museums are not concretized, but rather are ready for external shifts over time and space. Students in the *museum origins* course, for example, examine the changing meaning over time of enduring aspects of museums (such as workers, visitors, and collections). In *the museum system* course we use the concepts to discuss the death of some museums and what it means for a museum to be healthy.

In the program we use both analysis and synthesis to study museum systems. Analysis refers to breaking things apart in order to study the pieces; synthesis is the study of the whole. Quite often, students are taught how to break things apart but never put them back together. For complex systems, however, analysis is too reductionist and atomistic to be used alone.[22] One of our course-spanning assignments (in *the museum system*) is a system analysis and synthesis in which the conceptual language of inner and outer and external and internal must be used to critique an actual museum.

Embedded in the courses are notions of emergence and co-emergence. Emergence refers to the "creation of system-level patterns arising from on-going interactions of the system's agents" from which might emerge new systems, patterns, or phenomena.[23] There are multiple levels of emergence, including individual, group, and activity.[24] Co-emergence, in the context of learning, occurs when "the various components of curriculum action (e.g., students, teachers, texts, and processes) are understood to exist in a dynamic and mutually specifying relationship."[25] Our on-site museum studies laboratory (MuseLab) is a site for emergence; we have created several *organic* exhibits using a fast-moving design process that is sometimes inverted (starting with content, then finding the big idea and title last). Co-emergence is a foundational concept for our teaching but we also espouse such a concept for professionals in situ.

APPLICATION OF SYSTEMS THINKING
AND THE FUTURE OF MUSEUMS

We have presented a brief overview of how we have integrated systems thinking concepts into the curriculum of a museum studies program to better prepare students for future museum work. We believe that the use of systems thinking in the training of museum personnel will lead to the development of healthier museum systems by providing future professionals with better tools to understand and improve the institutions in which they work.

BIBLIOGRAPHY

Anderson, Virginia, and Lauren Johnson. *Systems Thinking Basics: From Concepts to Causal Loops.* Cambridge, MA: Pegasus, 1997.

Bell, Joshua A. "Museums as Relational Entities: The Politics and Poetics of Heritage." *Reviews in Anthropology* 41, no. 1 (2012): 70–92.

Bertalanffy, Ludwig von. *General System Theory: Foundations, Development, Applications.* New York: Braziller, 1969.

Clark, Andy. *Being There: Putting Brain, Body, and World Together Again.* Cambridge, MA: MIT Press, 1997.

Cleveland, John. "Complexity Theory: Basic Concepts and Application to Systems Thinking." Last modified March 27, 1994. Accessed July 18, 2016. http://www.slideshare.net/johncleveland/complexity-theory-basic-concepts.

Codynamics. "Introduction to the Basic Concepts of Complexity Science." Last modified 2004. Accessed September 24, 2015. http://www.codynamics.net/intro.htm.

Davis, A. Brent, and Dennis J. Sumara. *Complexity and Education.* Mahwah, NJ: Lawrence Erlbaum, 2006.

Davis, A. Brent, Dennis J. Sumara, and Thomas E. Kieren. "Cognition, Co-emergence, Curriculum." *Journal of Curriculum Studies* 28, no. 2 (1996): 151.

Doll, William E. "Complexity and the Culture of Curriculum." *Educational Philosophy and Theory* 40, no. 1 (2012): 10–29.

Haines, Stephen G. "Understanding Systems Thinking and Learning." In *The Manager's Pocket Guide to Systems Thinking and Learning.* Amherst, MA: HRD Press, 1998.

Hayles, Katherine. *Chaos and Order: Complex Dynamics in Literature and Science.* Chicago: University of Chicago Press, 1991.

Humphrey, Phillip S. Lecture, University of Kansas–Lawrence, 1976.

———. "The Nature of University Natural History Museums." In *Natural History Museums: Directions for Growth*, edited by Paisley S. Cato and Clyde Jones, 5–11. Lubbock: Texas Tech University Press, 1991.

Hussain, Hanin, Lindsey Conner, and Elaine Mayo. "Envisioning Curriculum as Six Simultaneities." *Complicity: An International Journal of Complexity and Education* 11, no. 1 (2014): 63.

Keene, Suzanne. *Managing Conservation in Museums.* Oxford: Butterworth-Heinemann, 2002.

Latham, Kiersten F. "The Invisibility of Collections Care Work." *Collections* 3, no. 1 (2007): 103–12.

———. "Lumping, Splitting and the Integration of Museum Studies with LIS," *Journal of Education for Library and Information Science* 56, no. 2 (2015): 130–40.

Latham, Kiersten F., and John E. Simmons. *Foundations of Museum Studies: Evolving Systems of Knowledge.* Santa Barbara, CA: Libraries Unlimited, 2014.

Lissack, Michael R. "Mind Your Metaphors: Lessons from Complexity Science." *Long Range Planning* 30, no. 2 (1997): 294–98.

Lockwood, Thomas. *Design Thinking: Integrating Innovation, Customer Experiences and Brand Value.* New York: Allworth, 2010.

Mitleton-Kelly, Eve. *Complex Systems and Evolutionary Perspectives on Organisations: The Application of Complexity Theory to Organisations.* Amsterdam: Pergamon, 2003.

Stewart, David, and Algis Mickunas. *Exploring Phenomenology: A Guide to the Field and Its Literature.* Chicago: American Library Association, 1990.

Sturmberg, Joachim P. "'Returning to Holism': An Imperative for the Twenty-First Century." In *The Value of Systems and Complexity Sciences for Healthcare*, edited by Joachim P. Strumberg, 3–19. New York: Springer, 2016.

Wood, Elizabeth E., and Kiersten F. Latham. *The Objects of Experience: Transforming Visitor-Object Encounters in Museums.* Walnut Creek, CA: Left Coast Press, 2014.

———. "The Thickness of Things: Exploring the Curriculum of Museums through Phenomenological Touch." *Journal of Curriculum Theorizing* 27, no. 2 (2011): 51–65.

NOTES

1. Kiersten F. Latham, "Lumping, Splitting and the Integration of Museum Studies with LIS," *Journal of Education for Library and Information Science* 56, no. 2 (2015): 130–40.

2. Joachim P. Sturmberg, "'Returning to Holism': An Imperative for the Twenty-First Century," in *The Value of Systems and Complexity Sciences for Healthcare*, ed. Joachim P. Strumberg (New York: Springer, 2016), 3–19.

3. Philip S. Humphrey (lecture, University of Kansas–Lawrence, 1976); Philip S. Humphrey, "The Nature of University Natural History Museums," in *Natural History Museums: Directions for Growth*, ed. Paisley S. Cato and Clyde Jones (Lubbock: Texas Tech University Press, 1991), 5–11.

4. Humphrey, lecture.

5. Suzanne Keene, *Managing Conservation in Museums* (Oxford: Butterworth-Heinemann, 2002).

6. Kiersten F. Latham and John E. Simmons, *Foundations of Museum Studies: Evolving Systems of Knowledge* (Santa Barbara, CA: Libraries Unlimited, 2014).

7. Joshua A. Bell, "Museums as Relational Entities: The Politics and Poetics of Heritage," *Reviews in Anthropology* 41, no. 1 (2012): 70–92.

8. Stephen G. Haines, "Understanding Systems Thinking and Learning," in *The Manager's Pocket Guide to Systems Thinking and Learning* (Amherst, MA: HRD Press, 1998).

9. Kiersten F. Latham, "The Invisibility of Collections Care Work," *Collections* 3, no. 1 (2007): 103–12.

10. Ludwig von Bertalanffy, *General System Theory: Foundations, Development, Applications* (New York: Braziller, 1969).

11. William E. Doll, "Complexity and the Culture of Curriculum," *Educational Philosophy and Theory* 40, no. 1 (2012): 10–29.

12. John Cleveland, "Complexity Theory: Basic Concepts and Application to Systems Thinking," last modified March 27, 1994, accessed July 18, 2016, http://www.slideshare.net/johncleveland/complexity-theory-basic-concepts.

13. Brent Davis and Dennis Sumara, *Complexity and Education* (Mahwah, NJ: Lawrence Erlbaum, 2006).

14. Doll, "Complexity and the Culture of Curriculum"; Katherine Hayles, *Chaos and Order: Complex Dynamics in Literature and Science* (Chicago: University of Chicago Press, 1991).

15. Doll, "Complexity and the Culture of Curriculum."

16. Ibid.

17. Codynamics, "Introduction to the Basic Concepts of Complexity Science," last modified 2004, accessed on September 24, 2015, http://www.codynamics.net/intro.htm.

18. Elizabeth E. Wood and Kiersten F. Latham, *The Objects of Experience: Transforming Visitor-Object Encounters in Museums* (Walnut Creek, CA: Left Coast Press, 2014).

19. Elizabeth E. Wood and Kiersten F. Latham, "The Thickness of Things: Exploring the Curriculum of Museums through Phenomenological Touch," *Journal of Curriculum Theorizing* 27, no. 2 (2011): 51–65.

20. Codydynamics, "Introduction to Basic Concepts."

21. Cleveland, "Complexity Theory."

22. Andy Clark, *Being There: Putting Brain, Body, and World Together Again* (Cambridge, MA: MIT Press, 1997).

23. Hanin Hussain, Lindsey Conner, and Elaine Mayo, "Envisioning Curriculum as Six Simultaneities," *Complicity: An International Journal of Complexity and Education* 11, no. 1 (2014): 63.

24. Ibid.

25. A. Brent Davis, Dennis J. Sumara, and Thomas E. Kieren, "Cognition, Co-emergence, Curriculum." *Journal of Curriculum Studies* 28, no. 2 (1996): 151.

20

Toward a Learning Museum and Systems Intelligence

Yuha Jung

In this edited book, we introduced systems thinking as a theory for museum management and operations. While systems thinking may seem like a mere idea, we strived to make it come to life by showing real museum examples that applied systems thinking to their various functions and areas. As demonstrated in each chapter and explained in our introduction (chapter 1), we did not use the word *system* in the sense that it is a machine or controlled mechanism.[1] It refers to a complex, interdependent, and open web of things, people, and relationships that are also part of a larger social, cultural, and natural environment that is continually in the state of flux.[2] As articulated in many chapters throughout this book, a museum is an open system that has interdependent things, departments, and people and it is necessarily part of its larger communities—influencing and being influenced by changes happening internally and externally. To manage complex and open museum organizations successfully, museums should be constantly learning to interact with the changing parts, perspectives, needs, and interests of webs of relationships. However, this is not the case for most museums.

While interdependent relationships within museums and their communities are growing, most museums tend to be hierarchical, highly controlled, compartmentalized, centralized, mechanical, and museum oriented as opposed to visitor and community oriented. These museums are felt to be irrelevant to most community members and tend to serve a very specific type of people, generally those that are white, wealthy, and well educated. This is due to museums not understanding their complex interdependence among their departments and people and with their communities. Senge refers to this as systems ignorance.[3] Systems ignorance describes the tendency of people consistently producing the same results that are not intended and often hurtful, yet not being able to fix them in a sustainable way. Museums do not want to be irrelevant, seen as elitist, not accessible, and producing knowledge that is not valued by its communities. Yet, many continue to do so. If they desire a different result, they must change how they operate using a completely new paradigm. Meadows et al. described systems thinking succinctly in that without understanding the underlying structures of a system and how its parts influence each other, we cannot manage the whole system effectively.[4] With this thinking as a new paradigm, museums can be systems intelligent.

However, thinking or theory alone without action cannot change the continuing undesirable results. Practice is always informed by theory, whatever that theory might be and whether the practitioner realizes it or not, and a known theory does not mean much until it is applied in reality.[5] According to Senge, all people have an innate systems thinking ability; he suggests that people should go observe where systems thinking is implemented successfully and study why in order to learn from best practices.[6] The chapters in this book allow the reader to do this by acting as best practices that could be applied to other museums with the adaptation and consideration necessary for a different context and uniqueness of a museum.

CHARACTERISTICS OF SYSTEMS-BASED MUSEUM PRACTICES

The vantage points for exploring systems-based museum practices represented in each section of the book included management and leadership, personnel management, exhibitions and programs, external communications, community engagement, fundraising and financial sustainability, and physical spaces. While presenting these chapters in separate sections might be seen as going against what is rooted in systems thinking, we did this intentionally in the hope that applying systems thinking in museum practices can start small, without having to be a museum-wide practice initially. Once that is successful, it can be applied to the larger museum practices, thinking inclusively about the museum's diverse roles and functions, multiple stakeholders, and the variety of perspectives. By looking at the strategies adopted by the many museums featured in this book, any museum considering implementing new practices or procedures based on systems thinking, either small or large, can find ideas about the characteristics of a successful systems thinking museum. Most of these characteristics are found collectively in many different chapters and are mentioned below.

Borrowing the term *learning organizations* from Senge, museums that are systems intelligent are *learning museums*.[7] Learning museums and their professionals understand that in order to pay attention to many relationships and apply their perspectives in practice, the hierarchical and highly controlled management and governing structure should be revised to be based on *collective leadership*, *network of relationships*, and *multidirectional communication* systems. Without these flexible and organic ways to manage museums and interact among various departments and with their communities, they may produce exhibitions and programs that are based on just a few people's vision and expertise. Even though unintentional, this limited scope would not be relevant to most community members, and could even increase the isolation and disconnect of the museum from its community.

Looking more closely at systems museum structure internally, most learning museums adopt a *team-based approach* that includes diverse levels and positions of museum workers from different departments. They understand that museum functions and departments are interconnected and each department's work informs all others' in achieving a collective vision. In this case, leadership is not just defined by the position one holds but by one's ability and experience to carry out a project; therefore it is often rotated depending on the nature of the project. Team members are empowered as they can work on projects that match their passions and skills, collaborating on achieving the collective goals with other staff members.

More flexible and organic management systems of learning museums allow them to listen to multiple perspectives and accommodate the needs and interests of communities. Therefore, learning museums are *visitor centered* and *community oriented*. They understand that museums are part of their larger communities and strive to listen to what their visitors and community members want from the museum and to find what is relevant to local issues and concerns in creating exhibitions and programs and generating knowledge. In this case, museums and their objects are no longer at the center of museum work; they alone do not mean much unless their work and meanings are interconnected with those of the visitors and local communities.

As they understand the importance of serving local communities, systems intelligent museums also strive for *cultural relevance*, trying to be socially inclusive and engaging people in collective actions that are important to local communities. They constantly communicate with their communities through demographic studies, visitor and non-visitor studies, evaluation methods, and other formal and informal conversation and engagement. In some progressive cases, community members are part of creating exhibitions and programs in a profound and complete manner based on the museums' deep understanding of their communities.

Learning museums expect the unexpected—they understand that museums cannot stay at a stale equilibrium and should keep reaching to be at *dynamic equilibrium*,[8] that is, constantly changing to be better and learning to act as changes occur. Therefore, they act *interdependently* to achieve the resources needed for *long-term sustainability*. For example, they rely on diverse funding sources and relationships that can support the museum for many years to come. In this case, sustainability means not simply existing, but thriving in a dynamic way that embraces change. Therefore, they remain flexible and have a comprehensive mechanism to deal with emerging challenges and opportunities.

Lastly, when museums apply systems thinking in their day-to-day practices, the result will be that they are *learning museums* that are continuously learning together to be better and more relevant for their communities. Becoming a learning museum cannot happen without a *paradigm change* within the whole museum and having a different mindset as museum professionals. Otherwise, the practices and characteristics described above will not be continued beyond a single project or two or incorporated into the day-to-day practices in the future. Therefore, to promote learning museums, people who work within them should be trained and educated in systems thinking. This can happen through teaching future museum professionals about systems thinking and professional development workshops.

EDUCATING FUTURE SYSTEMS THINKERS FOR MUSEUMS

If museums are truly to be learning organizations, people who run them should understand systems thinking, in other words, be systems intelligent. One of the ways is to get an advanced degree in a higher education institution. Kiersten Latham and John Simmons, in chapter 19, did an excellent job at presenting how museum studies programs in higher education institutions can be designed using systems thinking in both content and pedagogical approaches. This book can be used as a text in museum studies and related courses to educate future museum professionals and scholars to be systems intelligent. Another way is through professional development and deep reflection within museums as demonstrated by Douglas Worts (chapter 8) and Randi Korn (chapter 5). By using this book, museum studies students, museum professionals, and scholars can see the best practices and imagine how they can apply these strategies in their current and future careers as museum professionals and researchers. As Ann Rowson Love has shown in her reflection and action steps at each section end, museums can also use this book to reflect on their practice and adopt action steps based on systems thinking, the new paradigm for practices.

WHAT'S NEXT?

As mentioned in chapter 1, systems thinking is still new to museums and there is a long way to go until this paradigm is fully understood and integrated into the day-to-day management and operation of museums. As more museums and scholars pay attention to systems thinking as applied to museums, more research is needed in this area. We intend to "alter, expand, and improve"[9] systems thinking in museums through further application and research. The world is changing quickly, with unexpected social issues and new demands on many communities. Like any paradigm that exists, systems thinking is neither perfect nor an answer to all the challenges that communities face. But, as demonstrated through the stories, analyses, theories, and applications shared in this book, a connected museum can lead its communities in meeting those challenges by being an active-learning and socially engaged place where people are empowered to make changes in their lives and society together.

NOTES

1. Peter Checkland, "Soft Systems Methodology: A Thirty Year Retrospective," *Systems Research and Behavioral Science* 17, no. S1 (2000): 11–58.

2. Peter Senge, "Being Better in the World of Systems," speech at the 30th Anniversary Seminar of the Systems Analysis Laboratory, Aalto University, Finland, November 2014, https://www.youtube.com/watch?v=0QtQqZ6Q5-o; Sally Helgesen, *The Web of Inclusion: A New Architecture for Building Great Organizations* (New York: Doubleday, 1995).

3. Senge, "Being Better."

4. Donella H. Meadows, Dennis L. Meadows, Jorgen Randers, and William W. Behrens III, *The Limits to Growth: A Report for the Club of Rome's Project on the Predicament of Mankind* (New York: Universe, 1972).

5. Senge, "Being Better."

6. Ibid.

7. Peter Senge, *The Fifth Discipline: The Art and Practice of the Learning Organization* (New York: Doubleday, 1990).

8. Ludwig von Bertalanffy, "The Theory of Open Systems in Physics and Biology," *Science* 111, no. 2872 (1950): 23–29.

9. Meadows et al., *Limits to Growth*, 22.

Index

inclusion: interdisciplinary content advisors, 164, 199; non-museum voices, 163, 165
Indianapolis Museum of Art, 33
infrastructure, 57, 122, 149, 162, 184–185, 205
Inner and Outer Museum Model, 220–224
innovation, 17, 62, 82–94, 157, 186, 199, 221
Institute for Museum and Library Services (IMLS), 20, 198
institutional change, 11–13, 79, 124, 126
Integrated Postsecondary Education Data System (IPEDS), 20
intentional practice, 49–57, 68: alignment questions, 55, 57, 62
intentional practice quadrants: align, 55–56; evaluate, 53–54, 56 plan, 53–54; reflect, 54–55
interconnected network/system, 5, 27
internal system, 101, 157, 181, 222, 225
International Council of Museums (ICOM), 18
internships, 38, 70, 79
interventions, 32, 66, 89, 106, 112–114, 122, 132, 197
Internal Revenue Service (IRS), 19–20, 173
Israel Museum of Jerusalem (IMJ), 11, 150–154, 168

Janes, Robert, 4, 13, 34

Kent State University, 12, 219, 221
Kuhn, Thomas S., 37–38

Laszlo, Ervin, 30–31
leadership: delegated, 48, 62–63; directors, 38, 47, 53, 59, 68–69, 75–76, 133, 161, 184–185, 197; empowered female, 109; project management, 63–64, 103–104, 162–163, 231; risk, 76–77; shared, 6, 13, 31, 68, 230; structures, 47; team-based, 68. *See also* Chief Executive Officer, management, and teams
learning organization: co-learning; 6, 10; environment, 32, 49; museum, 13, 229–232; stagnant environment, 3, 32, 49
leverage points, 32, 82–89, 94

limitations, 18–19, 135, 142
living culture, 82–84
living systems, 13, 110–112, 225
the lone creative, 38, 42

management: business, 6; change, 121; executive team, 63–64; financial, 171–172, 176, 191; hierarchical, 27, 61; nonprofit, 183; organic, 4, 231; project management, 61, 63, 99, 101, 104; reshaping, 47; restructuring, 39; risk, 65, 71–76, 94; senior, 74–75; shared, 135; soft, 4; structures, 9–10; top down, 47, 59; traditional, 4–5, 38–39, 42, 82, 158. *See also* enterprise risk management, intentional practice, leadership, and Talent Management
marginalized voices, 6, 8, 196. *See also* diversity
Mary Brogan Museum of Art and Science (MOAS), 171–177
Mattingly, Mary, 110–114
Meadows, Donella, H., 31–32, 208, 230
meaning-making, 56, 163–165, 208
metrics: community, 19, 21–25; of success, 56
mindful museum, 4, 13
mission, vision, and values, 39, 46, 82–89, 97, 111, 126, 135, 150–154, 158, 224: investment in, 161; shared, 8–10, 48, 61–62, 64, 91, 231; social, 142, statements, 52; symbolic, 133
muscle memory, 73, 79
Musée Carnavalet, 122, 124
Musée national des beaux-arts du Québec (MNBAQ), 122, 126
Musée royal d'Afrique centrale, 122, 124, 126
museologist, 38, 197
museum: collections, 219; communication, 11, 219; ecosystem, 3, 5, 7, 9, 11, 13, 17, 19–20, 158, 220; experience, 5–6, 33, 39, 97, 198, 205–207, 213, 225; franchising, 183–184; functions, 9, 38–39, 42, 81, 223, 231; mission, 153; nomadism, 121; origins, 219, 225; practitioners, 3, 7; studies, 6–7, 13, 21,

About the Editors and the Contributors

THE EDITORS

Yuha Jung, PhD, is an assistant professor of arts administration at the University of Kentucky. She holds an MA in museum studies from Syracuse University, MPA from the University of Georgia, and PhD in art education from Pennsylvania State University with an emphasis on museum education and management. Her current research interests center on the incorporation of systems theory and organizational studies in arts and museum management and education. She has published numerous papers in the areas of culture diversity, engaging diverse audiences, systems theory, organizational culture, and informal learning in arts and cultural institutions.

Ann Rowson Love, PhD, is the coordinating faculty member for the museum education and visitor-centered exhibitions program in the Department of Art Education at Florida State University. She is also faculty liaison to the John and Mable Ringling Museum of Art. Love has been a museum educator, curator, and administrator for over twenty-five years. She presents and publishes widely on curatorial collaboration, visitor studies, and art museum interpretation.

THE CONTRIBUTORS

Caroline Angel Burke is the vice president of education, visitor experience, and collections, responsible for all educational programs, exhibits, interpretation, media development, and curatorial collections at the Edward M. Kennedy Institute for the United States Senate. Previously, she was senior project manager in exhibits at the Museum of Science, Boston, and program manager for the museum's adult and special programs, and has worked in curatorial, project management, educational, and visitor service management positions at a variety of museums and their support industries in the US and UK. She has a BA in history and anthropology from Northeastern University and a master's degree in Museum Studies from the University of Leicester.

Swarupa Anila is the director of interpretive engagement at the Detroit Institute of Arts. She is responsible for the strategic planning and execution of visitor-centered interpretation for exhibitions and permanent collections. She is a nationally recognized leader in the field, presents and publishes on interpretive practice, and has developed award-winning work. Anila has a BA from the University of Michigan and is a PhD candidate in postcolonial theory in literary and visual culture at Wayne State University. Anila currently serves on the editorial board for *Exhibition*, the journal of the National Association for Museum Exhibition.

Paul Bowers has led exhibition development and major projects from within and outside major institutions over the past twenty years. Since joining Museums Victoria, Melbourne in 2013, Bowers has instigated an evolution of exhibition development practice, creating new roles focusing on experience and audience, and renewing the development process around public offer planning, inception, creation, and delivery.

Sibelle C. Diniz, PhD, is an assistant professor in the Department of Economics at Federal University of Minas Gerais, Brazil. Her research interests are cultural economics, urban and regional economics, and social and solidarity economy.

Tom Duncan is an architect and exhibition designer for museums and heritage sites. He combines professional practice with academic research and teaching and is a PhD candidate at the University of Leicester, School of Museum Studies. His research investigates how the contemporary museum master plan can combine the spatial qualities of architecture with the experiential and storytelling qualities of the visitor experience. Based in Berlin, Germany, he is a founding partner, together with Noel McCauley, of the studio Duncan McCauley, working for clients such as the Victoria and Albert Museum in London and the State Museums of Berlin.

Victoria Eudy is a PhD candidate in the museum education and visitor-centered exhibitions program at Florida State University. Before coming to Florida State University, Victoria received her MAEd in art education from the University of Georgia. Her current research focus is the application of systems thinking in digital strategy development and implementation process in the art museum.

Diomira Maria Cicci Pinto Faria, PhD, is a professor of tourism economics in the Department of Geography at Federal University of Minas Gerais, Brazil. Her research interests are tourism, culture, economics, and regional development. She has authored and coauthored books and papers in her field.

Guido Ferilli is assistant professor and director of the Cultural Industries and Complexity Observatory at IULM University in Milan. His research focuses on economics, applied quantitative methods to the social sciences, and European programs. He researches and consults internationally in the fields of cultural policy design and local development.

Cora Fisher is a former curator at the Southeastern Center for Contemporary Art (SECCA) and is a freelance art writer originally from New York City. At SECCA she organized fifteen exhibitions and several publications, and launched a North Carolina Artist Salon Series, 12 x 12. She holds a BFA from the Cooper Union School of Art and an MA from the Center for Curatorial Studies at Bard College.

Amy Hamilton Foley has been with the Detroit Institute of Arts for over twenty years and has worked on more than 100 exhibitions, ranging from major internationally organized projects to more local endeavors. She leads exhibition planning and implementation to ensure the successful sequencing, management, and integration of all activities related to exhibitions and major gallery reinstallation projects. She has an MA in arts administration from Goucher College and a BA in art history from Bates College. She is a long-standing member of both the American and International Exhibition Organizers (IEO) groups and has recently joined the board of the IEO.

Kathy Fox has, over the last fifteen years, combined her passion for museums and the design process through a variety of complex museum exhibition projects for Museums Victoria. Fox holds a master of design by research degree and a bachelor of industrial design degree from RMIT University, as well as a bachelor of science degree from the University of Melbourne.

Sendy Ghirardi is a PhD student at IULM University in Milan. She graduated from IULM University with a thesis on participatory museum practices.

Amy Gilman, PhD, was named deputy director of the Toledo Museum of Art in 2016. In this role, she oversees the museum's art collections, development, leadership fellowships, and finances. Gilman came to the Toledo in 2005 as associate curator of modern and contemporary art after earning her doctorate in art history at Case Western Reserve University. In 2011 she became the associate director of the museum, managing curatorial, education, communications, and visitor engagement. She has been a member of the senior leadership team involved with the recent strategic plan and staff restructuring.

Patrick Greene, PhD, OBE, is a former chief executive officer of Museums Victoria. He is the chair of the National Cultural Heritage Committee, a member of the Council of Australasian Museum Directors and Australian World Heritage Advisory

Committee, and an ambassador for Club Melbourne, the organization established to attract international conferences to the Melbourne Convention Centre. He is an adjunct professor in the Centre for Cultural Heritage Asia Pacific of Deakin University and a professorial fellow of the University of Melbourne.

Natalia Grincheva, PhD, is a research fellow at the Transformative Technologies Research Unit at the University of Melbourne, where she works on a number of research projects exploring how new media technologies challenge and innovate contemporary art and cultural practices, policies, and diplomacy. Grincheva has a strong academic record in the fields of museum studies and digital diplomacy through her international field work in many countries. Based on her research finding on digital programs implemented by the largest internationally recognized museums in North America, Europe, and Asia, she is currently working on her first monograph, *Online Museums as Sites of Cultural Diplomacy*.

Randi Korn is the founding director of Randi Korn & Associates, (RK&A), a company that implements evaluations, audience research, and impact planning strategies. Korn focuses on intentional planning, a methodology that helps museums plan for and demonstrate impact. Korn uses intentional planning and evaluation to help museums clarify, measure, and communicate their value. Prior to starting RK&A in 1988, Korn held a variety of museum positions, including executive director, exhibition designer, interpretive planner, and evaluator. She lectures widely, has taught for eighteen years at the George Washington University, and served on the Visitor Studies Association board and as a research commissioner for the National Art Education Association.

Kiersten F. Latham, PhD, is an associate professor in the School of Library and Information Science (LIS) at Kent State University where she developed and teaches the specialization in museum studies from an LIS perspective. In addition to academic work, she has worked in, on, and about museums in various capacities for over twenty years, serving as a director, educator, researcher, collections manager, curator, volunteer, and consultant. Her research interests convene around the meaning of museum objects—especially regarding emotion, perception, sensation, and spirituality—and the conceptual foundations of museums as knowledge systems. Latham also runs the experimental MuseLab—a place for thinking, doing, and learning about museal things.

Ana Flávia Machado is an associate professor in the Department of Economics of Federal University of Minas Gerais, Brazil (UFMG) and currently is the director of Espaço do Conhecimento UFMG (Knowledge Museum UFMG). Her research focus is on culture, museums, and education. She organized a book in creative economy and has authored and coauthored many chapters and academic papers in her research field.

Susan Mann was the assistant director of the art department for the Mary Brogan Museum of Art and Science in Tallahassee, Florida, when the museum closed in 2012. She is currently a doctoral student in museum education and visitor-centered exhibitions at Florida State University. She began as an art educator specializing in elementary art education. In Washington State, she was involved with the Allied Arts Education Project in Bellingham, serving as the chair of the Arts Education Committee. Mann's museum experience includes working with the Florida State University Museum of Fine Arts and the Whatcom Museum of History and Art.

Rodrigo C. Michel is currently in the doctoral program in economics at Federal University of Minas Gerais, Brazil. His work focuses on creative and cultural economics, especially the cinematography industry and the production of music. He also has research experience in industrial organization and innovation.

Lynn Miller joined the Toledo Museum of Art in 2013 as the director of human resources. In 2016, she was promoted to assistant director, where she is responsible for protective services and facilities, and oversees all aspects of people resources, including diversity and inclusion initiatives. Miller earned her bachelor's degree in psychology from Bowling Green State University and has studied human resources and organizational design at the graduate level. Prior to coming to the museum, Miller held human resource leadership positions at several private sector organizations including Thomson Reuters, Domino's Pizza, and PeopleSoft.

Robin Nelson is a PhD candidate in public administration at the University of Ottawa, focusing on public policy. She has a master's degree in museum studies from the University of Toronto. Her research interests, developed from experiences working in community museums, are in subnational cultural policy, community museums, and policy instrumentation.

Bárbara Freitas Paglioto holds a degree in economics from the Federal University of Minas Gerais, Brazil (UFMG) and a master's degree in economics from CEDE-PLAR/UFMG. She has been a member of the research group in cultural economics of FACE/UFMG since 2012 with a research focus on economics of museums, consumption of culture, and creative economy.

Jonathan Paquette, PhD, is an associate professor at the School of Political Studies at the University of Ottawa in Ontario, Canada. His work focuses on institutional transformations in the museum sector and on museum policy. Paquette is an executive editor of the *Journal of Arts Management, Law, and Society.*

Monica Parker-James has more than two decades of experience in nonprofit program and project management in both formal and informal education settings. As an exhibit project manager for the Museum of Science, Boston, she was responsible for managing the development of permanent and traveling exhibits. Parker-James holds a master of science degree from Boston University. She currently serves as the director of strategic affiliations for Boston University's School of Medicine.

Nii Quarcoopome, PhD, is the department head of Africa, Oceania, and Indigenous Americas and co-chief curator at the Detroit Institute of Arts, where he has collaborated with the museum's interpretive educators to reinstall the African gallery. In 2010, he directed the groundbreaking exhibition *Through African Eyes: The European in African Art, 1500–Present*, which attracted major national funding and won the American Alliance of Museums' highest honor for overall excellence and a Detroit City Council Resolution. He has a PhD in art history from the University of California–Los Angeles.

Deborah Randolph, PhD, is the curator of education at the Southeastern Center for Contemporary Art in Winston-Salem, North Carolina. She holds a PhD in education from the University of North Carolina at Chapel Hill. Her research interests include relational capacity building in arts integration, the arts and social justice, and community activated exhibition programming.

Pier Luigi Sacco is a professor of economic policy at IULM University in Milan, senior researcher at MetaLAB (at) Harvard, and visiting scholar at Harvard University. He researches and consults internationally in the fields of cultural economics, game theory, and strategic policy design. He is a member of the editorial board and scientific committee of the *International Journal of Cultural and Creative Industries, Creative Industries Journal, Quality and Quantity,* and *Mind and Society.*

John E. Simmons was a zoo keeper, collections manager, and director of the Museum Studies Program at the University of Kansas, where he received the Chancellor's Award for Outstanding Mentoring of Graduate Students. His books include *Cuidado, Manejo y Conservación de las Colecciones Biológicas; Things Great and Small: Collections Management Policies; Fluid Preservation: A Comprehensive Reference; Foundations of Museum Studies: Evolving Systems of Knowledge;* and *Museums: A History.* He runs Museologica, a consulting company, is an adjunct curator of collections at the Earth and Mineral Sciences Museum and Art Gallery at the Pennsylvania State University, and is an adjunct museum studies instructor at Kent State University.

Juyeon Song is a PhD candidate in arts administration at Florida State University. Song received her BSBA with a concentration in finance and marketing from the University of Massachusetts. She began her professional career as a financial analyst in the Korean equity market. Juyeon received her MBA from KDI (Korea Development Institute) School and an MS in management from Georgia Tech. After graduation, Song worked as a portfolio manager at the Culture and Art Promotion

Endowment in the Arts Council Korea. Her research interests are capital structures and strategic decisions utilized in conjunction with managing the intangible assets used as resources in arts and cultural organizations.

Morgan Szymanski is a second-year museum education and visitor-centered exhibitions master's student at Florida State University. She currently works in the Education Department at the Museum of Florida History in Tallahassee, Florida. She is interested in bringing a multidisciplinary approach to educational programming at the museum.

Neville K. Vakharia is an assistant professor and research director in Drexel University's graduate arts administration program, teaching courses in management, strategic planning, entrepreneurship, and related subjects while leading research projects that seek to strengthen the arts, cultural, and creative sector. His research centers on the role that technology, innovation, and knowledge play in building sustainable, resilient, and relevant organizations and communities. Prior to Drexel, he spent over twenty years in leadership roles in the corporate, nonprofit, and foundation sectors. He currently serves on the boards of several nonprofit organizations and is an advisor to many emerging creative and social enterprises.

Gabriel Vaz de Melo is a master's student in CEDEPLAR/UFMG, Brazil. He is interested in cultural economics and digital economy, and currently participates in the research group in cultural economics at the same institution. He has a bachelor's degree in economics from the Federal University of Minas Gerais (UFMG).

Pat Villeneuve is a professor and director of arts administration in the Department of Art Education at Florida State University, where she has developed graduate programs in museum education and visitor-centered exhibitions. Villeneuve is the editor of the book *From Periphery to Center: Art Museum Education in the 21st Century* and recipient of the National Art Education Association National Museum Educator of the Year Award in 2009. She has published and presented extensively nationally and internationally and has developed supported interpretation, a model for visitor-centered exhibitions.

Douglas Worts is a culture and sustainability specialist with WorldViews Consulting in Toronto, Canada. Worts approaches culture broadly, *as how we live our lives* seeing museums as potential facilitators in forging an emerging *culture of sustainability*. His professional work combines a more than thirty-five-year career in museums with over two decades of exploring how culture shapes and directs the prospects for global human sustainability. Within Worts's museum career, experimental exhibits and audience research, coupled with organizational design and change management, have been of central importance. Systems thinking is fundamental within his work. Worts has published, taught, and lectured widely.